First Page of the Carolina Charter of 1663

NORTH CAROLINA CHARTERS AND CONSTITUTIONS 1578–1698

MATTIE ERMA EDWARDS PARKER, *Editor*

Carolina Charter Tercentenary Commission
RALEIGH, NORTH CAROLINA
1963

MEMBERS OF THE

CAROLINA CHARTER TERCENTENARY COMMISSION

FRANCIS E. WINSLOW, *Chairman*

Henry Belk
Mrs. Doris Betts
Chalmers G. Davidson
Lambert Davis
Mrs. Everett L. Durham
William C. Fields
William Carrington Gretter, Jr.
Grayson Harding
Mrs. James M. Harper, Jr.
Mrs. Ernest L. Ives
Dr. Henry W. Jordan
Mrs. Kauno A. Lehto
James G. W. MacLamroc
Mrs. Harry McMullan
Paul Murray
Dan M. Paul
Robert H. Spiro, Jr.
David Stick
J. P. Strother
Mrs. J. O. Tally, Jr.
Rt. Rev. Thomas H. Wright

EX OFFICIO MEMBERS

Robert L. Stallings, *Director*
State Department of Conservation and Development

Charles F. Carroll
State Superintendent of Public Instruction

Christopher Crittenden, *Director*
State Department of Archives and History

EXECUTIVE SECRETARY

Brig. Gen. John D. F. Phillips, USA (Ret.)

Acknowledgment is hereby made to the Mary Reynolds Babcock Foundation for the donation of funds to assist in the publication of this series.

Foreword

The Carolina Charter Tercentenary Commission is making a valuable and notable contribution in initiating a new series of THE COLONIAL RECORDS OF NORTH CAROLINA. This series will be of great value to the people of the State—and, indeed, to the population of the United States in general—in making available source materials that will serve as a basis for scholarly studies, school history texts, historical dramas, works of fiction, articles in magazines and newspapers, the marking and preservation of historic sites, the planning and preparation of historical museum exhibits, and many other programs and activities in the realm of history. Without making use of such source materials, painstakingly and accurately reproduced, it is impossible for our people to gain a true and undistorted picture of their past.

This new series is definitely needed. The first and only other series of THE COLONIAL RECORDS OF NORTH CAROLINA, compiled and edited by the devoted William L. Saunders and published by the State in ten volumes, was issued some three-quarters of a century ago, and since that time practically all writing in the field of North Carolina Colonial history has been based, in whole or in part, on that notable work. Since that day, however, many other records relating to North Carolina before 1776 have been discovered, and new inventions, processes, and products, such as the photocopy and microfilm, have made it possible to secure facsimile rather than handwritten copies with which the editor can work. In addition, there have been improvements in editorial standards and in printing, and new types of paper have been developed which, according to the best estimates, will last for many centuries. The State of North Carolina is taking advantage of all these advances and changed conditions in producing this new publication.

The Carolina Charter Tercentenary Commission is to be commended, and the State of North Carolina and its people are to be congratulated, for taking this step, which is essential if our citizens are to know and appreciate their rich historical heritage.

Christopher Crittenden, Director
State Department of Archives and History

Raleigh, N. C.
June 15, 1962

Table of Contents

Acknowledgments

Like most other books, this volume represents the combined effort of many people, including especially the members and staff of the Carolina Charter Tercentenary Commission, but also others.

The initiation of a new series of North Carolina colonial records was proposed to the Carolina Charter Tercentenary Commission by its Committee on Scholarly Activities. The Committee has given the project strong support. Some of its members have served on the Advisory Editorial Board, and others have given the editor aid of various sorts. The Executive Committee of the Carolina Charter Tercentenary Commission has made the colonial records project an important feature of its program and, together with the General Assembly, has taken the action needed to provide the funds necessary to launch the undertaking. The Executive Committee has continued as the guiding force of the project, and its members have assisted on many matters. The Advisory Editorial Board has helped plan the series and has aided in determining editorial policies. The members of the Board have read portions of the manuscript for this book and have raised questions leading to improvements which otherwise might not have been made. As a group and as individuals, they have responded generously to all requests for advice. General John D. F. Phillips, Executive Secretary of the Charter Commission, has advanced the work in numerous ways. He has handled the administrative matters related to the publication, has made valuable suggestions regarding editorial matters, and has been available for consultation at all times. Likewise, the other members of the Commission staff have afforded the daily co-operation needed for successful prosecution of the work.

Without the aid of other agencies, however, publication of this volume would not have been possible. The British Public Record Office supplied reproductions of most of the documents in this book and granted permission to publish material subject to crown copyright. The North Carolina State Department of Archives and History permitted transcription and publication of the charter of 1663 and made available its facilities for other aspects of the work. The staff of the Department has been generous in providing assistance. The North Carolina State Library has fulfilled numerous requests for aid. Members of the staff have graciously made investigations regarding materials needed and have borrowed from other libraries the books which they could not supply. Other agencies which have provided aid include the libraries of North Carolina State College, The University of North Carolina, Duke University, Princeton University, and Cornell University, The Library of Congress, and The Jamestown Foundation.

Several individuals who are not officially associated with the work have given valuable assistance. Dr. Lester J. Cappon, of the Institute of Early American History and Culture, and Dr. W. Edwin Hemphill, of the South Carolina Archives Department, attended the first meeting of the Advisory Editorial Board as visiting consultants. They aided in forming preliminary plans for this volume. Dr. Julian P. Boyd, Editor of *The Papers of Thomas Jefferson*, lent his manual of style and other materials, which have been invaluable guides in formulating office procedures and editorial policies. Mr. John K. Nelson, of The University of North Carolina, who was in London when the book was begun, arranged for photostatic reproductions of manuscripts to be sent from the British Public Record Office. Mr. Louis S. Manarin, of the North Carolina Confederate Centennial Commission, made available helpful material on editorial method.

The task of preparing this volume has been shared by the editor with four others, who, for varying periods of time, have been members of the editorial staff. These four are Mrs. Violet W. Quay, editorial assistant, and Mrs. Nan H. Barrow, Mrs. Audrey M. Piner, and Mrs. Carol B. Teachout, stenographers. They transcribed the documents and participated in most other aspects of the work. They not only have been the editor's fellow workers, but they also have served as her consultants. Mrs. Quay and Mrs. Piner prepared the index. Mr. James K. Huhta, who joined the editorial staff after the volume was practically completed, has read the Introduction to the volume and made helpful suggestions for improving it.

Two other people have been closely involved in the preparation of this book and have contributed to its completion. John Mason Parker has read much of the manuscript and made many suggestions which led to improvements. He and John Edwards Parker have borne with patience the inconvenience of having a "working" wife and mother, and they have provided her the help that was necessary for her to work on this book.

The editor is grateful to all who have aided in producing this volume. Although others have helped in many ways, responsibility for all shortcomings rests with the editor, who made the final decisions.

Mattie Erma Edwards Parker
Raleigh, North Carolina
July 30, 1962

Sources

The following list of books and articles used in preparing this volume is given in acknowledgment of the editor's indebtedness to those whose work provided information needed to produce this book.

Abbot, William W., *A Virginia Chronology, 1585–1783* (E. G. Swem, ed., *Jamestown 350th Anniversary Booklets*). Williamsburg, Va., 1957.

Andrews, Charles McLean, *The Colonial Period of American History*. 4 vols. New Haven, 1934–1938.

Andrews, Charles McLean, *Guide to the Materials for American History, to 1783, in the Public Record Office of Great Britain.* 2 vols. Washington, D. C., 1912–1914.

Barnes, Viola, "Land Tenure in English Colonial Charters of the Seventeenth Century," *Essays in Colonial History Presented to Charles McLean Andrews by His Students.* New Haven, 1931.

Bassett, John Spencer, "Constitutional Beginnings of North Carolina, 1663–1729," *Johns Hopkins University Studies in Historical and Political Science*, XII, No. 3 (1894).

Bemiss, Samuel M., *The Three Charters of the Virginia Company of London, with Seven Related Documents; 1606–1621* (E. G. Swem, ed., *Jamestown 350th Anniversary Historical Booklets*). Williamsburg, Va., 1957.

Brown, Louise Fargo, *The First Earl of Shaftesbury*. New York, 1933.

Cheves, Langdon, "The Shaftesbury Papers and Other Records Relating to Carolina," *South Carolina Historical Society Collections*, V (1897).

Craven, Wesley Frank, *The Virginia Company of London, 1606–1624* (E. G. Swem, ed., *Jamestown 350th Anniversary Historical Booklets*). Williamsburg, Va., 1957.

Crittenden, C. Christopher, "The Surrender of the Charter of Carolina," *The North Carolina Historical Review*, I (October, 1924), 383–402.

Davis, Junius, "Locke's Fundamental Constitutions," *The North Carolina Booklet*, VII, No. 1 (July, 1907).

Giuseppi, M. S., *Guide to the Manuscripts Preserved in the Public Record Office.* 2 vols. London, 1923–1924.

Guess, William Conrad, "County Government in Colonial North Carolina," *The James Sprunt Historical Publications*, XI, No. 1 (1911).

Hatch, Charles E., Jr., *The First Seventeen Years, Virginia, 1607–1624* (E. G. Swem, ed., *Jamestown 350th Anniversary Historical Booklets*). Williamsburg, Va., 1957.

Kingsbury, Susan M., ed., *The Records of the Virginia Company of London.* 4 vols. Washington, D. C., 1906–1935.

Lee, Enoch Lawrence, Jr., "History of the Lower Cape Fear: The Colonial Period." Unpublished Ph.D. dissertation, The University of North Carolina, 1961.

Lefler, Hugh Talmage, *North Carolina: The History of a Southern State.* Chapel Hill, N. C., 1954.

Maitland, F. W., *The Constitutional History of England.* Cambridge, 1908.

Maxwell-Lyte, H. C., *Historical Notes on the Use of the Great Seal of England.* London, 1926.

McCrady, Edward, *The History of South Carolina Under the Proprietary Government, 1670–1719,* New York, 1897.

Morgan, Lawrence N., "Land Tenure in Proprietary North Carolina," *The James Sprunt Historical Publications,* XII, No. 1 (1912).

Paschal, Herbert R., "Proprietary North Carolina: A Study in Colonial Government." Unpublished Ph.D. dissertation, The University of North Carolina, 1961.

Powell, William Stevens, *The Carolina Charter of 1663: How It Came to North Carolina and Its Place in History.* Raleigh, N. C., 1954.

Powell, William Stevens, ed., *Ye Countie of Albemarle in Carolina: A Collection of Documents, 1664–1675.* Raleigh, N. C., 1958.

Public Record Office, *The Thirty-Third Annual Report of the Deputy Keeper of the Public Records.* London, 1872.

Quinn, David Beers, *Raleigh and the British Empire* (A. L. Rowse, ed., *Teach Yourself History Library*). New York, 1949.

Quinn, David Beers, ed., *The Roanoke Voyages, 1584–1590.* 2 vols. London, 1955.

Quinn, David Beers, ed., *The Voyages and Colonizing Enterprises of Sir Humphrey Gilbert.* 2 vols. London, 1940.

Raper, Charles Lee, *North Carolina: A Study in English Colonial Government.* New York, 1904.

Rivers, William James, *A Sketch of the History of South Carolina to the Close of the Proprietary Government by the Revolution of 1719.* Charleston, S. C., 1856.

Salley, Alexander S., "The Fundamental Constitutions of Carolina," *The Proceedings of the South Carolina Historical Association,* IV (1934), 25–31.

Saunders, William L., *The Colonial Records of North Carolina.* 10 vols. Raleigh, N. C., 1886–1890.

Introduction to the Volume

Two groups of documents are contained in this volume. The first consists of charters issued by English sovereigns authorizing colonization of areas now in North Carolina, and the second comprises the constitutions issued by the lords proprietors of Carolina. These documents have been chosen for the initial volume of the new series of *The Colonial Records of North Carolina* because of their relation to the Carolina Charter of 1663 as well as for their significance in the early history of North Carolina. Inasmuch as the occasion for initiating this series is the three hundredth anniversary of the Carolina Charter, it seems appropriate to begin the publication with the charters and constitutions relating to colonial North Carolina.

The eight charters included in this book provided, in succession, the legal basis for the establishment of English colonies in the area now called North Carolina, and they authorized government for colonies in that region. Although settlers actually lived on North Carolina soil under authority of only three of these charters, all are significant in North Carolina history. As a series, they show trends in the development of English colonization policies affecting the North Carolina area, and individually each had an influence on the history of that region. For example, establishment of a popular assembly in Virginia, under the third charter of the Virginia Company, set precedent for establishing such a body in North Carolina. Furthermore, the first permanent settlers in the North Carolina area came from Virginia and settled under governmental and land policies which derived from provisions of the Virginia Company's charters. Because the ideas and practices of early North Carolina settlers were influenced by those of the Virginia colonists, the proprietors of Carolina later found it difficult to establish certain of their own policies in the northern part of their province. For many decades the North Carolina colony was affected by neighboring Virginia.

If regarded as legal instruments, the documents here called charters were in fact *letters patent.* Although there were differences between the charter and letters patent, in form, use, and issuance procedure, these differences were minor, and the practice of issuing charters was discontinued during the reign of Henry VIII, before any of the documents in this book were issued. After discontinuance of the charter, letters patent were used for the purposes which the charter formerly served. The term *charter,* however, was retained, but in popular rather than technical usage, to designate those letters patent which granted liberties, privileges, immunities, and exemptions, or which conferred extensive land grants. It is in this sense that the term is used in this volume.

Governmental authority conferred by charters was stated in general terms; the details were left to the grantees. Thus, the charters of the proprietors of Carolina, under which North Carolina became organized as a colony, conferred authority to create governmental agencies and to assign them functions. The proprietors undertook to implement two comprehensive plans of government for Carolina, the Concessions and Agreement, in 1665, and the Fundamental Constitutions of Carolina, in 1669. These plans of government have been called constitutions in this book, but there is an important difference between them and the written constitutions now in effect in the United States. In theory, at least, modern constitutions represent the will of the people, from whom they derive validity, and the word *constitution* is associated popularly with the idea of democratic government. The colonial constitutions of Carolina, however, were not instruments of democratic government. They were promulgated by the lords proprietors and represented their authority; their validity was derived from the proprietors, and ultimately from the English crown. Otherwise, the plans for governing colonial Carolina bore similarities to modern constitutions. They provided a governmental structure, assigned functions to the agencies composing this structure, and guaranteed to individuals certain rights and privileges. Because of these similarities, plans for government of colonial Carolina are called constitutions, which was the designation given by the proprietors.

The provisions of the charters and constitutions can be understood best in the light of ideas current in England when the documents were drafted. Three concepts are especially significant in this respect: the theory of effective occupation on which England based her claims in the New World; the feudal concepts on which English land law of the sixteenth and seventeenth centuries was based; and the ideas of individual rights and limited governmental authority which were developing in England during the period of American colonization.

The theory of effective occupation was advanced by the English to counter Spanish claims to a virtual monopoly of trade and political dominion in the New World. By the time England entered the colonization movement, Spain already had an extensive empire in Central and South America and claimed North America as well. Spain based her claims on discoveries of Spanish explorers and on the Treaty of Tordesillas, made in 1494. This treaty adjusted differences between Spain and Portugal over the location of a line of demarcation which had been established earlier to divide "heathen lands" between those two countries. Under the treaty, Portugal claimed right to a monopoly on trade and colonization in Africa, Asia, and the eastern part of South America (Brazil), and Spain claimed North America and the greater part of South America. England, however, refused to recognize claims based on the line of demarcation or on exploration, for she contended that nations had right only to those lands which they actually occupied. In accordance with this theory, England conceded to other countries those regions which they had settled, but she claimed for herself the right to conduct trade and establish colonies in unoccupied regions.

Advocacy of the theory of effective occupation made it necessary for England to occupy American territory to which she wished to establish title. Therefore, English charters granting land in America were contingent on the establish-

ment of colonies. The Gilbert and Raleigh grants were limited to six years, at the end of which they were to expire unless colonies had been established. When the Virginia Company appeared incapable of handling colonies efficiently, the crown nullified the charters of the company. Although the Heath charter contained no time limitation, the crown declared it void after a number of years had passed without colonies having been established. These actions were not capricious, but were in conformity with the theory of effective occupation.

English grants of territory in America also conformed to the land law of England, which was based on feudal concepts. In English legal theory, the sovereign was the ultimate owner of all land over which he ruled, and every landholder was legally a tenant of the king, directly or indirectly. The great lords who held large tracts of land in England, as well as those who held charters granting land in America, were direct tenants of the king. They sub-let land to others, who subdivided it further, and so the process, called *subinfeudation*, continued. For several centuries, all direct tenants of the king were tenants *in capite*, or "in chief." They held land *ut de corona*, or "as of the crown," and were subject to burdensome feudal dues and services. By the time America was colonized, however, another form of direct tenure from the sovereign had developed, and many of the king's direct tenants held land *ut de manore*, or "as of the manor." Tenants "as of the manor" were not subject to such burdensome obligations as were tenants "in chief." Under each form of tenure there were several modes of holding, or sets of obligations to be performed by the tenant, any of which might be specified. By the sixteenth century, however, all but two modes of holding had fallen into disuse. The two that remained were *knight's service* and *free and common socage*. Tenants who held by knight's service owed the king homage, fealty, military service, and a number of other obligations. Tenants in free and common socage also might owe the king a number of services and payments, but their main obligation was a fixed annual rental, in money or goods, and they did not owe military service. The most desirable tenure directly from the king, therefore, was "as of the manor," in free and common socage, and the least desirable was "in chief," by knight's service. When land was granted "as of the manor," one of the royal manors was named in order to specify the particular obligations assumed by the tenant, for these obligations were not uniform. The manor of East Greenwich, which is named in several charters in this volume, was most commonly specified in grants of land in England and America, although others sometimes were named.

The charters involving land now in North Carolina vary as to form of tenure conferred. The type of tenure is not clearly stated in the Gilbert and Raleigh charters, though it appears to have been "in chief," by knight's service. The first charter of the Virginia Company did not confer rights of land ownership on the company, which was granted only the authority to parcel out land to settlers, who then were to receive royal grants "as of the manor," in free and common socage. In its later charters, however, the company itself was granted land "as of the manor," in free and common socage, but it could sub-grant only in the same tenure. Thus, all three of the Virginia Company's charters guaranteed land to colonists on liberal terms. Sir Robert Heath, on the other hand, held his grant

under the most burdensome form of tenure, "in chief," by knight's service, but he could sub-grant land on any terms he wished. The lords proprietors also were given the right to sub-grant land in whatever tenure they chose, but, unlike Heath, they held the province "as of the manor," in free and common socage. This difference between the Heath grant and the proprietors' charters was due to the fact that Parliament had abolished tenures "in chief," and also knight's service, before the proprietors' charters were issued. The lords proprietors, however, were exempted from all statutes restricting tenure; therefore, they could grant land under the old tenures.

The importance of land policies in the colonies is easily overlooked today, for land no longer is the primary form of wealth. In the English colonies in America, however, land was practically the only form of wealth, and the terms under which it could be obtained were vitally important, both in attracting settlers and promoting their well-being. Many colonists came to America because of the scarcity of agricultural land in England, where fields were being converted to pasturage for sheep, to provide wool for the growing textile industry. Such settlers were attracted to colonies where they could obtain land with minimum restrictions and rents. Promoters of colonies also were interested primarily in land, especially if they were members of the English landed class, which had been adversely affected by economic changes that were bringing prosperity to other classes, such as the merchants. The expenses of landowners were increasing, because of inflation and higher living standards, while their income was being diminished by loss of feudal dues and services that had become obsolescent. As a result of these conditions, some landowners obtained charters and promoted colonies in America, hoping to replenish their fortunes by exacting rental dues and services which they no longer could obtain in England. Thus, land policies were significant to promoters and settlers, but the interests of the two groups were in opposition to each other.

Feudal law and practices current in England also were reflected in other features of the charters. Feudalism was an intricate way of life, in which government, land rights, social stratification, religion, and almost all other aspects of society were closely interwoven. By the time America was colonized, feudalism had disintegrated to some extent in England, but many of its institutions and practices remained. Legal thought lagged behind social change, and it was dominated by feudal ideas, some of which no longer were pertinent to actual conditions. Many remnants of feudalism, in law and institutions, were incorporated in the charters affecting North Carolina, and later in the constitutions issued by the proprietors. One such holdover from feudalism, the interdependence of land rights and government, is evident in those provisions in the charters which authorized establishment of manors and manorial courts.

The manor, which was the basic feudal unit, continued to be important in seventeenth-century England. Lords of manors still had governmental authority over their tenants and continued to hold manorial courts. Two of these seignioral courts, the view of frankpledge and the court baron, were private institutions, and were not courts of record. Both were assemblies of the freehold tenants of the manor, presided over by the lord or his steward. The court baron dealt with civil

matters, chiefly those arising from uses and abuses of tenancies; the view of frankpledge dealt with conduct. A third manorial court, the court leet, with jurisdiction over petty criminal offenses and minor civil matters, was a court of record. Although it operated under authority of the sovereign and enforced the king's peace, the court leet was held by the lord of the manor or his steward. Establishment of all three of these institutions was authorized by some of the charters, including those of the lords proprietors, and provisions for them were made in the Fundamental Constitutions.

Although the early Carolina colonists were accustomed to manors and manorial courts, they were not accustomed to all the features of feudalism which the proprietors' charters authorized. Like several other American charters, the lords proprietors' patents contained the bishop-of-Durham clause, which gave the proprietors as much power in Carolina as the bishop of Durham ever had possessed in his county. Many of the feudal practices authorized by this provision had long been obsolete in England.

Durham was one of three English counties palatine, over which feudal lords once possessed almost regal authority. These three, Durham, Chester, and Lancaster, were located on the borders, and their lords were responsible for protecting England from invaders. The lords of these counties may have been allowed their extraordinary authority in compensation for the protection they afforded, or their power may have developed because it was needed to provide protection in these remote regions. The bishop of Durham, who was feudal lord of this county, retained his special powers longer than the lords of Chester and Lancaster, probably because his office and power were not hereditary. Although the bishop's authority over Durham had been greatly diminished by the seventeenth century, this decrease in power was not reflected in the American charters containing the bishop-of-Durham clause, which conferred authority equivalent to that which the bishop had possessed when his power was at its height. The grant of extensive feudal power conferred on the proprietors of Carolina in the bishop-of-Durham clause is significant because it largely accounts for the extreme feudal features of the Fundamental Constitutions of Carolina, which were designed to implement the authority conferred by this provision.

A third English concept incorporated in the charters was the developing idea that individuals could be protected by law against the abuse of authority by the government. All of the charters concerned with North Carolina territory contained provisions requiring that laws made for colonies be consonant with the laws of England and that the rights of Englishmen be accorded to settlers in America. The "liberties, franchises, and immunities" which the charters guaranteed to colonists were by no means the equivalent of modern democracy, nor of the individual rights and freedoms set forth in modern constitutions. They included little more than property rights and protective procedures in courts, for such modern liberties as freedom of speech, press, religion, and assembly had not been obtained by citizens of England when the charters were issued. Nevertheless, the idea that individuals had rights which their government was bound by law to respect was incorporated in all the charters concerned with North Carolina territory. In addition, the Heath grant and the patents of the lords proprietors

provided that the colonists were to have voice in lawmaking. Thus, the charters took account of the concept that government operated under law and that citizens themselves should have a part in lawmaking.

Obviously, those provisions of charters limiting governmental authority were contradictory to provisions conferring almost absolute authority upon the grantees. As the charters did not specify the ways in which such contradictions were to be reconciled, the grantees were left free to reconcile them as they chose. The proprietors of Carolina, concerned with their own rights rather than the rights of settlers, often paid little more than nominal attention to limitations on their power. Nevertheless, the fact that the concept of limitations upon governmental authority was embedded in the charters was important to the inhabitants of Carolina, who at times called this to the attention of the proprietors, either by formal action or by rebellion. Eventually, the idea of restrictions upon governmental authority became a factor in bringing about the American Revolution, and when North Carolina and the other American colonies became independent of England, written constitutions were adopted, which, like the charters, imposed limitations on the power of governmental officials.

The issuance of a charter, or *letters patent,* was a complicated procedure, which began with a *petition* to the crown from those desiring a grant. Appropriate officials then considered the petition and decided whether or not the proposed charter should be issued; frequently, they held consultation with the petitioner and reached agreement as to the provisions of the grant. After the provisions had been determined, a *warrant* was drawn, bearing the king's signature and giving directions for preparation of the proposed charter. The warrant was sent to the patent office, where the first copy of the charter, called the *king's bill,* was prepared. The king's bill contained the complete wording of the patent, except that the formal phrases, or *protocols,* were omitted. It was sent first to the official who had issued the warrant, who obtained the royal signature, or *sign manual,* on the bill. Then it was sent to the signet office, where it served as authority for preparation of a second copy, called the *signet bill,* which was sealed with the sovereign's small seal, the signet. The king's bill was retained in the signet office, and the signet bill was sent to the privy seal office, where it served as authority for preparation of a third copy, called the *writ of privy seal,* on which the privy seal was placed. The writ of privy seal was sent to the lord chancellor and was signed by him. It then served as authorization for proper officials to prepare final copies of the charter, or *letters patent,* including the protocols, and to transmit them to the lord chancellor. Two final copies usually were prepared. Occasionally, the sovereign's signature was placed on the letters patent, at the top of the first page, but usually it was not, for the royal sign manual was mandatory only on the king's bill; the sovereign's seals, which were the signet, privy seal, and great seal, served in place of his signature on the other copies. The great seal was affixed to the final copies by the lord chancellor, attended by three clerks; it was appended by a ribbon at the bottom of the document. The sealed letters patent were then sent to the patentees, and the writ of privy seal was sent to the chancery, where it was entered on the *patent roll.* The entire process by which a charter was issued was often referred to as *passing through the seals.*

Photostatic reproductions of enrollments on the patent roll were followed in transcribing six of the charters in this volume. The first charter issued to the lords proprietors of Carolina, in 1663, was transcribed from a copy believed by experts to be a final copy, that is, the charter itself. Although the 1663 charter was issued in duplicate, a list of the fees paid for issuance indicates that the duplicate was not so extensively decorated as the original. The elaborately decorated copy transcribed for this volume appears to be the original charter rather than the duplicate.[1] The Heath charter was transcribed from a photostatic reproduction of a copy of an *exemplification*, or attested copy, of the charter, made in 1631, two years after the charter was issued. The exemplification was transcribed instead of the enrollment because the latter is in Latin. All of the manuscripts reproduced for use in transcribing the charters are in the British Public Record Office. The first charter of the lords proprietors is owned by the state of North Carolina and is in the custody of the State Department of Archives and History. With one exception, the constitutions also were transcribed from photostatic reproductions of manuscripts in the British Public Record Office. A microfilm reproduction of a contemporary printed copy was used for the March 1, 1670, Fundamental Constitutions.

One manuscript used in preparing this volume should be mentioned particularly, although it was not transcribed, as another copy of the same document was considered more suitable. This manuscript, which is a copy of the August 17, 1682, version of the Fundamental Constitutions, contains marginal notes referring to the March 1, 1670, version as "the third Constitutions." So far as other known records indicate, the March 1, 1670, version is the second set of the Constitutions issued by the proprietors. Therefore, the notes on the 1682 manuscript suggest the possibility that there were more than the five versions now known. These notes, however, may be related to notes contained in another manuscript, that from which the July 21, 1669, version was transcribed for this volume.[2] In effect, the 1669 manuscript consists of two versions of the Constitutions, for it contains notes showing revisions made in forty-one of the one hundred and eleven articles that had been written. Although some of these revisions were incorporated in the March 1, 1670, version, some were not, and both forms given in the 1669 manuscript differ in other respects from the March 1, 1670, version. Nothing found in the course of preparing this volume indicates definitely when the 1669 manuscript was revised; the alterations could have been made before the formal adoption of the Constitutions, on July 21, 1669, or afterward. It may be, however, that the writer of the notes in the 1682 manuscript considered the two forms shown in the 1669 manuscript the first and second Constitutions, and, therefore, the March 1, 1670, version as "the third Constitutions."

---

[1] See William L. Saunders, *The Colonial Records of North Carolina* (Raleigh, 1886–1890), I, 115, for itemized list of fees paid by the proprietors for their charters.

[2] The following publications contain literal transcriptions of the July 21, 1669, manuscript: *The Thirty-Third Annual Report of the Deputy Keeper of the Public Records* (London, 1872), Appendix 3, 258–269. Langdon Cheves, Ed., *The Shaftesbury Papers and Other Records Relating to Carolina* (*Collections of the South Carolina Historical Society*, V [1896]), 93–117.

In transcribing the July 21, 1669, manuscript, departure has been made from the practice followed by others editing this document, who published literal transcriptions showing the appearance of the manuscript, insofar as this could be done on a printed page. In this volume, a transcription is given of the constitutions as originally written in the manuscript, as well as could be determined, with footnotes and brackets indicating changes which appear contemporary with the original. This version is followed by transcriptions of those articles that were altered later, giving the revised form of those articles.

All of the photostatic reproductions of manuscripts secured in preparing this volume have been deposited with the State Department of Archives and History. These include two manuscripts that were not transcribed: the copy of the August 17, 1682, Fundamental Constitutions referred to above, and the patent-roll copy of the Heath charter. These documents are subject to crown copyright and are reproduced in this volume by permission of the Controller of Her Majesty's Stationery Office. Similar permission is necessary for further reproduction.

Although subsequent volumes in this series will be prepared primarily for scholars, this volume has been planned for the general reader as well as the scholar. For this reason, the "modernized" editorial method has been used, with some modifications. Editorial rules have been kept flexible, however, so that the text could be followed faithfully, despite "modernization," and so that some of the "flavor" of the documents could be kept. For example, the spellings of proper names have been retained, including variations, although in other respects spelling has been modernized and has been made uniform within each document. Within the volume as a whole uniformity in spelling has not been attempted. Instead, those modern spellings requiring the least change have been adopted for each document. Most obsolete and archaic words have been replaced by their present-day equivalents, but a few have been kept, to convey some of the original "flavor." The capitalization in the documents has been retained, although a few capitals have been added. Indentation in transcriptions of the constitutions is the same as that in the documents transcribed, but indentation has been supplied in transcriptions of the charters. Punctuation has been modernized or supplied in all documents. Both indentation and punctuation, however, have been adapted in some measure to existing capitalization and punctuation, which has resulted in different treatments of some passages which in other respects are identical. As interpretation is the chief basis of the punctuation supplied, the transcriptions in this volume necessarily represent the editor's interpretations of the documents. This, of course, should be borne in mind by those using the volume, as different interpretations of some passages may be made.

A few "slips of the pen" have been "silently" corrected, but most errors have been reproduced, some without comment and some accompanied by comments or emendations in brackets or footnotes. Although the copies which were used in preparing the volume have been compared with other copies or transcriptions of the documents, no attempt has been made to indicate variations. Occasionally, however, the wording of other contemporary copies has been given in brackets or footnotes for the sake of clarification. Effort has been made to keep annotation to the minimum required to clarify the documents.

CHARTERS

Charter to Sir Humphrey Gilbert

June 11, 1578

INTRODUCTION

England made no effort to colonize America until the latter part of the sixteenth century, for she lacked the needed resources and was torn by internal dissension. During the reign of Elizabeth I, however, the English nation achieved a fair degree of unity and obtained sufficient sea-power, capital, and population to attempt overseas colonization.

Interest in America was aroused among Englishmen in 1563, when Jean Ribault arrived to solicit aid for a colony of French Huguenots which he had established on the southeastern coast of North America. Publication that year of Ribault's account of his experiences in "Florida" gave Englishmen their first opportunity to read in their own language the details of a visit to the New World. Interest in America was further stimulated by the exploits of English "sea dogs," such as John Hawkins, Richard Grenville, and Francis Drake, who raided Spanish shipping and settlements in the New World. Plans for sending English colonies to America were discussed in the 1560's, but no serious colonization effort was begun until 1578, when Sir Humphrey Gilbert obtained a charter from Queen Elizabeth, granting him the right to discover and settle "remote heathen and barbarous lands, countries, and territories, not actually possessed of any Christian prince or people. . . ."

Gilbert's charter conferred extensive rights of ownership and trade in America. It also authorized Gilbert to govern as he saw fit any colonies that he might establish, provided that the laws he made conformed to the laws of England. These rights and authority, however, were not to become permanent unless a colony was established within the six-year term of the grant.

There is no indication that Gilbert's plans or expeditions directly involved territory now in North Carolina. Gilbert established no colonies in America; from the standpoint of immediate achievement, his efforts failed. Nevertheless, the activities that Gilbert began, and which his associates continued, resulted in the establishment, soon after his death, of colonies on Roanoke Island, in present-day North Carolina. Although these colonies were not permanent, they demon-

strated that Englishmen could live in America, and they provided experience which made possible the later establishment of permanent settlements.

The Gilbert charter is significant, not merely to North Carolina but to the entire United States, for it was the formal beginning of English colonization in America. The long series of activities which it launched eventually resulted in a new nation, with language and institutions drawn primarily from England.

Gilbert was lost in a storm at sea, in 1583, on his way home from Newfoundland, where disasters had forced him to abandon plans to select a site for a settlement. After his death, his associates tried to prepare another expedition before the charter expired. When it became evident that preparations could not be completed in time, another charter was requested and granted. The next English expedition was made under authority of a grant to Walter Raleigh, who was Gilbert's half-brother, and his associate in colonization activities.

THE DOCUMENT

ELIZABETH, by the grace of God, etc. To all people to whom these presents shall come, greeting:

Know ye, that, of our especial grace, certain science, and mere motion, we have given and granted, and, by these presents, for us, our heirs and successors, do give and grant, to our trusty and well-beloved servant, Sir Humfrey Gilberte, of Compton, in our County of Devon, Knight, and to his heirs and Assigns, forever, free liberty and licence from time to time, and at all times forever hereafter, to discover, search, find out, and view such remote heathen and barbarous lands, Countries, and territories, not actually possessed of any Christian Prince or people, as to him, his heirs and Assigns, and to every or any of them, shall seem good;

And the same to have, hold, occupy, and enjoy, to him, his heirs and Assigns, forever, with all commodities, jurisdictions, and royalties, both by sea and land.

And the said Sir Humfrey, and all such as, from time to time, by licence of us, our heirs and successors, shall go or travel thither, to inhabit or remain there, to build and fortify, at the discretion of the said Sir Humfrey, and of his heirs and Assigns; the statutes or Acts of Parliament made against fugitives, or against such as shall depart, remain, or continue out of our Realm of England without licence, or any other Act, statute, law, or matter whatsoever to the contrary in any wise notwithstanding.

And we do likewise, by these presents, for us, our heirs and successors, give full authority and power to the said Sir Humfrey, his heirs and Assigns, and every of them, that he and they, and every or any of them, shall and may, at all and every time and times hereafter, have, take, and lead in the said voyages, to travel thitherward or to inhabit there with him and them; and them,[1] and every or any of them, such and so many of our subjects as shall willingly accompany him and them, and every or any of them, with sufficient shipping and furniture for their transportations;

So that none of the same persons, nor any of them, be such as hereafter shall be specially restrained by us, our heirs or successors.

---

[1] Repetition of *and them* may have been unintentional. It does not occur in the corresponding passage in the Walter Raleigh charter. In that document, however, a similar repetition does occur in a closely related passage that is not in the Gilbert charter. In both instances, the sense and punctuation would be slightly different without the repetition.

And further, that he, the said Sir Humfrey, his heirs and Assigns, and every or any of them, shall have, hold, occupy, and enjoy, to him, his heirs and assigns, and every of them, forever, all the soil of all such lands, Countries, and Territories so to be discovered or possessed as aforesaid; and of all Cities, Castles, Towns, villages, and places in the same; with the rights, royalties, and jurisdictions, as well marine as other, within the said lands or Countries, or the Seas thereunto adjoining; to be had or used with full power to dispose thereof, and of every part thereof, in fee simple or otherwise, according to the order of the laws of England, as near as the same conveniently may be, at his and their will and pleasure, to any person then being, or that shall remain, within the allegiance of us, our heirs and successors; reserving always, to us, our heirs and successors, for all services, duties, and demands, the fifth part of all the ore of gold and silver that, from time to time, and at all times, after such discovery, subduing, and possessing, shall be there gotten;

All which lands, Countries, and Territories shall forever be held by the said Sir Humfrey, and his heirs and assigns, of us, our heirs and successors, by homage and by the said payment of the said fifth part before reserved only, for all services.

And moreover, we do, by these presents, for us, our heirs and successors, give and grant licence to the said Sir Humfrey Gilberte, his heirs and Assigns, and every of them, that he and they, and every or any of them, shall and may, from time to time, and at all times forever hereafter, for his and their defence, encounter, expulse, repel, and resist, as well by Sea as by land, and by all other ways whatsoever, all and every such person and persons whatsoever as, without the special licence and liking of the said Sir Humfrey, and of his heirs or Assigns, shall attempt to inhabit within the said Countries, or any of them, or within the space of two hundred leagues near to the place or places, within such Countries as aforesaid, if they shall not be before planted or inhabited, within the limits aforesaid, with the subjects of any Christian Prince being in Amity with her Majesty, where the said Sir Humfrey, his heirs or assigns, or any of them, or his or their, or any of their, Associates or companies, shall, within six years next ensuing, make their dwellings or abidings; or that shall enterprise or attempt, at any time hereafter, unlawfully to annoy, either by Sea or land, the said Sir Humfrey, his heirs or Assigns, or any of them, or his or their, or any of their, companies;

Giving and granting, by these presents, further power and authority to the said Sir Humfrey, his heirs and Assigns, and every of

them, from time to time, and at all times forever hereafter, to take and surprise, by all manner means whatsoever, all and every those person and persons, with their ships, vessels, and other goods and furniture, which, without the licence of the said Sir Humfrey, or his heirs or Assigns, as aforesaid, shall be found trafficking into any harbor or harbors, Creek or Creeks, within the limits aforesaid; The subjects of our Realms and dominions, and all other persons in amity with us, being driven by force of tempest or shipwreck only excepted;

And those persons, and every of them, with their ships, vessels, goods, and furniture, to detain and possess as of good and lawful prize,[2] according to the discretion of him, the said Sir Humfrey, his heirs and Assigns, and every or any of them.

And, for uniting in more perfect league and amity of such Countries, lands, and Territories, so to be possessed and inhabited as aforesaid, with our Realms of England and Ireland, and for the better encouragement of men to this enterprise, we do, by these presents, grant and declare that all such Countries, so hereafter to be possessed and inhabited as aforesaid, from thenceforth shall be of the allegiance of us, our heirs and successors; and we do grant to the said Sir Humfrey, his heirs and Assigns, and to all and every of them, and to all and every other person and persons being of our allegiance, whose names shall be noted or entered in some of our Courts of record within this our Realm of England, and that, with the assent of the said Sir Humfrey, his heirs or Assigns, shall now in this journey for discovery, or in the second journey for conquest hereafter, travel to such lands, Countries, and territories as aforesaid, and to their, and every of their, heirs, that they, and every or any of them, being either born within our said Realms of England or Ireland, or in any other place within our allegiance, and which hereafter shall be inhabiting within any the lands, Countries, and territories with such licence as aforesaid, shall and may have and enjoy all the privileges of free denizens and persons native of England and within our allegiance; in such like ample manner and form as if they were born and personally resident within our said Realm of England; Any law, custom, or usage to the contrary notwithstanding.

And forasmuch as, upon the finding out, discovering, and inhabiting of such remote lands, Countries, and Territories as aforesaid, it shall be necessary, for the safety of all men that shall adventure themselves in

[2] *Price* in the manuscript. *Price* formerly meant *a person or thing captured or seized by force, especially in war.* This meaning was taken on by *prize,* which is a by-form of *price.*

those journeys or voyages, to determine to live together in Christian Peace and Civil quietness, each with other, whereby every one may, with more pleasure and profit, enjoy that whereunto they shall attain with great pain and peril, we, for us, our heirs and successors, are likewise pleased and contented, and, by these presents, do give and grant to the said Sir Humfrey, and his heirs and Assigns, forever, that he and they, and every or any of them, shall and may, from time to time forever hereafter, within the said mentioned remote Lands and Countries, and in the way by the Seas thither and from thence, have full and mere power and authority to correct, punish, pardon, govern, and rule, by their, and every or any of their, good discretions and policies, as well in causes Capital or criminal as civil, both marine and other, all such, our subjects and others, as shall, from time to time hereafter, adventure themselves in the said journeys or voyages, habitative or possessive, or that shall, at any time hereafter, inhabit any such lands, Countries, or territories as aforesaid, or that shall abide within two hundred leagues of any the said place or places where the said Sir Humfrey, or his heirs or assigns, or any of them, or any of his or their Associates or companies, shall inhabit within six years next ensuing the date hereof; according to such statutes, laws, and ordinances as shall be, by him, the said Sir Humfrey, his heirs and Assigns, and every or any of them, devised or established for the better government of the said people, as aforesaid;

So always, that the said statutes, laws, and ordinances may be, as near as conveniently may, agreeable to the form of the laws and policy of England;

And also, so as they be not against the true Christian faith or religion, now professed in the Church of England; nor in any wise to withdraw any of the subjects or people of those lands or places from the allegiance of us, our heirs or successors, as their immediate sovereigns under God.

And further, we do, by these presents, for us, our heirs and successors, give and grant full power and authority to our trusty and well-beloved Counsellor, Sir William Cycill, Knight, Lord Burghley, our High Treasurer of England, and to the Lord Treasurer of England of us, our heirs and successors, for the time being, and to the Privy Council of us, our heirs and successors, or any four of them, for the time being, that he, they, or any four of them shall and may, from time to time, and at all times hereafter, under his or their hands or seals, by virtue of these presents, authorize and licence the said Sir Humfrey Gilbert, his heirs and assigns, and every or any of them, by him and themselves, or by

their, or any of their, sufficient Attorneys, deputies, Officers, Ministers, factors, and servants, to embark and transport out of our Realms of England and Ireland all or any of his or their, or any of their, goods, and all or any the goods of his and their Associates and companies, and every or any of them; with such other necessaries and commodities of any our Realms as to the said Lord Treasurer, or four of the Privy Council of us, our heirs or successors, for the time being, as aforesaid, shall be, from time to time, by his or their wisdoms or discretions, thought meet and convenient for the better relief and support of him, the said Sir Humfrey, his heirs and Assigns, and every or any of them, and of his and their, and every or any of their, said Associates and companies; Any Act, statute, law, or other thing to the contrary in any wise notwithstanding.

Provided always, and our will and pleasure is, and we do hereby declare to all Christian Kings, Princes, and states, that, if the said Sir Humfrey, his heirs or Assigns, or any of them, or any other by their licence or appointment, shall, at any time or times hereafter, rob or spoil, by sea or by land, or do any Act of unjust and unlawful hostility to any of the subjects of us, our heirs and successors, or any of the subjects of any King, Prince, ruler, Governor, or state, being then in perfect league and Amity with us, our heirs or successors, and that, upon such Injury, or upon just complaint of any such Prince, Ruler, Governor, or state, or their subjects, we, our heirs or successors, shall make open proclamation within any the Ports of our Realm of England commodious:

That the said Sir Humfrey, his heirs or Assigns, or any others to whom these our letters patents may extend, shall, within the term to be limited by such proclamation, make full restitution and satisfaction of all such Injuries done, So as both we and the said Princes, or others so complaining, may hold us and them selves fully contented; and that, if the said Sir Humfrey, his heirs and Assigns, shall not make, and cause to be made, satisfaction accordingly, within such time so to be limited, That then it shall be lawful to us, our heirs and successors, to put the said Sir Humfrey, his heirs, Assigns, and Adherents, and all the inhabitants of the said places to be discovered as is aforesaid, or any of them, out of our allegiance and protection;

And that, from and after such time of putting out of protection, the said Sir Humfrey, his heirs, assigns, Adherents, and others, so to be put out;

And the said places within their habitation, possession, and rule shall be out of our protection and allegiance, and free for all princes

and others to pursue with hostility, as being not our subjects, nor by us any way to be avowed, maintained, or defended, nor to be held as any of ours, nor to our protection or dominion or allegiance any way belonging.

For that express mention, etc.

In witness whereof, etc.

Witness, our self, at Westminster, the eleventh day of June, the twentieth year of our reign.

per ipsam Reginam, etc.

[Transcribed from a photostatic copy of the enrollment of the charter on the patent roll. Manuscript in the British Public Record Office, London. Reference C. 66/1178. Photostatic copy deposited in the State Department of Archives and History, Raleigh, North Carolina.]

Charter to Walter Raleigh

March 25, 1584

INTRODUCTION

On March 25, 1584, shortly before the Gilbert grant was due to expire, Queen Elizabeth issued a charter to Gilbert's half-brother, Walter Raleigh. In effect, this grant was a six-year extension of Gilbert's charter, although Newfoundland was excluded from the Raleigh grant.

About a month after the Raleigh charter was sealed, two ships, commanded by Philip Amadas and Arthur Barlowe, sailed for the southeastern coast of North America, where a site for a colony was to be selected. In July, the expedition landed on one of the island barriers off the coast of modern North Carolina. On behalf of Raleigh, Amadas and Barlowe took formal possession in the name of the Queen and explored the surrounding territory, including Roanoke Island, which lies between Pamlico and Albemarle sounds. After the return of this expedition, Raleigh obtained Elizabeth's permission to name the newly possessed land Virginia in her honor; this name came to be applied by the English to much of the Atlantic coast. Raleigh was knighted in recognition of his achievement and in return for the honor he had accorded the Queen.

In 1585, Raleigh sent out a colony, with Ralph Lane as governor, which settled on Roanoke Island. This was the first English colony to settle in America. About a year later, the colonists returned to England, for they had not received needed supplies and reinforcements. A supply ship arrived only a few weeks after the colonists' departure, and soon afterward a relief expedition under Richard Grenville arrived. Grenville left a small garrison to hold possession and retain Raleigh's rights, but the garrison left the island and disappeared, after an attack by Indians.

In late July, 1587, another colony sent by Raleigh arrived off Hatteras and settled on Roanoke Island. Its governor, John White, was an artist who had been a member of the Lane colony and had made paintings and maps of the Roanoke region and other places in America. White and his colonists had expected to settle in the Chesapeake region, which was considered a more favorable location than Roanoke, but they were forced to remain at Roanoke Island, for Simon Fernandez, master of the largest ship in the expedition, refused to take them

farther. On August 18, Governor White's daughter, Eleanor, the wife of Ananias Dare, gave birth to a child, Virginia, the first child born of English colonists in America.

At the urging of the other colonists, White returned to England in late August to expedite the shipping of supplies, with the understanding that the colonists would move to the mainland and would leave at Roanoke Island directions for finding them. War with Spain prevented White's return until 1590, when he found Roanoke Island deserted; the only clues to the colonists' location were the letters CRO carved on a tree and the word CROATOAN carved at the entrance to the colonists' fort. Further search by White was prevented by damage to the ships in the expedition and by an unfavorable wind. No other immediate effort to find the lost colony is recorded, and later attempts, which appear to have been desultory, were unsuccessful. The fate of the colonists has never been learned. For many years, however, the colony was presumed in England to be in existence, and Raleigh's rights in "Virginia" were considered established.

After hostilities with Spain subsided, English interest in America was revived. Raleigh's associates sent commercial expeditions to the New England area and made an unsuccessful attempt to establish a colony in that region. Raleigh's own interest in North America during this period was chiefly commercial. In 1602, he sent ships to the Cape Fear area to trade with the Indians and to obtain a cargo of timber and medicinal plants. The following year, he sent an expedition to the Chesapeake region. This expedition quickly returned to England because of the death of its leader, Bartholomew Gilbert, at the hands of Indians. By the time the ships reached England, Raleigh had been imprisoned on charges of high treason, based on claims that he had conspired with Spain to prevent the ascension of James I to the throne at Elizabeth's death. Upon his conviction of this offense, Raleigh's rights under his charter were forfeited to the crown, and "Virginia" was at the disposal of the new sovereign, James I.

THE DOCUMENT

ELIZABETH, by the grace of God, etc. To all people to whom these presents shall come, greeting:

Know ye, that, of our especial grace, certain science, and mere motion, we have given and granted, and, by these presents, for us, our heirs and successors, do give and grant, to our trusty and well-beloved servant, Walter Raleighe, Esquire, and to his heirs and assigns, forever, free liberty and license from time to time, and at all times forever hereafter, to discover, search, find out, and view such remote heathen and barbarous Lands, Countries, and territories, not actually possessed of any Christian Prince and inhabited by Christian people, as to him, his heirs and assigns, and to every or any of them, shall seem good; and the same to have, hold, occupy, and enjoy, to him, his heirs and assigns, forever; with all prerogatives, commodities, jurisdictions, and royalties, privileges, Franchises, and pre-eminences, there or thereabouts, both by sea and land, whatsoever we, by our letters patents, may grant, and as we, or any of our noble Progenitors, have heretofore granted to any person or persons, bodies politic or corporate.

And the said Walter Raleigh, his heirs and assigns, and all such as, from time to time, by license of us, our heirs and successors, shall go or travel thither, to inhabit or remain there, to build and fortify, at the discretion of the said Walter Raleighe, his heirs and assigns; the statutes or acts of Parliament made against fugitives, or against such as shall depart, remain, or continue out of our Realm of England without license, or any other Act, statute, law, or ordinance whatsoever to the contrary in any wise notwithstanding.

And we do likewise, by these presents, of our grace especial, mere motion, and certain knowledge, for us, our heirs and successors, give and grant full authority, liberty, and power to the said Walter Raleighe, his heirs and assigns, and every of them, That he and they, and every or any of them, shall and may, at all and every time and times hereafter, have, take, and lead in the said voyages, to travel thitherward or to inhabit there with him or them, and every or any of them, such and so many of our subjects as shall willingly accompany him and them; and them,[1] and every or any of them, to whom also, by these presents, we do give full liberty, power, and authority in that behalf; and also, to

---

[1] Repetition of *and them* may have been inadvertent, although the occurrence of a similar repetition in the Gilbert charter suggests that the wording was intended as written. The sense and punctuation would be slightly different without the repetition.

have, take, employ, and use sufficient shipping and furniture for their transportations and Navigations in that behalf;

So that none of the same persons, nor any of them, be such as hereafter shall be restrained by us, our heirs or successors.

And further, that he, the said Walter Raleighe, his heirs and assigns, and every of them, shall have, hold, occupy, and enjoy, to him, his heirs and assigns, and every of them, forever, all the soil of all such lands, Countries, and territories so to be discovered or possessed as aforesaid; and of all Cities, Castles, towns, villages, and places in the same; with the rights, royalties, franchises, and Jurisdictions, as well marine as other, within the said Lands or Countries, or the seas thereunto adjoining; to be had or used with full power to dispose thereof, and of every part, in fee simple or otherwise, according to the order of the laws of England, as near as the same conveniently may be, at his and their will and pleasure, to any person then being, or that shall remain, within the allegiance of us, our heirs and successors;

Reserving always, to us, our heirs and successors, for all services, duties, and demands, the fifth part of all the ore of Gold and silver that, from time to time, and at all times, after such discovery, subduing, or possessing, shall be there gotten or obtained;

All which lands, Countries, and territories shall forever be held by the said Walter Raleigh, his heirs and assigns, of us, our heirs and successors, by homage and by the said payment of the said fifth part before reserved only, for all service.

And moreover, we do, by these presents, for us, our heirs and successors, give and grant license to the said Walter Raleighe, his heirs and assigns, and every of them, that he and they, and every or any of them, shall and may, from time to time, and at all times forever hereafter, for his and their defence, encounter, expulse, repel, and resist, as well by sea as by land, and by all other ways whatsoever, all and every such person and persons whatsoever as, without the special license and liking of the said Walter Raleighe, and of his heirs and assigns, shall attempt to inhabit within the said Countries, or any of them, or within the space of two hundred leagues near to the place or places, within such Countries as aforesaid, if they shall not be before planted or inhabited, within the limits aforesaid, with the Subjects of any Christian Prince being in amity with us, where the said Walter Raleighe, his heirs or assigns, or any of them, or his or their, or any of their, Associates or Company, shall, within six years next ensuing, make their dwellings or abidings; or that shall enterprise or attempt, at any time hereafter, unlawfully to annoy,

either by sea or land, the said Walter Raleigh, his heirs or Assigns, or any of them, or his or their, or any of their, companies;

Giving and granting, by these presents, further power and authority to the said Walter Raleighe, his heirs and Assigns, and every of them, from time to time, and at all times forever hereafter, to take and surprise, by all manner means whatsoever, all and every those person and persons, with their ships, vessels, or other goods and furniture, which, without the license of the said Walter Raleighe, or his heirs or assigns, as aforesaid, shall be found trafficking into any harbor or harbors, Creek or Creeks, within the limits aforesaid; the subjects of our Realms and Dominions, and all other persons in amity with us, trading to the New found lands for fishings, as they heretofore have commonly used, or being driven by force of tempest or shipwreck, only excepted;

And those persons, and every of them, with their ships, vessels, goods, and furnitures, to detain and possess as of good and lawful prize,[2] according to the discretion of him, the said Walter Raleigh, his heirs and assigns, and every or any of them.

And, for uniting in more perfect League and amity of such Countries, Lands, and territories, so to be possessed and Inhabited as aforesaid, with our Realms of England and Ireland, and the better encouragement of men to this enterprise, we do, by these presents, grant and declare that all such Countries, so hereafter to be possessed and inhabited as is aforesaid, from thenceforth shall be of the allegiance of us, our heirs and successors.

And we do grant to the said Walter Raleighe, his heirs and assigns, and to all and every of them, and to all and every other person and persons being of our allegiance, whose names shall be noted or entered in some of our Courts of Record within this our Realm of England, and that, with the assent of the said Walter Raleighe, his heirs and assigns, shall, in his Journeys for discovery, or in the Journeys for Conquest hereafter, travel to such lands, Countries, and territories as aforesaid, and to their, and every of their, heirs, that they, and every or any of them, being either born within our said Realm of England or Ireland, or in any other place within our allegiances, And which hereafter shall be Inhabiting within any the lands, Countries, and territories with such license as aforesaid, shall and may have and enjoy all the privileges of free Denizens and persons native of England and within our allegiance; in such

---

[2] *Price* in the manuscript. *Price* formerly meant *a person or thing captured or seized by force, especially in war.* This meaning was taken on by *prize,* which is a by-form of *price.*

like ample manner and form as if they were born and personally resident within our said Realm of England; Any law, Custom, or usage to the Contrary notwithstanding.

And forasmuch as, upon the finding out, discovering, or Inhabiting of such remote lands, Countries, and territories as aforesaid, it shall be necessary, for the safety of all men that shall adventure themselves in those Journeys or voyages, to determine to live together in Christian peace and Civil quietness, each with other, whereby every one may, with more pleasure and profit, enjoy that whereunto they shall attain with great pain and peril, we, for us, our heirs and successors, are likewise pleased and contented, and, by these presents, do give and grant to the said Walter Raleighe, his heirs and assigns, forever, that he and they, and every or any of them, shall and may, from time to time forever hereafter, within the said mentioned remote Lands and Countries, in the way by the Seas thither and from thence, have full and mere power and authority to correct, punish, pardon, govern, and rule, by their, and every or any of their, good discretions and policies, as well in causes Capital or Criminal as Civil, both marine and other, all such, our subjects and other, as shall, from time to time hereafter, adventure themselves in the said Journeys or voyages, or that shall, at any time hereafter, inhabit any such lands, Countries, or territories as aforesaid, or that shall abide within two hundred leagues of any the said place or places where the said Walter Raleigh, or his heirs or assigns, or any of them, or any of his or their Associates or Companies, shall Inhabit within six years next ensuing the date hereof; according to such statutes, laws, and ordinances as shall be, by him, the said Walter Raleighe, his heirs and assigns, and every or any of them, devised or established for the better government of the said people, as aforesaid;

So always, that the said statutes, laws, and ordinances may be, as near as conveniently they may be, agreeable to the form of the laws, statutes, government, or policy of England; and also, so as they be not against the true Christian faith or Religion, now professed in the Church of England; nor in any wise to withdraw any of the subjects or people of those lands or places from the allegiance of us, our heirs and successors, As their immediate Sovereigns under God.

And further, we do, by these presents, for us, our heirs and successors, give and grant full power and authority to our trusty and well-beloved Counsellor, Sir William Cecill, Knight, Lord Burghley, our High Treasurer of England, and to the Lord Treasurer of England of us, our heirs and successors, for the time being, and to the Privy council

of us, our heirs and successors, or any four or more of them, for the time being, That he, they, or any four or more of them shall and may, from time to time, and at all times hereafter, under his or their hands or seals, by virtue of these presents, authorize and license the said Walter Raleighe, his heirs and assigns, and every or any of them, by him and themselves, or by their, or any of their, sufficient Attorneys, Deputies, Officers, ministers, factors, and servants, to embark and transport out of our Realms of England and Ireland, or the Dominions thereof, all or any of his or their, or any of their, goods, and all or any the goods of his and their associates and Companies, and every or any of them; with such other necessaries and commodities of any our Realms as to the said Lord Treasurer, or four or more of the Privy Council of us, our heirs or Successors, for the time being, as aforesaid, shall be, from time to time, by his or their wisdoms or discretions, thought meet and convenient for the better Relief and support of him, the said Walter Raleighe, his heirs and assigns, and every or any of them, and of his or their, and every or any of their, associates and Companies; Any Act, statute, law, or other thing to the Contrary in any wise notwithstanding.

Provided always, and our will and pleasure is, And we do hereby declare to all Christian Kings, Princes, and states, that, if the said Walter Raleigh, his heirs or assigns, or any of them, or any other by their license or appointment, shall, at any time or times hereafter, rob or spoil, by sea or by land, or do any act of unjust and unlawful hostility to any the subjects of us, our heirs and successors, or to any of the subjects of any King, Prince, Ruler, Governor, or state, being then in perfect League and amity with us, our heirs and successors, And that, upon such Injury, or upon just Complaint of any such Prince, Ruler, Governor, or state, and their subjects, we, our heirs and successors, shall make open proclamation within any the ports of our Realm of England commodious:

That the said Walter Raleighe, his heirs or assigns, or any other to whom these our letters patents may extend, shall, within the term to be limited by such proclamation, make full restitution and satisfaction of all such injuries done, so as both we and the said Princes, and others so Complaining, may hold us and themselves fully contented;

And that, if the said Walter Raleigh, his heirs and assigns, shall not make, or cause to be made, satisfaction accordingly, within such times so to be limited, That then it shall be lawful to us, our heirs and successors, to put the said Walter Raleighe, his heirs, assigns, and adherents, and all the Inhabitants of the said places to be discovered as aforesaid, or any of them, out of our allegiance and protection;

And that, from and after such time of putting out of protection of, the said Walter Raleigh, his heirs, assigns, and adherents, and others, so to be put out; and the said places within their habitation, possession, and rule shall be out of our protection and allegiance, and free for all Princes and others to pursue with hostility as being not our subjects, nor by us any way to be avouched, maintained, or defended, nor to be held as any of ours, nor to our protection or Dominion or alliance any way belonging.

For that express mention of the clear yearly value or certainty of the premises, or any part thereof, or of any other gifts or grants by us, or any our Progenitors or predecessors, to the foresaid Walter Raleighe before this time made, in these presents be not expressed, or any other grant, ordinance, provision, proclamation, or restraint to the contrary thereof before this time made, given, ordained, or provided, or any other thing, cause, or matter whatsoever in any wise notwithstanding.

In witness whereof, etc. Witness, our self, at Westminster, the five and twentieth day of March.

per breve de privato sigillo

[Transcribed from a photostatic copy of the enrollment of the charter on the patent roll. Manuscript in the British Public Record Office, London. Reference: C. 66/1237. Photostatic copy deposited in the State Department of Archives and History, Raleigh, North Carolina.]

Charter to the Virginia Company

April 10, 1606

INTRODUCTION

On April 10, 1606, King James I granted a charter conferring rights in America upon two closely associated groups known as the Virginia Company. The territory included in this grant was a strip one hundred miles wide extending along the Atlantic coast from the mouth of the Cape Fear River through about half of the modern state of Maine. One of the groups, consisting chiefly of residents of London, was allotted the southern portion of this region, which included most of the coastal section of modern North Carolina. The other group, chiefly from Bristol, Exeter, and Plymouth, was assigned the northern portion of the territory granted.

The Virginia Company received its charter only about three years after the last expedition sent to "Virginia" by Raleigh. The company, which was an outgrowth of the Gilbert and Raleigh colonization activities, included among its members some of the participants in those enterprises. Among these were Raleigh Gilbert, who was Sir Humphrey's youngest son, and the younger Richard Hakluyt, who had been an ardent supporter of the earlier undertakings. Sir Thomas Smith, the foremost merchant of London, who also had supported some of the earlier expeditions, took a prominent role in directing the new enterprise.

Organizers of the Virginia Company utilized in various ways the experience gained by Gilbert and Raleigh. Conscious of the financial weakness of the earlier enterprises, which were supported chiefly by land owners, they sought support from the wealthy merchant class. Instead of organizing as small groups of "associates," such as those which had supported Gilbert and Raleigh, the Virginia Company promoters formed one large company. This afforded advantages in legal status as well as in resources. The new company also benefitted from geographical knowledge obtained by earlier expeditions. Without further exploration, the London group sent its colony to the Chesapeake region, which had been recommended by the Lane colonists as a favorable site.

The crown granted less extensive privileges to the Virginia Company than those which had been granted to Gilbert and Raleigh. The territory involved in the new charter was restricted to a prescribed region. The company was not

given the right to own land, although it could parcel out land among settlers, to be granted to them by patents from the king. Governmental authority over colonies was reserved by the crown, to be exercised by a council resident in London, appointed and instructed by the king. The authority of the company chiefly consisted of recruiting, transporting, and supplying colonists, conducting trade, and handling other financial matters. Colonists were guaranteed the rights of Englishmen at home, such as trial by jury, habeas corpus, and the right to own and inherit property, but they were not given right to participate in government.

In May, 1607, a colony sent out by the London group of the Virginia Company reached the Chesapeake region. The colonists settled on a peninsula (that later became an island) near the mouth of the James River, in the present-day state of Virginia. Known first as James Fort and later as Jamestown, this settlement became the first permanent English colony in America. Its members explored the area to the south, which is now part of North Carolina, and made some effort to find Raleigh's lost colonists. About fifty years later, colonists from the Virginia settlements moved into the Albemarle Sound region, near the site of the former Roanoke colonies, and became the first permanent settlers in the area later named North Carolina.

Experience with the Jamestown colony soon indicated need for changes in the charter. The London group petitioned for a new grant, which was issued in 1609.

THE DOCUMENT

JAMES, by the grace of God, etc.

Whereas, our loving and well-disposed subjects, Sir Thomas Gates and Sir George Somers, Knights; Richarde Hackluit, Clerk, prebendary of Westminster; and Edwarde Maria Winghfeilde, Thomas Hannam, and Raleighe Gilberde, Esquires; William Parker and George Popham, Gentlemen, and divers others of our loving subjects have been humble suitors unto us that we would vouchsafe unto them our licence to make habitation, plantation, and to deduce a Colony of sundry of our people into that part of America commonly called Virginia, and other parts and territories in America, either appertaining unto us or which are not now actually possessed by any Christian Prince or people, situate, lying, and being all along the sea Coasts between four and Thirty degrees of northerly latitude from the equinoctial line and Five and Forty degrees of the same latitude, and in the Main land between the same Four and Thirty, and Five and Forty degrees, and the Islands thereunto adjacent, or within one hundred Miles of the Coast thereof;

And to that end, and for the more speedy accomplishment of their said intended plantation and habitation there, are desirous to divide themselves into two several Colonies and Companies: the one consisting of certain Knights, Gentlemen, Merchants, and other Adventurers of our City of London and elsewhere, which are, and from time to time shall be, joined unto them which do desire to begin their plantations and habitations in some fit and convenient place between Four and Thirty, and one and Forty degrees of the said latitude, all along the Coast of Virginia and Coasts of America aforesaid; and the other consisting of sundry Knights, Gentlemen, Merchants, and other Adventurers of our Cities of Bristol and Exeter, and of our town of Plymouth, and of other places, which do join themselves unto that Colony which do desire to begin their plantations and habitations in some fit and convenient place between Eight and thirty degrees and Five and Forty degrees of the said latitude, all along the said Coast of Virginia and America, as that Coast lies:

We, greatly commending, and graciously accepting of, their desires to the furtherance of so noble a work, which may, by the providence of Almighty God, hereafter tend to the glory of His Divine Majesty, in propagating of Christian religion to such people as yet live in darkness and miserable ignorance of the true knowledge and worship of God, and may in time bring the infidels and savages living in those parts to hu-

man civility and to a settled and quiet government, do, by these our letters Patents, graciously accept of, and agree to, their humble and well-intended desires;

And do, therefore, for us, our heirs and successors, grant and agree that the said Sir Thomas Gates, Sir George Sumers, Richarde Hackluit, and Edwarde Maria Winghfeilde, Adventurers of and for our City of London, and all such others as are or shall be joined unto them of that Colony, shall be called the first Colony;

And they shall and may begin their said first plantation and seat of their first abode and habitation at any place upon the said Coast of Virginia or America where they shall think fit and convenient, between the said four and thirty, and one and Forty degrees of the said latitude;

And that they shall have all the lands, woods, soil, Grounds, havens, ports, Rivers, Mines, Minerals, Marshes, waters, Fishings, Commodities, and hereditaments whatsoever, from the said first seat of their plantation and habitation, by the space of Fifty Miles of English statute measure, all along the said Coast of Virginia and America towards the west and southwest, as the Coast lies, with all the Islands within one hundred Miles directly over against the same sea Coast;

And also, all the lands, soil, Grounds, havens, Ports, Rivers, Mines, Minerals, Woods, Marshes, Waters, Fishings, Commodities, and hereditaments whatsoever, from the said place of their first plantation and habitation, for the space of Fifty like English Miles, all along the said Coast of Virginia and America towards the East and Northeast, as the Coast lies, together with all the Islands within one hundred Miles directly over against the same sea Coast;

And also, all the lands, woods, soil, Grounds, havens, ports, Rivers, Mines, Minerals, Marshes, Waters, Fishings, Commodities, and hereditaments whatsoever, from the same Fifty Miles every way on the sea Coast, directly into the main land, by the space of One hundred like English miles;

And shall and may inhabit and remain there; and shall and may also build and fortify within any the same, for their better safeguard and defence, according to their best discretions and the direction of the Council of that Colony; and that no other of our subjects shall be permitted or suffered to plant or inhabit behind or on the backside of them towards the Main land, without the express licence or consent of the Council of that Colony thereunto in writing first had or obtained.

And we do likewise, for us, our heirs and successors, by these presents, grant and agree that the said Thomas Hannam and Raleighe

Gilberde, William Parker and George Popham, and all others of the town of Plymouth in the County of Devon, or elsewhere, which are or shall be joined unto them of that Colony, shall be called the second Colony; and that they shall and may begin their said first plantation and seat of their first abode and habitation at any place upon the said Coast of Virginia and America where they shall think fit and convenient, between Eight and Thirty degrees of the said latitude and Five and Forty degrees of the same Latitude;

And that they shall have all the lands, soil, Grounds, havens, Ports, Rivers, Mines, Minerals, woods, Marshes, waters, Fishings, Commodities, and hereditaments whatsoever, from the first seat of their plantation and habitation, by the space of Fifty like English Miles, as is aforesaid, all along the said Coast of Virginia and America towards the west and southwest, or towards the south, as the Coast lies, and all the Islands within one hundred Miles directly over against the said sea Coast;

And also, all the lands, soil, Grounds, havens, ports, Rivers, Mines, Minerals, Woods, Marshes, Waters, Fishings, Commodities, and hereditaments whatsoever, from the said place of their first plantation and habitation, for the space of Fifty like Miles, all along the said Coast of Virginia and America towards the East and Northeast, or towards the North, as the Coast lies, and all the Islands also within one hundred Miles directly over against the same sea Coast;

And also, all the lands, soil, Grounds, havens, ports, Rivers, woods, Mines, Minerals, Marshes, waters, Fishings, Commodities, and hereditaments whatsoever, from the same Fifty Miles every way on the sea Coast, directly into the main land, by the space of one hundred like English Miles;

And shall and may inhabit and remain there; and shall and may also build and fortify within any the same, for their better safeguard, according to their best discretions and the direction of the Council of that Colony; and that none of our subjects shall be permitted or suffered to plant or inhabit behind or on the back of them towards the Main land, without the express licence or consent of the Council of that Colony in writing thereunto first had and obtained;

Provided always, and our will and pleasure herein is, that the plantation and habitation of such of the said Colonies as shall last plant themselves, as aforesaid, shall not be made within one hundred like English Miles of the other of them that first began to make their plantation, as aforesaid.

And we do, also, ordain, establish, and agree, for us, our heirs and

successors, that each of the said Colonies shall have a Council, which shall govern and order all matters and Causes which shall arise, grow, or happen to or within the same several Colonies, according to such laws, ordinances, and Instructions as shall be in that behalf given and signed with our hand, or sign manual, and pass under the privy seal of our Realm of England;

Each of which Councils shall consist of Thirteen persons, and to be ordained, made, and removed from time to time according as shall be directed and comprised in the same Instructions; and shall have a several seal for all matters that shall pass or concern the same several Councils; Each of which seals shall have the King's Arms engraved on the one side thereof and his portrait on the other;

And that the seal for the Council of the said first Colony shall have engraved round about on the one side these words: *Sigillum Regis Magne Britanie Francie et Hibernie;* on the other side, this Inscription round about: *Pro Consilio Prime Colonie Virginie;*

And the seal for the Council of the said second Colony shall also have engraved round about the one side thereof the foresaid words: *Sigillum Regis Magne Britanie Francie et Hibernie;* and on the other side: *Pro Consilio Secunde Colonie Virginie;*

And that, also, there shall be a Council established here in England, which shall, in like manner, consist of thirteen persons, to be for that purpose appointed by us, our heirs and successors, which shall be called our Council of Virginia;

And shall, from time to time, have the superior managing and direction only of and for all matters that shall or may concern the government as well of the said several Colonies as of and for any other part or place within the aforesaid precincts of Four and thirty, and Five and Forty degrees above mentioned; which Council shall, in like manner, have a seal for matters concerning the Council, with the like Arms and portrait as aforesaid, with this inscription engraved round about the one side: *Sigillum Regis Magne Britanie Francie et Hibernie;* and round about the other side: *Pro Consilio Suo Virginie.*

And moreover, we do grant and agree, for us, our heirs and successors, that the said several Councils of and for the said several Colonies shall, and lawfully may, by virtue hereof, from time to time, without interruption of us, our heirs or successors, give and take order to dig, mine, and search for all manner of Mines of Gold, silver, and Copper, as well within any part of their said several Colonies as of the said Main

lands on the backside of the same Colonies; and to have and enjoy the Gold, silver, and Copper to be gotten thereof, to the use and behoof of the same Colonies and the plantations thereof; yielding therefor, yearly, to us, our heirs and successors, the Fifth part only of all the same Gold and silver, and the Fifteenth part of all the same Copper, so to be gotten or had as is aforesaid; without any other manner of profit or Account to be given or yielded to us, our heirs or successors, for or in respect of the same;

And that they shall, or lawfully may, establish and cause to be made a coin, to pass current there between the people of those several Colonies, for the more ease of traffic and bargaining between and amongst them and the natives there, of such metal and in such manner and form as the same several Councils there shall limit and appoint.

And we do likewise, for us, our heirs and successors, by these presents, give full power and authority to the said Sir Thomas Gates, Sir George Sumers, Richarde Hackluit, Edwarde Maria Winghfeilde, Thomas Hannam, Raleighe Gilberde, William Parker, and George Popham, and to every of them, and to the said several Companies, plantations, and Colonies, that they, and every of them, shall and may, at all and every time and times hereafter, have, take, and lead in the said voyage, and for and towards the said several plantations and Colonies, and to travel thitherward, and to abide and inhabit there, in every of the said Colonies and Plantations, such and so many of our subjects as shall willingly accompany them, or any of them, in the said voyages and plantations, with sufficient shipping and furniture of Armour, Weapons, ordnance, powder, victuals, and all other things necessary for the said plantations and for their use and defence there;

Provided always, that none of the said persons be such as hereafter shall be specially restrained by us, our heirs or successors.

Moreover, we do, by these presents, for us, our heirs and successors, give and grant Licence unto the said Sir Thomas Gates, Sir George Sumers, Richarde Hackluite, Edwarde Maria Winghfeilde, Thomas Hannam, Raleighe Gilberde, William Parker, and George Popham, and to every of the said Colonies, that they, and every of them, shall and may, from time to time, and at all times forever hereafter, for their several defences, encounter or expulse, repel, and resist, as well by sea as by land, by all ways and means whatsoever, all and every such person and persons as, without especial Licence of the said several Colonies and plantations, shall attempt to inhabit within the said several precincts

and limits of the said several Colonies and plantations, or any of them, or that shall enterprise or attempt, at any time hereafter, the hurt, detriment, or annoyance of the said several Colonies or plantations;

Giving and granting, by these presents, unto the said Sir Thomas Gates, Sir George Somers, Richarde Hackluite, and Edwarde Maria Winghfeilde, and their Associates of the said first Colony, and unto the said Thomas Hannam, Raleighe Gilberde, William Parker, and George Popham, and their Associates of the said second Colony, and to every of them, from time to time, and at all times forever hereafter, power and authority to take and surprise, by all ways and means whatsoever, all and every person and persons, with their ships, vessels, Goods, and other furniture, which shall be found trafficking into any harbor or harbors, Creek, Creeks, or place within the limits or precincts of the said several Colonies and plantations, not being of the same Colony, until such time as they, being of any Realms or Dominions under our obedience, shall pay or agree to pay to the hands of the Treasurer of that Colony, within whose limits and precincts they shall so traffic, two and a half upon any hundred of any thing so by them trafficked, bought, or sold; and being strangers, and not subjects under our obeisance, until they shall pay Five upon every hundred of such Wares and Commodities as they shall traffic, buy, or sell within the precincts of the said several Colonies, wherein they shall so traffic, buy, or sell as aforesaid; which sums of money or benefit, as aforesaid, for and during the space of one and Twenty years next ensuing the date hereof, shall be wholly employed to the use, benefit, and behoof of the said several plantations where such traffic shall be made; And after the said one and Twenty years ended, the same shall be taken to the use of us, our heirs and successors, by such officer and Minister as by us, our heirs and successors, shall be thereunto assigned or appointed.

And we do further, by these presents, for us, our heirs and successors, give and grant unto the said Sir Thomas Gates, Sir George Sumers, Richarde Hackluit, and Edwarde Maria Winghfeilde, and to their Associates of the said first Colony and plantation, and to the said Thomas Hannam, Raleighe Gilberde, William Parker, and George Popham, and their Associates of the said second Colony and plantation, that they, and every of them, by their Deputies, Ministers, and Factors, may transport the Goods, Chattels, Armour, munition, and furniture needful to be used by them, for their said Apparel, defence, or otherwise in respect of the said plantations, out of our Realms of England and Ireland, and all other our dominions, from time to time, for and during the time of

seven years next ensuing the date hereof, for the better relief of the said several Colonies and plantations, without any Custom, subsidy, or other duty unto us, our heirs or successors, to be yielded or paid for the same.

Also, we do, for us, our heirs and successors, declare, by these presents, that all and every the persons, being our subjects, which shall dwell and inhabit within every or any of the said several Colonies and plantations, and every of their children which shall happen to be born within the limits and precincts of the said several Colonies and plantations, shall have and enjoy all liberties, Franchises, and Immunities within any of our other Dominions, to all intents and purposes as if they had been abiding and born within this our Realm of England, or any other of our said Dominions.

Moreover, our gracious will and pleasure is, and we do, by these presents, for us, our heirs and successors, declare and set forth, that if any person or persons which shall be of any of the said Colonies and plantations, or any other which shall traffic to the said Colonies and plantations, or any of them, shall, at any time or times hereafter, transport any wares, Merchandise, or Commodities out of our Dominions with a pretence and purpose to land, sell, or otherwise dispose the same within any the limits and precincts of any of the said Colonies and plantations, And yet, nevertheless, being at the sea or after he has landed the same within any of the said Colonies and plantations, shall carry the same into any other foreign Country with a purpose there to sell or dispose of the same, without the licence of us, our heirs or successors, in that behalf first had or obtained, That then, all the Goods and Chattels of the said person or persons so offending and transporting, together with the said ship or vessel wherein such transportation was made, shall be forfeited to us, our heirs and successors.

Provided always, and our will and pleasure is, and we do hereby declare to all Christian Kings, Princes, and states, that if any person or persons which shall hereafter be of any of the said several Colonies and plantations, or any other by his, their, or any of their Licence or appointment, shall, at any time or times hereafter, rob or spoil, by sea or by land, or do any Act of unjust and unlawful hostility to any the subjects of us, our heirs or successors, or any of the subjects of any King, Prince, Ruler, Governor, or state, being then in league or Amity with us, our heirs or successors, and that, upon such Injury, or upon just complaint of such Prince, Ruler, Governor, or state, or their subjects, we, our heirs or successors, shall make open proclamation within any the ports of our Realm of England commodious for that purpose: that the said person or per-

sons having committed any such Robbery or spoil shall, within the term to be limited by such Proclamations, make full restitution or satisfaction of all such Injuries done, so as the said Princes, or others so complained, may hold themselves fully satisfied and contented; and that, if the said person or persons having committed such robbery or spoil shall not make, or cause to be made, satisfaction, accordingly with such time so to be limited, That then it shall be lawful to us, our heirs and successors, to put the said person or persons having committed such robbery or spoil, and their procurers, Abettors, or Comforters, out of our allegiance and protection; and that it shall be lawful and free for all Princes and others to pursue with hostility the said Offenders, and every of them, and their, and every of their, procurers, Aiders, Abettors, and comforters in that behalf.

And finally, we do, for us, our heirs and successors, grant and agree to and with the said Sir Thomas Gates, Sir George Sumers, Richarde Hackluit, and Edwarde Maria Winghfeilde, and all others of the said first Colony:

That we, our heirs or successors, upon petition in that behalf to be made, shall, by letters Patents, under the great [Seal] of England, give and grant unto such persons, their heirs and Assigns, as the Council of that Colony, or the most part of them, shall for that purpose nominate and assign, all the lands, tenements, and hereditaments which shall be within the precincts limited for that Colony, as is aforesaid;

To be held of us, our heirs and successors, as of our Manor of East Greenwich, in the County of Kent, in free and Common Soccage only, and not in Capite.

And do, in like manner, grant and agree, for us, our heirs and successors, to and with the said Thomas Hannam, Raleighe Gilberd, William Parker, and George Popham, and all others of the said second Colony:

That we, our heirs or successors, upon petition in that behalf to be made, shall, by letters Patents, under the great Seal of England, give and grant unto such persons, their heirs and Assigns, as the Council of that Colony, or the most part of them, shall for that purpose nominate and assign, all the lands, tenements, and hereditaments which shall be within the precincts limited for that Colony, as is aforesaid;

To be held of us, our heirs and successors, as of our Manor of East Greenwich, in the County of Kent, in free and Common Soccage only, and not in Capite.

All which lands, tenements, and hereditaments, so to be passed by

the said several letters Patents, shall be, by sufficient Assurance from the same patentees, so distributed and divided amongst the undertakers for the plantation of the said several Colonies and such as shall make their plantation in either of the said several Colonies, in such manner and form, and for such estates, as shall be ordered and set down by the Council of the same Colony, or the most part of them, respectively, within which the same lands, tenements, and hereditaments shall lie or be.

Although express mention, etc.

In witness whereof, etc.

Witness, our self, at Westminster, the tenth day of April.

per breve de privato sigillo, etc.

[Transcribed from a photostatic copy of the enrollment of the charter on the patent roll. Manuscript in British Public Record Office, London. Reference: C. 66/1709. Photostatic copy deposited in the State Department of Archives and History, Raleigh, North Carolina.]

Charter to the Virginia Company of London

May 23, 1609

INTRODUCTION

A charter issued to the London group of the Virginia Company passed the great seal on May 23, 1609. This group was now incorporated as the Treasurer and Company of Adventurers and Planters of the City of London for the First Colony in Virginia.

The new charter granted additional territory and conferred upon the company rights of ownership over this and the territory formerly assigned to the London group; it also gave the company the right to sub-grant land to settlers and shareholders. This charter abolished the old royal council and placed direction of company affairs and the government of colonies in the hands of an elective treasurer and council. Although members who were to serve as the first treasurer and council were named in the charter, shareholders in the company were given the right to elect officers to replace them when vacancies occurred. These changes gave the company authority over its own affairs, including the government of colonies, and raised the status of the average shareholder. The new charter also revised the financial structure of the company, which made the company more attractive to prospective shareholders.

Acting under their new authority to govern colonies, the treasurer and council of the company abolished the local council at Jamestown, which had been ineffective, and placed a governor with an advisory council in charge of the colony. The governors, who had almost dictatorial powers, brought order to the colony, but they paid little regard to the "liberties, franchises, and immunities" of settlers.

Despite the changes effected under the new charter, the company failed to prosper. Settlers at Jamestown died from disease and starvation. Ships sent to supply and reinforce the colonists were wrecked. The financial resources of the company continued to be inadequate. Stockholders became discontented at lack of profits and lack of influence. Desire to establish a new colony in the Bermuda Islands was thwarted, for the Bermudas lay outside the boundaries of the grant. In an attempt to solve these problems, another charter was granted in 1612.

THE DOCUMENT

JAMES, by the grace of God, etc. To all, etc.

Whereas, at the humble suit and request of sundry our loving and well-disposed subjects intending to deduce a Colony and to make habitation and plantation of sundry of our people in that part of America commonly called Virginia, and other parts and Territories in America, either appertaining unto us or which are not actually possessed of any Christian Prince or people within certain bounds and Regions, we have formerly, by our letters patents, bearing date the tenth of April in the Fourth year of our reign of England, France, and Ireland, and the nine and thirtieth of Scotland, granted to Sir Thomas Gates, Sir George Somers, and others, for the more speedy accomplishment of the said plantation and habitation, that they should divide themselves into two Colonies, the one, consisting of divers knights, Gentlemen, Merchants, and others of our City of London, called the First Colony, And the other, of sundry knights, gentlemen, and others of the Cities of Bristol, Exeter, the town of Plymouth, and other places, called the second Colony; And have yielded and granted main, and sundry privileges and liberties, to each Colony, for their quiet settling and good government therein, as by the said letters patents more at large appears;

Now, forasmuch as divers and sundry of our loving subjects, as well Adventurers as planters of the said First Colony, which have already engaged them selves in furthering the business of the said plantation, and do further intend, by the assistance of Almighty God, to prosecute the same to a happy end, have of late been humble suitors unto us that, in respect of their great charges and the adventure of many of their lives, which they have hazarded in the said discovery and plantation of the said Country, we would be pleased to grant them a further enlargement and explanation of the said grant, privileges, and liberties, and that such Councillors and other officers may be appointed amongst them to manage and direct their affairs, and are willing and ready to adventure with them, as also, whose dwellings are not so far remote from the City of London but that they may, at convenient times, be ready at hand to give advice and assistance upon all occasions requisite:

We, greatly affecting the effectual prosecution and happy success of the said plantation, and commending their good desires therein, for their further encouragement in accomplishing so excellent a work, much pleasing to God and profitable to our Kingdoms, Do, of our special grace, and certain knowledge, and mere motion, for us, our heirs and

successors, give, grant, and confirm to our trusty and well-beloved subjects: Robert, Earl of Salisburie; Thomas, Earl of Suffolke; Henrie, Earl of Southampton; William, Earl of Pembroke; Henrie, Earl of Lincoln; ——,[1] Earl of Dorsett; Thomas, Earl of Exeter; Phillipp, Earl of Mountgomery; Robert, Lord Viscount Lisle; Theoplilus, Lord Howard of Walden; James Mountague, Lord Bishop of Bathe and Welles; Edward, Lord Zouche; Thomas, Lord Lawarr; William, Lord Mounteagle; Raphe, Lord Ewre; Edmond, Lord Sheffeild; Grey, Lord Shandis; ——, Lord Compton; John, Lord Petre; John, Lord Stanhope; George, Lord Carew; Sir Humfrey Welde, Lord Mayor of London; George Percie, Esquire; Sir Edward Cecill, knight; Sir George Wharton, knight; Franncis West, Esquire; Sir William Waade, knight; Sir Henrie Nevill, knight; Sir Thomas Smithe, knight; Sir Oliver Cromwell, knight; Sir Peter Manwood, knight; Sir Dru Drurie, knight; Sir John Scott, knight; Sir Thomas Challoner, knight; Sir Robert Drurie, knight; Sir Anthonye Cope, knight; Sir Horatio Veere, knight; Sir Edward Conwaie, knight; Sir William Browne; Sir Maurice Barkeley, knight; Sir Roberte Maunsell, knight; Sir Amias Preston, knight; Sir Thomas Gates, knight; Sir Anthonie Ashley, knight; Sir Michaell Sandes, knight; Sir Henrie Carew, knight; Sir Stephen Soame, knight; Sir Calisthenes Brooke, knight; Sir Edward Michelborne, knight; Sir John Ratcliffe, knight; Sir Charles Willmott, knight; Sir George Moore, knight; Sir Hugh Wirrall, knight; Sir Thomas Dennys, knight; Sir John Hollis, knight; Sir William Godolphin, knight; Sir Thomas Monnson, knight; Sir Thomas Ridgwaie, knight; Sir John Brooke, knight; Sir Roberte Killigrew, knight; Sir Henrie Peyton, knight; Sir Richard Williamson, knight; Sir Ferdinando Weynman, knight; Sir William St. John, knight; Sir Thomas Holcrofte, knight; Sir John Mallory, knight; Sir Roger Ashton, knight; Sir Walter Cope, knight; Sir Richard Wigmore, knight; Sir William Cooke, knight; Sir Herberte Crofte, knight; Sir Henrie Fanshawe, knight; Sir John Smith, knight; Sir Franncis Wolley, knight; Sir Edward Waterhouse, knight; Sir Henrie Sekeford, knight; Sir Edwarde Sandes, knight; Sir Thomas Wayneman, knight; Sir John Trevor, knight; Sir Warrwick Heale, knight; Sir Robert Wroth, knight; Sir John Townesende, knight; Sir Christopher Perkins, knight; Sir Daniell Dun, knight; Sir Henrie Hobarte, knight; Sir Franncis Bacon, knight; Sir Henrie Mountague, knight; Sir Georg Coppin, knight; Sir Samuell Sandes, knight; Sir Thomas Roe, knight; Sir George Somers, knight; Sir Thomas Freake, knight; Sir

[1] A blank in the manuscript is indicated thus: ——.

Thomas Horwell, knight; Sir Charles Kelke, knight; Sir Baptist Hickes, knight; Sir John Wattes, knight; Sir Roberte Carey, knight; Sir William Romney, knight; Sir Thomas Middleton, knight; Sir Hatton Cheeke, knight; Sir John Ogle, knight; Sir Cavallero Meycot, knight; Sir Stephen Riddlesden, knight; Sir Thomas Bludder, knight; Sir Anthonie Aucher, knight; Sir Robert Johnson, knight; Sir Thomas Panton, knight; Sir Charles Morgan, knight; Sir Stephen Powle, knight; Sir John Burlacie, knight; Sir Christofer Cleane, knight; Sir George Hayward, knight; Sir Thomas Dane, knight; Sir Thomas Dutton, knight; Sir Anthonie Forest, knight; Sir Robert Payne, knight; Sir John Digby, knight; Sir Dudley Digges, knight; Sir Rowland Cotton, knight; Doctor Mathewe Sutcliffe; Doctor ____ Meddowes; Doctor ____ Turner; Doctor ____ Poe; Captain ____ Pagnam; Captain Jeffrey Holcrofte; Captain ____ Raunne; Captain Henrie Spry; Captain ____ Shelpton; Captain ____ Sparkes; Thomas Wyatt; Captain ____ Brinsley; Captain William Courtney; Captain ____ Herbert; Captain ____ Clarke; Captain ____ Dewhurst; Captain John Blundell; Captain Frier; Captain Lewis Orwell; Captain Edward Lloyd; Captain Slingesby; Captain ____ Huntley; Captain ____ Orme; Captain Woodhouse; Captain ____ Mason; Captain Thomas Holcroft; Captain John Cooke; Captain ____ Hollis; Captain William Proude; Captain Henrie Woodhouse; Captain Richard Lindeley; Captain ____ Dexter; Captain William Winter; Captain ____ Herle; Captain John Bingham; Captain ____ Burray; Captain Thomas Conwey; Captain ____ Rookwood; Captain William Lovelace; Captain John Ashley; Captain Thomas Wynne; Captain Thomas Mewtis; Captain Edward Harwood; Captain Michaell Evered; Captain ____ Connoth; Captain ____ Miles; Captain ____ Pigott; Captain Edward Maria Wingfeild; Captain Christopher Newporte; Captain John Siclemore, alias Ratcliffe; Captain John Smith; Captain John Martyn; Captain Peter Wynne; Captain Waldoe; Captain Thomas Wood; Captain Thomas Button; George Bolls, Esquire, Sheriff of London; William Crashawe, Bachelor of Divinity; William Seabright, Esquire; Christopher Brookes, Esquire; John Bingley, Esquire; Thomas Watson, Esquire; Richard Percivall, Esquire; John Moore, Esquire; Hugh Brooker, Esquire; David Waterhouse, Esquire; Anthonie Aucher, Esquire; Roberte Bowyer, Esquire; Raphe Ewens, Esquire; Zacharie Jones, Esquire; George Calvert, Esquire; William Dobson, Esquire; Henry Reynoldes, Esquire; Thomas Walker, Esquire; Anthonie Barnars, Esquire; Thomas Sandes, Esquire; Henrie Sandes, Esquire; Richard Sandes, son of Sir Edwin Sandes; William Oxenbridge, Esquire; John Moore, Esquire; Thomas Wilson, Esquire; John Bullocke, Esquire; John

Waller; Thomas Webb; Jehughe Robinson; William Brewster; Robert Evelyn; Henrie Dabenie; Richard Hacklewte, Minister; John Eldred, Merchant; William Russell, Merchant; John Merrick, Merchant; Richard Bannester, Merchant; Charles Anthonie, Goldsmith; John Banckes; William Evans; Richard Humble; Robert Chamberleyne, Merchant; Thomas Barber, Merchant; Richard Penxtell, Merchant; John Fletcher, Merchant; Thomas Nicholls, Merchant; John Stoakes, Merchant; Gabriell Archer; Franncis Covell; William Bonham; Edward Harrison; John Wolstenholme; Nicholas Salter; Hugh Evans; William Barners; Otho Mawdett; Richard Staper, Merchant; John Elkin, Merchant; William Coyse; Thomas Perkin, Cooper; Humfrey Ramell, Cooper; Henry Jackson; Roberte Shingleton; Christopher Nicholls; John Harper; Abraham Chamberlaine; Thomas Shipton; Thomas Carpenter; Anthonie Crewe; George Holman; Robert Hill; Cleophas Smithe; Raphe Harrison; John Farmer; James Brearley; William Crosley; Richard Cockes; John Gearinge; Richard Strough, Ironmonger; Thomas Langton; Griffith Hinton; Richard Ironside; Richard Deane; Richard Turner; William Leveson, Mercer; James Chatfeilde; Edward Allen; Tedder Robertes; Heldebrand Sprinson; Arthure Mouse; John Gardener; James Russell; Richard Casewell; Richard Evanns; John Hawkins; Richard Kerrill; Richard Brooke; Mathewe Scrivener, gentleman; William Stallendge, gentleman; Arthure Venn, gentleman; Sanndes Webb, gentleman; Michaell Phettiplace, gentleman; William Phetiplace, gentleman; Ambrose Brusey, gentleman; John Taverner, gentleman; George Pretty, gentleman; Peter Latham, gentleman; Thomas Monnford, gentleman; William Cantrell, gentleman; Richard Wiffine, gentleman; Raphe Mooreton, gentleman; John Cornellis; Martyn Freeman; Raphe Freeman; Andreau Moore; Thomas White; Edward Perkin; Roberte Offley; Thomas Whitley; George Pitt; Roberte Parkehurste; Thomas Morris; Peter Vaulore; Jeffrey Duppa; John Gilbert; William Hancock; Mathew Bromrigg; Francis Tirrell; Randall Carter; Othowell Smithe; Thomas Honnyman; Marten Bonde, Haberdasher; Joan Mousloe; Roberte Johnson; William Younge; John Woddall; William Felgate; Humfrey Westwood; Richard Champion; Henrie Robinson; Franncis Mapes; William Sambatch; Rauley Crashawe; Daniell Tucker; Thomas Grave; Hugh Willestone; Thomas Culpepper of Wigsell, Esquire; John Culpepper, gentleman; Henrie Lee; Josias Kirton, gentleman; John Porie, gentleman; Henrie Collins; George Burton; William Atkinson; Thomas Forrest; John Russell; John Houlte; Harman Harrison; Gabriell Beedell; John Beedell; Henrie Daukes; George Scott; Edward Fleetewood, gentleman; Richard Rogers, gentleman; Arthure

Robinson; Robert Robinson; John Huntley; John Grey; William Payne; William Feilde; William Wattey; William Webster; John Dingley; Thomas Draper; Richard Glanvile; Arnolde Lulls; Henrie Rowe; William Moore; Nicholas Grice; James Monnger; Nicholas Andrewes; Jerome Haydon, Ironmonger; Phillipp Durrant; John Quales; John West; Mathew Springeham; John Johnson; Christopher Hore; Thomas Sned; George Barkeley; Arthure Pett; Thomas Careles; William Barkley; Thomas Johnson; Alexander Bentes; Captain William Kinge; George Sandes, gentleman; James White, gentleman; Edmond Wynn; Charles Towler; Richard Reynoldes; Edward Webb; Richard Maplesden; Thomas Levers; David Bourne; Thomas Wood; Raphe Hamer; Edward Barnes, Mercer; John Wright, Mercer; Roberte Middleton; Edward Litsfeild; Katherine West; Thomas Webb; Raphe Kinge; Roberte Coppine; James Askewe; Cristopher Nicholls; William Bardwell; Alexander Childe; Lewes Tate; Edward Ditchfeilde; James Swifte; Richard Widdowes, Goldsmith; Edmonde Brudenell; John Hanford; Edward Wooller; William Palmer, haberdasher; John Badger; John Hodgson; Peter Monnsill; John Carrill; John Busbridge; William Dunn; Thomas Johnson; Nicholas Benson; Thomas Shipton; Nathaniell Wade; Randoll Wettwood; Mathew Dequester; Charles Hawkins; Hugh Hamersley; Abraham Carthwright; George Bennett; William Cattor; Richard Goddart; Henrie Cromwell; Phinees Pett; Roberte Cooper; Henrie Neice; Edward Wilkes; Roberte Bateman; Nicholas Farrar; John Newhouse; John Cason; Thomas Harris, gentleman; George Etheridge, gentleman; Thomas Mayle, gentleman; Richard Stratford; Thomas ——; Richard Cooper; John Westrowe; Edward Welshe; Thomas Brittaine; Thomas Knowls; Octavian Thorne; Edmonde Smyth; John March; Edward Carew; Thomas Pleydall; Richard Lea; Miles Palmer; Henrie Price; John Josua, gentleman; William Clawday; Jerome Pearsye; John Bree, gentleman; William Hampson; Christopher Pickford; Thomas Hunt; Thomas Truston; Christopher Lanman; John Haward, Clerk; Richarde Partridge; Allen Cotton; Felix Wilson; Thomas Colethurst; George Wilmer; Andrew Wilmer; Morrice Lewellin; Thomas Jedwin; Peter Burgoyne; Thomas Burgoyne; Roberte Burgoyne; Roberte Smithe, Merchant-tailor; Edward Cage, Grocer; Thomas Canon, gentleman; William Welby, Stationer; Clement Wilmer, gentleman; John Clapham, gentleman; Giles Frannces, gentleman; George Walker, Sadler; John Swinehowe, Stationer; Edward Bushoppe, Stationer; Leonard White, gentleman; Christopher Barron; Peter Benson; Richard Smyth; George Prockter, Minister; Millicent Ramesden, widow; Joseph Soane; Thomas

Hinshawe; John Baker; Roberte Thorneton; John Davies; Edward Facett; George Nuce, gentleman; John Robinson; Captain Thomas Wood; William Browne, Shoemaker; Roberte Barker, Shoemaker; Roberte Penington; Francis Burley, Minister; William Quick, Grocer; Edward Lewes, Grocer; Laurence Campe, Draper; Aden Perkins, Grocer; Richard Shepparde, Preacher; William Sheckley, Haberdasher; William Tayler, Haberdasher; Edward Lukyn, gentleman; John Francklyn, Haberdasher; John Southicke; Peter Peate; George Johan, Ironmonger; George Yardeley, gentleman; Henrie Shelley; John Pratt; Thomas Church, Draper; William Powell, gentleman; Richard Frithe, gentleman; Thomas Wheeler, Draper; Franncis Hasilerigg, gentleman; Hughe Shippley, gentleman; John Andrewes, the elder, of Cambridge; Franncis Whistler, gentleman; John Vassall, gentleman; Richard Howle; Edward Barkeley, gentleman; Richard Knerisborough, gentleman; Nicholas Exton, Draper; William Bennet, Fishmonger; James Hawood, Merchant; Nicholas Isaak, Merchant; William Gibbs, Merchant; ____ Bushopp; Barnard Michell; Isaake Michell; John Streat; Edward Gall; John Marten, gentleman; Thomas Fox; Luke Lodge; John Woodleefe, gentleman; Rice Webb; Vincent Lowe; Samuell Burnam; Edmonde Pears, Haberdasher; Josua Goudge; John St. John; Edwarde Vaughan; William Dunn; Thomas Alcock; John Andrewes, the younger, of Cambridge; Samuell Smithe; Thomas Jerrard; Thomas Whittingham; William Cannynge; Paule Canninge; George Chandler; Henrye Vincent; Thomas Ketley; James Skelton; James Montain; George Webb, gentleman; Josephe Newbroughesmith; Josias Mande; Raphe Haman, the younger; Edward Brewster, the son of William Brewster; Leonard Harwood, Mercer; Phillipp Druerdent; William Carpenter; Tristram Hill; Roberte Cockes, Grocer; Laurence Grene, Grocer; Daniell Winche, Grocer; Humfrey Stile, Grocer; Averie Dransfeild, Grocer; Edwarde Hodges, Grocer; Edward Beale, Grocer; Raphe Busby, Grocer; Raphe Busby, Grocer; [2] John Whittingham, Grocer; John Hide, Grocer; Mathew Shipperd, Grocer; Thomas Allen, Grocer; Richard Hooker, Grocer; Laurence Munckas, Grocer; John Tanner, Grocer; Peter Gate, Grocer; John Blunt, Grocer; Roberte Berrisford, Grocer; Roberte Berrisford, Grocer; [3] Thomas Wells, gentleman; John Ellis, Grocer; Henrie Colthurst, Grocer; John Cranage, Grocer; Thomas Jeninges, Grocer; Edmond Peshall, Grocer; Timothie Bathurst, Grocer; Gyles Parslowe, Grocer; Roberte Johnson, Grocer; William Janson, Vintner; Ezechiell Smith; Richard Murrettone; William Sharpe;

[2] Repetition in the manuscript.

[3] Repetition in the manuscript.

Roberte Ritche; William Stannerd, Innholder; John Stocken; William Strachey, gentleman; George Farmer, gentleman; Thomas Gypes, Cloth-worker; Abraham Dawes, gentleman; Thomas Brockett, gentleman; George Bathe, Fishmonger; John Dike, Fishmonger; Henrie Spranger; Richard Farringdon; Christopher Vertue, Vintner; Thomas Baley, Vintner; George Robins, Vintner; Tobias Hinson, Grocer; Urian Spencer; Clement Chitchelley; John Searpe, gentleman; James Cambell, Iron-monger; Christopher Clitherowe, Ironmonger; Phillipp Jacobson; Peter Jacobson of Andwarpe; William Barckley; Miles Banckes, Cutler; Peter Highley, Grocer; Henrie John, gentleman; John Stoakley, Merchant-tailor; the Company of Mercers; the Company of Grocers; the Company of Drapers; the company of Fishmongers; the company of Gold-smiths; the Company of Skinners; the company of Merchant-tailors; the Company of Haberdashers; the Company of Salters; the company of Iron-mongers; the company of Vintners; the company of Cloth-workers; the company of Dyers; the company of Brewers; the company of Leather-sellers; the company of Pewterers; the company of Cutlers; the Company of White-bakers; the company of Wax-chandlers; the company of Tallow-chandlers; the Company of Armorers; the company of Girdlers; the company of Butchers; the Company of Sadlers; the Company of Carpenters; the company of Cordwainers; the Company of Barber Chirurgeons; the company of Painter-stainers; the Company of Curriers; the company of Masons; the Company of Plumbers; the Company of Innholders; the company of Founders; the company of Poulterers; the company of Cooks; the company of Coopers; the company of Tilers and Bricklayers; the company of Bowyers; the company of Fletchers; the company of Blacksmiths; the company of Joiners; the company of Weavers; the company of Woolmen; the company of Woodmongers; the company of Scriveners; the company of Fruiterers; the company of Plasterers; the company of Brown-bakers; the company of Stationers; the company of Embroiderers; the company of Upholsterers; the company of Musicians; the company of Turners; the company of Basketmakers; the company of Glaziers; John Levett, Merchant; Thomas Nornicott, Cloth-worker; Richard Venn, Haberdasher; Thomas Scott, gentleman; Thomas Juxson, Merchant-tailor; George Hankinson; Thomas Leeyer, gentleman; Mathew Cooper; George Butler, gentleman; Thomas Lawson, gentleman; Edward Smith, Haberdasher; Stephen Sparrowe; John Jones, Merchant; ____ Reynoldes, Brewer; Thomas Plummer, Merchant; James Duppa, Brewer; Rowland Coytemore; William Sotherne; George Whittmoore, Haberdasher; Anthonie Gosoulde, the younger; John

Allen, Fishmonger; Symonde Yeomans, Fishmonger; Launcelot Davis, gentleman; John Hopkins, an Alderman of Bristoll; John Kettlebye, gentleman; Richard Chene, Goldsmith; George Hooker, gentleman; Roberte Sheninge, yeoman;

And to such and so many as they do, or shall hereafter, admit to be joined with them, in form hereafter in these presents expressed, whether they go in their persons to be planters there in the said plantation or whether they go not but do adventure their moneys, goods, or chattels, that they shall be one body, or commonalty, perpetual, and shall have perpetual succession, and one common Seal to serve for the said body, or commonalty; and that they, and their successors, shall be known, called, and incorporated by the name of the Treasurer and Company of Adventurers and planters of the City of London for the First Colony in Virginia.

And that they, and their successors, shall be, from henceforth forever, enabled to take, acquire, and purchase, by the name aforesaid, license for the same from us, our heirs or successors, first had and obtained, any manner of lands, tenements, and hereditaments, goods and chattels, within our Realm of England and dominion of Wales; and that they, and their successors, shall be likewise enabled, by the name aforesaid, to plead and to be impleaded before any of our judges or Justices in any our courts, and in any actions or suits whatsoever.

And we do, also, of our said special grace, certain knowledge, and mere motion, give, grant, and confirm unto the said Treasurer and Company, and their successors, under the reservations, limitations, and declarations hereafter expressed:

All those lands, Countries, and territories, situate, lying, and being in that place of America called Virginia, from the point of land called Cape or Point Comfort, all along the Seacoast to the Northward two hundred Miles; and from the said point of Cape Comfort, all along the Seacoast to the southward two hundred Miles; and all that space and circuit of land lying from the Seacoast of the precinct aforesaid up into the land, throughout from Sea to sea, West and Northwest; and also, all the Islands lying within one hundred Miles along the coast of both Seas of the precinct aforesaid; together with all the soils, grounds, havens, and ports, Mines, as well royal Mines of Gold and silver as other Minerals, pearls and precious stones, quarries, woods, rivers, waters, fishings, commodities, Jurisdictions, Royalties, privileges, franchises, and pre-eminences within the said territory and the precincts thereof whatsoever, and thereto or thereabouts, both by sea and land, being or in any sort belonging or ap-

pertaining, and which we, by our letters patents, may or can grant; and in as ample manner and sort as we, or any our noble Progenitors, have heretofore granted to any company, body politic or corporate, or to any adventurer or adventurers, undertaker or undertakers, of any discoveries, plantations, or traffic of, in, or into any foreign parts whatsoever; and in as large and ample manner as if the same were herein particularly mentioned and expressed;

To have, hold, possess, and enjoy all and singular the said lands, Countries, and territories, with all and singular other the premises heretofore by these granted or mentioned to be granted; to them, the said Treasurer and company, their successors and assigns, forever; to the sole and proper use of them, the said Treasurer and Company, their successors and assigns; to be held of us, our heirs and successors, as of our Manor of East Greenwich, in free and common Socage, and not in Capite;

Yielding and paying therefor, to us, our heirs and successors, the fifth part only of all Ore of gold and silver that, from time to time, and at all times hereafter, shall be there gotten, had, and obtained, for all manner of services.

And, Nevertheless, our will and pleasure is, and we do, by these presents, charge, command, warrant, and authorize, that the said Treasurer and Company, and their successors, or the major part of them which shall be present and assembled for that purpose, shall, from time to time, under their common Seal, distribute, convey, assign, and set over such particular portions of lands, tenements, and hereditaments, by these presents formerly granted, unto such our loving subjects, naturally born or Denizens or others, as well adventurers as planters, as by the said Company, upon a Commission of Survey and distribution executed and returned for that purpose, shall be named, appointed, and allowed; wherein, our will and pleasure is that respect be had as well of the proportion of the Adventure as to the special service, hazard, exploit, or merit of any person so to be recompensed, advanced, or rewarded.

And forasmuch as the good and prosperous success of the said plantation cannot but chiefly depend, next under the blessing of God and the support of our Royal authority, upon the provident and good direction of the whole enterprise by a careful and understanding Council, and that it is not convenient that all the adventurers shall be so often drawn to meet and assemble as shall be requisite for them to have meetings and conference about their affairs:

Therefore, we do ordain, establish, and confirm that there shall be perpetually one Council, here resident, according to the tenor of our

former letters Patents; which Council shall have a Seal for the better government and administration of the said plantation, besides the legal Seal of the Company or corporation, as in our former letters patents is also expressed.

And further, we establish and ordain that Henrie, Earl of Southampton; William, Earl of Pembrooke; Henrie, Earl of Lincoln; Thomas, Earl of Exeter; Roberte, Lord Viscount Lisle; Lord Theophilus Howard; James, Lord Bishop of Bathe and Wells; Edward, Lord Zouche; Thomas, Lord Laware; William, Lord Mounteagle; Edmunde, Lord Sheffeilde; Grey, Lord Shanndoys; John, Lord Stanhope; George, Lord Carew; Sir Humfrey Welde, Lord Mayor of London; Sir Edward Cecill; Sir William Waad; Sir Henrie Nevill; Sir Thomas Smith; Sir Oliver Cromwell; Sir Peter Manwood; Sir Thomas Challoner; Sir Henrie Hobarte; Sir Franncis Bacon; Sir George Coppin; Sir John Scott; Sir Henrie Carey; Sir Roberte Drurie; Sir Horatio Vere; Sir Edward Conwaye; Sir Maurice Berkeley; Sir Thomas Gates; Sir Michaell Sandes; Sir Roberte Mansfeild; Sir John Trevor; Sir Amyas Preston; Sir William Godolphin; Sir Walter Cope; Sir Robert Killigrewe; Sir Henrie Fanshawe; Sir Edwyn Sandes; Sir John Wattes; Sir Henrie Mountague; Sir William Romney; Sir Thomas Roe; Sir Baptiste Hickes; Sir Richard Williamson; Sir Stephen Powle; Sir Dudley Digges; Christopher Brooke; John Eldred; and John Wolstenholme shall be our Council for the said Company of Adventurers and planters in Virginia.

And the said Sir Thomas Smith we ordain to be Treasurer of the said Company; which Treasurer shall have authority to give order for the warning of the Council and summoning the company to their Courts and Meetings; and the said Council and Treasurer, or any of them, shall be from henceforth nominated, chosen, continued, displaced, changed, altered, and supplied, as death or other several occasions shall require, out of the Company of the said Adventurers, by the voice of the greater part of the said Council and adventurers in their assembly for that purpose;

Provided always, that every Councillor so newly elected shall be presented to the Lord Chancellor of England, or to the Lord High Treasurer of England, or the Lord Chamberlain of the household of us, our heirs and successors, for the time being, to take his oath of a Councillor to us, our heirs and successors, for the said Company and Colony in Virginia.

And we do, by these presents, of our especial grace, certain knowledge, and mere motion, for us, our heirs and successors, grant unto the said Treasurer and Company, and their successors, that, if it happen at

any time or times the Treasurer for the time being to be sick, or to have any such cause of absence from the City of London as shall be allowed by the said Council, or the greater part of them assembled, so as he cannot attend the affairs of that Company, In every such case, it shall and may be lawful for such Treasurer for the time being to assign, constitute, and appoint one of the Council for Company, to be likewise allowed by the Council, or the greater part of them assembled, to be the deputy Treasurer for the said Company; which Deputy shall have power to do and execute all things which belong to the said Treasurer, during such time as such Treasurer shall be either sick or otherwise absent upon cause allowed of by the said Council, or the Major part of them, as aforesaid, so fully and wholly, and in as large and ample manner and form, and to all intents and purposes, as the said Treasurer, if he were present himself, may or might do and execute the same.

And further, of our especial grace, certain knowledge, and mere motion, for us, our heirs and successors, we do, by these presents, give and grant full power and authority to our said Council here resident, as well at this present time as hereafter:

From time to time, to nominate, make, constitute, ordain, and confirm, by such name or names, style or styles, as to them shall seem good, and likewise to revoke, discharge, change, and alter, as well all and singular Governors, Officers, and Ministers which already have been made as also which hereafter shall be by them thought Fit and Needful to be made or used for the Government of the said Colony and plantation; and also, to make, ordain, and establish all manner of orders, laws, directions, instructions, forms, and Ceremonies of government and Magistracy fit and necessary for and concerning the government of the said Colony and plantation, and the same, at all times hereafter, to abrogate, revoke, or change, not only within the precincts of the said Colony but also upon the Seas in going and coming to and from the said Colony, as they, in their good discretions, shall think to be fittest for good of the adventurers and inhabiters there.

And we do also declare that, for divers reasons and considerations us thereunto especially moving, our will and pleasure is, and we do hereby ordain, that Immediately from and after such time as any such governor or principal Officer, so to be nominated and appointed by our said Council for the Government of the said Colony as aforesaid, shall arrive in Virginia and give notice unto the Colony there resident of our pleasure in this behalf, The government, power, and authority of the President and Council heretofore, by our former letters Patents, there established, and

all laws and constitutions by them formerly made, shall utterly cease and be determined; And all officers, Governors, and Ministers formerly constituted or appointed shall be discharged; Any thing in our said former letters Patents concerning the said plantation contained in anywise to the contrary notwithstanding;

Straightly charging and commanding the President and Council now resident in the said Colony, upon their allegiance, after knowledge given unto them of our will and pleasure, by these presents signified and declared, that they forthwith be obedient to such Governor or Governors as by our said Council here resident shall be named and appointed as aforesaid, and to all directions, orders, and commandments which they shall receive from them, as well in the present resigning and giving up of their authority, offices, charge, and places as in all other attendance as shall be by them from time to time required.

And we do further, by these presents, ordain and establish that the said Treasurer and Council here resident, and their successors, or any four of them assembled, the treasurer being one, shall, from time to time, have full power and authority to admit and receive any other person into their company, corporation, and freedom; And further, in a general assembly of the adventurers, with the consent of the greater part, upon good cause, to disfranchise and put out any person or persons out of the said Freedom and Company.

And we do also grant and confirm, for us, our heirs and successors, That it shall be lawful for the said Treasurer and Company, and their successors, by direction of the Governors there, to dig and to search for all manner of Mines of Gold, silver, copper, Iron, lead, Tin, and other Minerals, as well within the precinct aforesaid as within any part of the Main land not formerly granted to any other;

And to have and enjoy the Gold, silver, Copper, Iron, lead, and Tin, and all other minerals to be gotten thereby, to the use and behoof of the said Company of planters and Adventurers; yielding therefor and paying yearly unto us, our heirs and successors, as aforesaid.

And we do further, of our special grace, certain knowledge, and mere motion, for us, our heirs and successors, grant, by these presents, to and with the said Treasurer and Company, and their successors:

That it shall be lawful and Free for them, and their assigns, at all and every time and times hereafter, out of our Realm of England, and out of all other dominions, to take and lead into the said voyage, and for and towards the said plantation, and to travel thitherwards, and to abide and inhabit therein the said Colony and plantation, all such and so many of our

loving subjects, or any other strangers that will become our loving subjects and live under our allegiance, as shall willingly accompany them in the said voyage and plantation; with sufficient shipping, Armour, weapons, ordnance, Munition, powder, shot, victuals, and such Merchandise or wares as are esteemed by the wild people in those parts; clothing, implements, furniture, cattle, horses, and Mares; and all other things necessary for the said plantation, and for their use and defence, and trade with the people there, and in passing and returning to and from; without yielding or paying subsidy, custom, imposition, or any other tax or duties to us, our heirs or successors, for the space of seven years from the date of these presents;

Provided, that none of the said persons be such as shall be hereafter by special name restrained by us, our heirs or successors.

And, for their further encouragement, of our special grace and favour, we do, by these presents, for us, our heirs and successors, yield and grant to and with the said Treasurer and company, and their successors, and every of them, their factors and assigns, that they, and every of them, shall be free and quiet of all subsidies and customs in Virginia for the space of one and twenty years, and from all taxes and impositions forever, upon any goods or Merchandises, at any time or times hereafter, either upon importation thither or exportation from thence into our Realm of England, or into any other of our dominions, by the said Treasurer and company, and their successors, their deputies, factors, assigns, or any of them; except only the five pounds per Centum due for custom upon all such goods and Merchandises as shall be brought or imported into our Realm of England, or any other of these our dominions, according to the ancient trade of Merchants; which Five pounds per Centum only being paid, it shall be thenceforth lawful and Free for the said Adventurers the same goods and Merchandises to export and carry out of our said Dominions into foreign parts without any custom, tax, or other duty to be paid to us, our heirs or successors, or to any other our Officers or Deputies;

Provided, that the said goods and Merchandises be shipped out within thirteen months after their first landing within any part of those dominions.

And we do also confirm and grant to the said Treasurer and Company, and their successors, as also to all and every such governor, or other Officers and Ministers, as by our said Council shall be appointed to have power and authority of Government and command in or over the said Colony or plantation:

That they, and every of them, shall and lawfully may, from time to

time, and at all times forever hereafter, for their several defence and safety, encounter, expulse, repel, and resist, by force and arms, as well by sea as by land, and all ways and means whatsoever, all and every such person and persons whatsoever as, without the special license of the said Treasurer and Company, and their successors, shall attempt to inhabit within the said several precincts and limits of the said Colony and plantation; and also, all and every such person and persons whatsoever as shall enterprise or attempt, at any time hereafter, destruction, invasion, hurt, detriment, or annoyance to the said Colony and plantation, as is likewise specified in the said former grant;

And that it shall be lawful for the said Treasurer and Company, and their successors, and every of them, from time to time, and at all times hereafter, and they shall have full power and authority, to take and surprise, by all ways and means whatsoever, all and every person and persons whatsoever, with their ships, goods, and other furniture, trafficking in any harbor, Creek, or place within the limits or precincts of the said Colony and plantation, and, being allowed by the said Company [not] to be adventurers or planters of the said Colony, until such time as they, being of any Realms or dominions under our obedience, shall pay or agree to pay to the hands of the Treasurer, or of some other officer deputed by the said Governors in Virginia, over and above such subsidy and custom as the said Company is, or hereafter shall be, to pay, five pounds per Centum upon all Goods and Merchandises so brought in thither, and also, five per Centum upon all goods by them shipped out from thence; and being strangers, and not under our obedience, until they have paid, over and above such subsidy and custom as the same Treasurer and Company, and their successors, is, or hereafter shall be, to pay, ten pounds per Centum upon all such goods likewise carried in and out; Anything in the former letters patents to the contrary notwithstanding;

And the same sums of money and benefit as aforesaid, for and during the space of one and twenty years, shall be wholly employed to the benefit and behoof of the said Colony and plantation;

And after the said one and twenty years ended, the same shall be taken to the use of us, our heirs or successors, by such Officer and Minister as by us, our heirs or successors, shall be thereunto assigned and appointed, as is specified in the said former letters Patents.

Also, we do, for us, our heirs and successors, declare, by these presents, that all and every the persons, being our subjects, which shall go and inhabit within the said Colony and plantation, and every of their children and posterity which shall happen to be born within the limits

thereof, shall have, enjoy all liberties, Franchises, and immunities of Free Denizens and natural subjects within any of our other dominions, to all intents and purposes as if they had been abiding and born within this our Kingdom of England, or in any other of our Dominions.

And forasmuch as it shall be necessary for all such our loving subjects as shall inhabit within the said precincts of Virginia aforesaid to determine to live together in the fear and true worship of Almighty God, Christian Peace, and civil quietness, each with other, whereby every one may, with more safety, pleasure, and profit, enjoy that whereunto they shall attain with great pain and peril:

We, for us, our heirs and successors, are likewise pleased and contented, and, by these presents, do give and grant unto the said Treasurer and Company, and their successors, and to such Governors, officers, and Ministers as shall be, by our said Council, constituted and appointed, according to the natures and limits of their offices and places respectively:

That they shall and may, from time to time, forever hereafter, within the said precincts of Virginia, or in the way by the Seas thither and from thence, have full and absolute power and authority to correct, punish, pardon, govern, and rule all such the subjects of us, our heirs and successors, as shall, from time to time, adventure themselves in any voyage thither, or that shall, at any time hereafter, inhabit in the precincts and territory of the said Colony as aforesaid; according to such order, ordinances, constitutions, directions, and instructions as by our said Council, as aforesaid, shall be established; and in defect thereof, in case of necessity, according to the good discretions of the said Governors and officers respectively, as well in cases capital and criminal as Civil, both Marine and other;

So always, as the said statutes, ordinances, and proceedings, as near as conveniently may be, be agreeable to the laws, statutes, government, and policy of this our Realm of England.

And we do further, of our special grace, certain knowledge, and mere motion, grant, declare, and ordain that such principal Governor as, from time to time, shall duly and lawfully be authorized and appointed, in manner and form in these presents heretofore expressed, shall [have] full power and authority to use and exercise Martial law in cases of Rebellion or mutiny; in as large and ample manner as our lieutenants in our Counties within our Realm of England have, or ought to have, by force of their Commissions of lieutenancy.

And furthermore, if any person or persons, adventurers or planters, of the said Colony or any other, at any time or times hereafter, shall

transport any Moneys, goods, or Merchandises out of any our kingdoms with a pretence or purpose to land, sell, or otherwise dispose the same within the limits and bounds of the said Colony, and yet, nevertheless, being at Sea, or after he has landed within any part of the said Colony, shall carry the same into any other foreign Country with a purpose there to sell and dispose thereof, That then, all the goods and Chattels of the said person or persons so offending, and transported, together with the ship or vessel wherein such transportation was made, shall be forfeited to us, our heirs and successors.

And further, our will and pleasure is that in all questions and doubts that shall arise upon any difficulty of construction or interpretation of any thing contained either in this or in our said former letters Patents, the same shall be taken and interpreted in most ample and beneficial manner for the said Treasurer and Company, and their successors, and every member thereof.

And further, we do, by these presents, ratify and confirm unto the said Treasurer and Company, and their successors, all privileges, Franchises, liberties, and Immunities granted in our said former letters Patents, and not in these our letters patents revoked, altered, changed, or abridged.

And finally, our will and pleasure is, and we do further hereby, for us, our heirs and successors, grant and agree to and with the said Treasurer and Company, and their successors, That all and singular person and persons which shall, at any time or times hereafter, adventure any sum or sums of money in and towards the said plantation of the said Colony in Virginia, and shall be admitted, by the said Council and Company, as adventurers of the said Colony, in form aforesaid, and shall be enrolled in the book or Record of the adventurers of the said Company, shall and may be accounted, accepted, taken, held, and reputed adventurers of the said Colony, and shall and may enjoy all and singular grants, privileges, liberties, benefits, profits, commodities, advantages, and emoluments whatsoever; as fully, largely, amply, and absolutely as if they, and every of them, had been precisely, plainly, singularly, and distinctly named and inserted in these our letters Patents.

And lastly, because the principal effect which we can desire or expect of this action is the conversion and reduction of the people in those parts unto the true worship of God, and Christian Religion, in which respect we would be loath that any person should be permitted to pass that we suspected to affect the superstitions of the Church of Rome, we do hereby declare that it is our will and pleasure that none be permitted to pass in any voyage from time to time to be made into the said Country but

such as first shall have taken the oath of supremacy; For which purpose we do, by these presents, give full power and authority to the Treasurer for the time being and any three of the Council to tender and exhibit the said oath to all such persons as shall, at any time, be sent and employed in the said voyage.

Although express mention, etc. In witness whereof, etc.

T R apud XXIII die May.

per ipsum Regem

[Transcribed from a photostatic copy of the enrollment of the charter on the patent roll. Manuscript in the British Public Record Office, London. Reference: C. 66/1796. Photostatic copy deposited in the State Department of Archives and History, Raleigh, North Carolina.]

Charter to the Virginia Company of London

March 12, 1612

INTRODUCTION

A new charter was issued to the Virginia Company of London on March 12, 1612. It extended the territorial boundaries to include the Bermuda Islands and granted authority to establish a lottery to create a permanent fund to support colonies. It reduced the power of the treasurer and council and gave the ordinary stockholders a large degree of control over the affairs of the company and the government of colonies. The changes effected under the new charter placed the company on a regular joint-stock basis and increased its prestige.

The democratic element introduced into the control of the company was the most significant provision of the new charter. The organization of the company as thus established appears to have served as a model when the government of the Virginia colony was reorganized in 1618. An important feature of the reorganization of the colony was the establishment of a popular assembly, which held its first meeting on July 30, 1619. This assembly became a precedent for other English colonies in America, and provision for such a body was included in all the later charters involving the North Carolina area.

The affairs of the company improved for a time after the new charter was issued, but difficulties soon developed. Large numbers of colonists in Virginia died from disease, and many others were killed in an Indian massacre which occurred in 1622. Lotteries established by the company failed to provide the financial resources needed to support colonies, and the company reached the verge of bankruptcy. Bitter factional strife developed and further reduced the efficiency of the company. As a result of these conditions, the crown ordered an investigation, which led to *quo warranto* proceedings. On May 24, 1624, a decision was handed down in the Court of King's Bench revoking the charter of the Virginia Company of London.

Upon revocation of the charter, the Virginia possessions of the company reverted to the crown, and government of the colony was again in the hands of the king. The North Carolina area, in which no permanent settlement had been made, was again available for disposal by the crown.

THE DOCUMENT

JAMES, by the grace of God, etc. To all to whom, etc. Greeting:

Whereas, at the humble suit of divers and sundry our loving Subjects, as well Adventurers as Planters of the first Colony in Virginia, and for the propagation of Christian Religion and reclaiming of people barbarous to Civility and humanity, we have, by our letters patents, bearing date at Westminster the Three and Twentieth day of May in the seventh year of our Reign of England, France, and Ireland, and the two and Fortieth of Scotland, Given and granted unto them That they, and all such and so many of our loving subjects as should, from time to time, forever after, be joined with them as Planters or Adventurers in the said plantation, and their successors, forever, should be one body politic, incorporated by the name of the Treasurer and planters of the City of London for the first Colony in Virginia;

And whereas, also, for the greater good and benefit of the said Company, And for the better furnishing and establishing of the said plantation, we did further grant and Confirm, by our said letters patents, unto the said Treasurer and Company, and their successors, forever, All those lands, Countries, and Territories, situate, lying, and being in that part of America called Virginia, from the point of land called Cape or Point Comfort, all along the seacoast to the Northward two hundred Miles; And from the said point of Cape Comfort, all along the seacoast to the Southward two hundred miles; And all the space and Circuit of land lying from the seacoast of the precinct aforesaid up or into the land, throughout from sea to sea, west and Northwest; And also, all the Islands lying within one hundred miles along the Coast of both the seas of the precinct aforesaid; with divers other grants, liberties, franchises, pre-eminences, privileges, profits, benefits, and Commodities granted in and by our said letters patents to the said Treasurer and Company, and their successors, forever;

Now, forasmuch as we are given to understand that in these seas adjoining to the said Coast of Virginia, and without the Compass of those two hundred miles by us so granted unto the said Treasurer and Company as aforesaid, and yet not far distant from the said Colony in Virginia, there are or may be divers Islands lying desolate and uninhabited, some of which are already made known and discovered by the industry, travel, and expenses of the said Company, and others also are supposed to be, and remain as yet unknown and undiscovered, all and every of which it may

import the said Colony, both in safety and policy of trade, to populate and plant;

In regard whereof, as well for the preventing of peril as for the better Commodity and prosperity of the said Colony, They have been humble Suitors unto us that we would be pleased to grant unto them an Enlargement of our said former letters patents, as well for a more ample extent of their limits and territories into the seas adjoining to and upon the Coast of Virginia as also for some other matters and Articles concerning the better government of the said Company and Colony, In which point our said former letters patents do not extend so far as time and experience have found to be needful and Convenient:

We, therefore, tendering the good and happy success of the said plantation, both in respect of the general weal of human society as in respect of the good of our own estate and kingdoms, And being willing to give furtherance unto all good means that may advance the benefit of the said Company, and which may secure the safety of our loving subjects planted in our said Colony under the favour and protection of God Almighty And of our royal power and authority, have, therefore, of our especial grace, certain knowledge, and mere motion, given, granted, and Confirmed, and, for us, our heirs and successors, we do, by these presents, give, grant, and Confirm, unto the said Treasurer and Company of Adventurers and planters of the said City of London for the first Colony in Virginia, and to their heirs and successors, forever:

All and singular the said Islands, situate and being in any part of the said Ocean bordering upon the Coast of our said first Colony in Virginia, and being within three hundred leagues of any the parts heretofore granted to the said Treasurer and Company in our said former letters patents, as aforesaid, And being within or between the one and Forty, and thirty degrees of Northerly latitude; together with all and singular lands, grounds, havens, ports, Rivers, waters, fishings, Mines, and minerals, as well royal Mines of gold and silver as other Mines and Minerals, Pearls, precious stones, quarries, and all and singular other Commodities, jurisdictions, Royalties, privileges, franchises, and pre-eminences, both within the said tract of land upon the Main and also within the said Islands and seas adjoining, whatsoever, and thereunto or thereabouts, both by sea and land, being or situate, and which, by our letters patents, we may or can grant; and in as ample manner and sort as we, or any our noble progenitors, have heretofore granted to any person or persons, or to any Company, body politic or corporate, or to any Adventurer or Adventurers, undertaker or undertakers, of any discoveries, plantations, or traffic of,

in, or into any foreign parts whatsoever; and in as large and ample manner as if the same were herein particularly named, mentioned, and expressed;

Provided always, that the said Islands, or any the premises herein mentioned and by these presents intended and meant to be granted, be not already actually possessed or inhabited by any other Christian Prince or State, Nor be within the bounds, limits, or Territories of the Northern Colony, heretofore by us granted, to be planted by divers of our loving subjects in the North parts of Virginia;

To have and to hold, possess, and enjoy all and singular the said Islands in the said Ocean seas so lying and bordering upon the Coast or Coasts of the Territories of the said first Colony in Virginia as aforesaid; with all and singular the said soils, lands, and grounds, and all and singular other the premises heretofore by these presents granted or mentioned to be granted; to them, the said Treasurer and Company of Adventurers and planters of the City of London for the first Colony in Virginia, and to their heirs, successors, and assigns, forever; To the sole and proper use and behoof of them, the said Treasurer and Company, and their heirs, successors, and assigns, forever;

To be held of us, our heirs and successors, as of our Manor of East Greenwich, in free and Common Soccage, and not in Capite; yielding and paying therefor, to us, our heirs and successors, the fifth part of the Ore of all gold and silver which shall be there gotten, had, or obtained, for all manner of services whatsoever.

And further, our will and pleasure is, and we do, by these presents, grant and confirm, for the good and welfare of the said plantation, And that Posterity may hereafter know who have adventured, and not been sparing of their purses, in such a noble and generous action for the general good of their Country, and at the request and with the Consent of the Company aforesaid:

That our trusty and well-beloved subjects: George, Lord Archbishop of Canterbury; Gilbert, Earl of Shrewsberry; Mary, Countess of Shrewesbury; Elizabeth, Countess of Derby; Margarett, Countess of Comberland; Henry, Earl of Huntingdon; Edward, Earl of Beddford; Lucy, Countess of Bedford; Marie, Countess of Pembroke; Richard, Earl of Clanrickard; Lady Elizabeth Graie; William, Lord Viscount Cramborne; William, Lord Bishop of Duresme; Henry, Lord Bishop of Worceter; John, Lord Bishop of Oxonford; William, Lord Pagett; Dudley, Lord North; Franncis, Lord Norries; William, Lord Knollis; John, Lord Harrington; Robert, Lord Spencer; Edward, Lord Denny; William,

Lord Cavendishe; James, Lord Hay; Eleanor, Lady Cave; Mistress Elizabeth Scott, widow; Edward Sackvill, Esquire; Sir Henry Nevill of Aburgavenny, knight; Sir Robert Riche, knight; Sir John Harrington, knight; Sir Raphe Winwood, knight; Sir John Graie, knight; Sir Henry Riche, knight; Sir Henry Wotton, knight; Peregrine Berly, Esquire; Sir Edward Phelipps, knight, Master of the Rolls; Sir Moile Finche, knight; Sir Thomas Mansell, knight; Sir John St. John, knight; Sir Richard Spencer, knight; Sir Franncis Barrington, knight; Sir George Carie of Devoonshire, knight; Sir William Twisden, knight; Sir John Levesun, knight; Sir Thomas Walsingham, knight; Sir Edward Care, knight; Sir Arthure Manwaringe, knight; Sir Thomas Jermyn, knight; Sir Valentine Knightley, knight; Sir John Dodderidge, knight; Sir John Hungerford, knight; Sir John Stradling, knight; Sir John Bourchidd, knight; Sir John Bennett, knight; Sir Samuell Leonard, knight; Sir Franncis Goodwin, knight; Sir Wareham St. Legier, knight; Sir James Scudamore, knight; Sir Thomas Mildmaie, knight; Sir Percivall Harte, knight; Sir Percivall Willoughby, knight; Sir Franncis Leigh, knight; Sir Henry Goodere, knight; Sir John Cuttes, knight; Sir James Parrett, knight; Sir William Craven, knight; Sir John Sammes, knight; Sir Carey Raleigh, knight; Sir William Maynard, knight; Sir Edmund Bowyer, knight; Sir William Cornewallis, knight; Sir Thomas Beomont, knight; Sir Thomas Cumingsby, knight; Sir Henry Beddingfeild, knight; Sir David Murrcty, knight; Sir William Pole, knight; Sir William Throgmorton, knight; Sir Thomas Grantham, knight; Sir Thomas Stewkley, knight; Sir Edward Heron, knight; Sir Raph Shelten, knight; Sir Lewes Thesam, knight; Sir Walter Aston, knight; Sir Thomas Denton, knight; Sir Ewstace Hart, knight; Sir John Ogle, knight; Sir Thomas Dale, knight; Sir William Boulstrod, knight; Sir William Fleetwood, knight; Sir John Acland, knight; Sir John Hanham, knight; Sir Roberte Meller, knight; Sir Thomas Wilford, knight; Sir William Lower, knight; Sir Thomas Lerdes, knight; Sir Franncis Barneham, knight; Sir Walter Chute, knight; Sir Thomas Tracy, knight; Sir Marmaduke Darrell, knight; Sir William Harrys, knight; Sir Thomas Gerrard, knight; Sir Peter Freetchvile, knight; Sir Richard Trevor, knight; Sir Annas Bamfeild, knight; Sir William Smith of Essex, knight; Sir Thomas Hewett, knight; Sir Richard Smith, knight; Sir John Heyward, knight; Sir Christopher Harris, knight; Sir John Pettus, knight; Sir William Strode, knight; Sir Thomas Harfleet, knight; Sir Walter Vaughan, knight; Sir William Herrick, knight; Sir Samuell Saltonstall, knight; Sir Richard Cooper, knight; Sir Henry Fane, knight; Sir Franncis Egiok, knight; Sir Robert Edolph, knight; Sir Arthure Harries,

knight; Sir George Huntley, knight; Sir George Chute, knight; Sir Robert Leigh, knight; Sir Richard Lovelace, knight; Sir William Lovelace, knight; Sir Robert Yaxley, knight; Sir Franncis Wortley, knight; Sir Franncis Heiborne, knight; Sir Guy Palme, knight; Sir Richard Bingley, knight; Sir Ambrose Turvill, knight; Sir Nicholas Stoddard, knight; Sir William Gree, knight; Sir Walter Coverte, knight; Sir Thomas Eversfeild, knight; Sir Nicholas Parker, knight; Sir Edward Culpeper, knight; Sir William Ayliffe, knight; and Sir John Keile, knight; Doctor George Mountaine, Dean of Westminster; Lawrence Bohan, Doctor in Physic; Anthony Hinton, Doctor in Physic; John Pawlett; Arthure Jugram; Anthony Irby; John Weld; John Walter; John Harris; Anthony Dyott; William Ravenscrofte; Thomas Warre; William Hackwill; Lawrence Hide; Nicholas Hide; Thomas Stevens; Franncis Tate; Thomas Coventry; John Hare; Robert Askwith; George Sanndys; Franncis Jones; Thomas Wentworth; Henry Cromewell; John Arundell; John Culpeper; John Hoskins; Walter Fitzwilliams; Walter Kirkham; William Roscarrock; Richard Carmerdon; Edward Carue; Thomas Merry; Nicholas Lichfeild; John Middleton; John Smithe and Thomas Smith, the sons of Sir Thomas Smith; Peter Franke; George Gerrard; Gregory Sprynte; John Drake; Roger Puleston; Oliver Nicholas; Richard Nunnington; John Vaughan; John Evelin; Lamorock Stradling; John Riddall; John Kettleby; Warren Townshend; Lionell Cranfeild; Edward Salter; William Litton; Humfrey May; George Thorpe; Henry Sandys and Edwin Sandys, the sons of Sir Edwin Sanndys; Thomas Conway; Captain Owen Gwinn; Captain Giles Hawkridge; Edward Dyer; Richard Connock; Benjamin Brand; Richard Leigh and Thomas Pelham, Esquires; Thomas Digges and John Digges, Esquires, the sons of Sir Dudley Diggs, knight; Franncis Bradley; Richard Buckminster; Franncis Burley; John Procter; Alexannder Whitakers; Thomas Frake, the elder, and Henry Freake, the elder, Ministers of God's Word; The Mayor and Citizens of Chichester; the Mayor and Jurates of Dover; The Bailiffs, Burgesses, and Commonalty of Ipswich; The Mayor and Commonalty of Lyme Regis; The Mayor and Commonalty of Sandwich; The Wardens, Assistants, and Company of the Trinity house; Thomas Martin; Franncis Smaleman; Augustine Steward; Richard Tomlins; Humfrey Joblan; John Legate; Robert Backley; John Crowe; Edward Backley; William Flett; Henry Wolstenholme; Edmund Alleyn; George Tucker; Franncis Glanville; Thomas Gouge; John Evelin; William Hall; John Smithe; George Samms; John Robinson; William Tucker; John Wolstenholme and Henry Wolstenholme, sons of John Wolstenholme, Esquire; William Hodges;

Jonathan Mattall; Phinees Pett; Captain John Kinge; Captain William Beck; Giles Alington; Franncis Heiton and Samuell Holliland, gentlemen; Richard Chamberlaine; George Chamberlaine; Hewett Staper; Humfrey Handford; Raph Freeman; George Swinhoe; Richard Pigott; Elias Robertes; Roger Harris; Devereux Wogan; Edward Baber; William Greenewell; Thomas Stilles; Nicholas Hooker; Robert Garsett; Thomas Cordell; William Bright; John Reynoldes; Peter Bartley; John Willett; Humfry Smithe; Roger Dye; Nicholas Leate; Thomas Wale; Lewes Tate; Humfrey Merrett; Roberte Peake; Powell Isaackson; Sebastian Viccars; Jarvis Mundes; Richard Warner; Gresham Hogan Warner; Daniell Bernley; Andrew Troughton; William Barrett; Thomas Hodges; John Downes; Richard Harper; Thomas Foxall; William Haselden; James Harrison; William Burrell; John Hodsall; Richard Fisheborne; John Miller; Edward Cooke; Richard Hall, Merchant; Richard Hall, Anchor-smith; John Delbridge; Richard Francklin; Edmund Scott; John Britten; Robert Strutt; Edmund Pond; Edward James; Robert Bell; Richard Herne; William Ferrers; William Millett; Anthony Abdy; Roberte Gore; Benjamyn Decrow; Henry Timberley; Humfrey Basse; Abraham Speckart; Richard Moorer; William Compton; Richard Poulsonne; William Wolaston; John Beomont, Clothier; Alexannder Childe; William Fald, Fishmonger; Franncis Baldwin; John Jones, Merchant; Thomas Plomer, Edward Plomer, Merchants; John Stoickden; Robert Tindall; Peter Erundell; Ruben Bourne; Thomas Hampton and Franncis Carter, Citizens of London, who, since our said last letters patents, are become Adventurers, and have joined themselves with the former Adventurers and Planters of the said Company and society, shall from henceforth be reputed, deemed, and taken to be, and shall be, brethren and free members of the Company, and shall and may, respectively, and according to the proportion and value of their several Adventures, have, hold, and enjoy all such interest, right, title, privileges, pre-eminences, liberties, franchises, immunities, profits, and Commodities whatsoever; in as large, ample, and beneficial manner, to all intents, Constructions, and purposes, as any other Adventurers nominated and expressed in any our former letters patents, or any of them, have or may have by force and virtue of these presents, or any our former letters patents whatsoever.

And we are further pleased, and we do, by these presents, grant and Confirm, That Phillipp, Earl of Montgomery; William, Lord Paget; Sir John Harrington, knight; Sir William Cavendish, knight; Sir John Sammes, knight; Sir Samuell Sandys, knight; Sir Thomas Freke, knight; Sir William St. John, knight; Sir Richard Grobham, knight; Sir Thomas

Dale, knight; Sir Cavalliero Maycott, knight; Richard Martin, Esquire; John Bingley, Esquire; Thomas Watson, Esquire; and Arthure Jugram, Esquire, whom the said Treasurer and Company have, since the said letters patents, nominated, and set down as worthy and discreet persons fit to serve us as Councillors, to be of our Council for the said Plantation, shall be reputed, deemed, and taken as persons of our said Council for the said first Colony, in such manner and sort, to all intents and purposes, as those who have been formerly elected and nominated as our Councillors for that Colony, And whose names have been or are inserted and expressed in our said former letters patents.

And we do hereby ordain and grant, by these presents, That the said Treasurer and Company of Adventurers and planters aforesaid shall and may, once every week, or oftener at their pleasure, hold and keep a Court and assembly for the better ordering and government of the said plantation, and such things as shall Concern the same; And that any five persons of the said Council for the said first Colony in Virginia for the time being, of which Company the Treasurer, or his deputy, always to be one, and the number of fifteen others, at the least, of the generality of the said Company, assembled together in such Court or assembly in such manner as is and has been heretofore used and accustomed, shall be said, taken, held, and reputed to be, and shall be, a full and sufficient Court of the said Company for the handling, ordering, and dispatching of all such casual and particular occurrences and accidental matters of less consequence and weight as shall, from time to time, happen touching and concerning the said plantation;

And that, nevertheless, for the handling, ordering, and disposing of matters and affairs of great weight and importance, and such as shall or may in any sort concern the weal public and general good of the said Company and plantation, as, namely, the manner of government from time to time to be used, the ordering and disposing of the said possessions, and the settling and establishing of a trade there, or such like, there shall be held and kept every year, upon the last Wednesday save one of Hillary, Easter, Trinity, and Michaelmas Terms, forever, one great, general, and solemn assembly; which four several assemblies shall be styled and Called the four great and general Courts of the Council and Company of Adventurers for Virginia.

In all and every of which said great and general Courts so assembled, our will and pleasure is, and we do, for us, our heirs and successors, forever, give and grant to the said Treasurer and Company, and their successors, forever, by these presents:

That they, the said Treasurer and Company, or the greater number of them so assembled, shall and may have full power and authority from time to time, and at all times hereafter, to elect and choose discreet persons to be of our Council for the said first Colony in Virginia; and to nominate and appoint such officers as they shall think fit and requisite for the government, managing, ordering, and dispatching of the affairs of the said Company; and shall likewise have full power and authority to ordain and make such laws and ordinances for the good and welfare of the said plantation as to them from time to time shall be thought requisite and meet;

So always, as the same be not Contrary to the laws and statutes of this our Realm of England;

And shall, in like manner, have power and authority to expulse, disfranchise, and put out of and from their said Company and society, forever, All and every such person and persons as, having either promised or subscribed their names to become Adventurers to the said plantation of the said first Colony in Virginia, or having been nominated for Adventurers in these or any our letters patents, or having been otherwise admitted and nominated to be of the said Company, have, nevertheless, either not put in any adventure at all for and towards the said plantation or else have refused and neglected, or shall refuse and neglect, to bring in his or their adventure, by word or writing promised, within six months after the same shall be so payable and due.

And whereas, the failing and non-payment of such moneys as have been promised in adventure for the advancement of the said plantation has been often, by experience, found to be dangerous and prejudicial to the same, and much to have hindered the progress and proceeding of the said plantation;

And for that it seems to us a thing reasonable That such persons as, by their handwriting, have engaged themselves for the payment of their adventures, and afterwards neglecting their faith and promise, should be Compellable to make good and keep the same:

Therefore, our will and pleasure is that in any suit or suits Commenced or to be Commenced in any of our Courts at Westminster, or elsewhere, by the said Treasurer and Company, or otherwise, against any such persons, That our Judges for the time being, both in our Court of Chancery and at the Common Law, do favour and further the said suits so far forth as law and equity will in any wise suffer and permit.

And we do, for us, our heirs and successors, further give and grant to the said Treasurer and Company, and their successors, forever, That

they, the said Treasurer and Company, or the greater part of them for the time being so in a full and general Court assembled as aforesaid, shall and may, from time to time, and at all times hereafter forever, elect, choose, and permit into their Company and society any person or persons, as well strangers and aliens born in any parts beyond the seas wheresoever, being in amity with us, as our natural liege subjects born in any our Realms and Dominions;

And that all such persons so elected, chosen, and admitted to be of the said Company, as aforesaid, shall thereupon be taken, reputed, and held, and shall be, free members of the said Company; and shall have, hold, and enjoy all and singular freedoms, liberties, franchises, privileges, Immunities, benefits, profits, and Commodities whatsoever to the said Company in any sort belonging or appertaining; as fully, freely, and amply as any other Adventurer or adventurers, now being, or which hereafter at any time shall be, of the said Company, has, have, shall, may, might, or ought to have or enjoy the same, to all intents and purposes whatsoever.

And we do further, of our special grace, certain knowledge, and mere motion, for us, our heirs and successors, give and grant to the said Treasurer and Company, and their successors, forever, by these presents:

That it shall be lawful and free for them, and their assigns, at all and every time and times hereafter, out of any our Realms and Dominions whatsoever, to take, lead, Carry, and transport in and into the said voyage, and for and towards the said plantation of our said first Colony in Virginia, all such and so many of our loving subjects, or any other strangers that will become our loving subjects and live under our Allegiance, as shall willingly accompany them in the said voyage and plantation; with shipping, armour, weapons, ordnance, munition, powder, shot, victuals, and all manner of merchandises and wares, and all manner of clothing, implements, furniture, beasts, Cattle, horses, mares, and all other things necessary for the said plantation, and for their use and defence, and for trade with the people there, and in passing and returning to and fro; without paying or yielding any subsidy, Custom, or imposition, either inward or outward, or any other duty, to us, our heirs or successors, for the same, for the space of seven years from the date of these presents.

And we do further, for us, our heirs and successors, give and grant to the said Treasurer and Company, and their successors, forever, by these presents:

That the said Treasurer of the said Company, or his deputy for the

time being, or any two others of our said Council for the said first Colony in Virginia for the time being, shall and may, at all times hereafter, and from time to time, have full power and authority to administer and give the oath and oaths of supremacy and Allegiance, or either of them, to all and every person and persons which shall, at any time and times hereafter, go or pass to the said Colony in Virginia;

And further, That it shall be likewise lawful for the said Treasurer, or his deputy for the time, or any two others of our said Council for the said first Colony in Virginia for the time being, from time to time, and at all times hereafter, to administer such a formal oath as by their discretion shall be reasonably devised, as well unto any person or persons employed or to be employed in, for, or touching the said plantation, for their honest, faithful, and just discharge of their service in all such matters as shall be Committed unto them for the good and benefit of the said Company, Colony, and plantation, as also unto such other person or persons as the said Treasurer, or his deputy, with two others of the said Council, shall think meet, for the examination or clearing of the truth in any cause whatsoever concerning the said plantation, or any business from thence proceeding, or thereunto proceeding, or thereunto belonging.

And furthermore, whereas, we have been certified that divers lewd and ill disposed persons, both Sailors, Soldiers, Artificers, husbandmen, laborers, and others, having received wages, apparel, or other entertainment from the said Company, or having Contracted and agreed with the said Company, to go, or to serve, or to be employed in the said Plantation of the said first Colony in Virginia, have afterwards either withdrawn, hid, or concealed themselves, or have refused to go thither, after they have been so entertained and agreed withal;

And that divers and sundry persons also, which have been sent and employed in the said plantation of the said first Colony in Virginia, at and upon the charge of the said Company, and having there misbehaved themselves by mutinies, sedition, and other notorious misdemeanors, or having been employed or sent abroad by the Governor of Virginia, or his deputy, with some ship or pinnace for provisions for the said Colony, or for some discovery or other business and affairs concerning the same, have from thence, most treacherously, either come back again and returned into our Realm of England by stealth or without licence of our governor of our said Colony in Virginia for the time being, or have been sent hither as misdoers and offenders; and that many also of those persons, after their return from thence, having been questioned by our said Council here for such their misbehaviors and offences, by their insolent

and contemptuous Carriage in the presence of our said Council, have shown little respect and reverence, either to the place or authority in which we have placed and appointed them;

And others, for the colouring of their lewdness and misdemeanors Committed in Virginia, have endeavored them, by most vile and slanderous reports, made and divulged as well of the Country of Virginia as also of the government and estate of the said plantation and Colony, as much as in them lay, to bring the said voyage and plantation into disgrace and Contempt, By means whereof, not only the Adventurers and planters already engaged in the said plantation have been exceedingly abused and hindered, and a great number of other our loving and well-disposed subjects, otherwise well affected and inclining to join and adventure in so noble, Christian, and worthy an action, have been discouraged from the same, but also the utter overthrow and ruin of the said enterprise have been greatly endangered, which cannot miscarry without some dishonor to us and our kingdom;

Now, forasmuch as it appears unto us that these insolences, misdemeanors, and abuses, not to be tolerated in any Civil government, have for the most part grown and proceeded in regard of our said Council have not any direct power and authority by any express words in our former letters patents to Correct and chastise such offenders:

We, therefore, for the more speedy reformation of so great and enormous abuses and misdemeanors heretofore practised and Committed, and for the preventing of the like hereafter, do, by these presents, for us, our heirs and successors, give and grant to the said Treasurer and Company, and their successors, forever, that it shall and may be lawful for our said Council for the said first Colony in Virginia, or any two of them, whereof the said Treasurer, or his deputy for the time being, to be always one, by warrant under their hands, to send for, or cause to be apprehended, all and every such person and persons who shall be noted or accused or found, at any time or times hereafter, to offend or misbehave themselves in any the offences before mentioned and expressed;

And, upon the examination of any such offender or offenders, and just proof made, by oath taken before the Council, of any such notorious misdemeanors by them Committed as aforesaid, And also, upon any insolent, contemptuous, or unreverent Carriage and misbehavior to or against our said Council, shown or used by any such person or persons so called, convented, and appearing before them as aforesaid, That in all such cases, they, our said Council, or any two of them for the time being, shall and may have full power and authority either here to bind them over, with

good sureties for their good behaviour, and further therein to proceed to all intents and purposes as it is used in other like cases within our Realm of England, or else, at their discretion, to remand and send back the said offenders, or any of them, unto the said Colony in Virginia, there to be proceeded against and punished as the governor, deputy, and Council there for the time being shall think meet, or otherwise according to such laws and ordinances as are or shall be in use there for the well ordering and good government of the said Colony.

And, for the more effectual advancing of the said plantation, we do further, for us, our heirs and successors, of our especial grace and favour, by virtue of our prerogative Royal, and by the assent and Consent of the Lords and others of our Privy Council, give and grant unto the said Treasurer and Company full power and authority, free leave, liberty, and licence, to set forth, erect, and publish one or more lottery or lotteries, to have continuance and to endure and be held for the space of one whole year next after the opening of the same; and after the end and expiration of the said term, the said lottery or lotteries to continue and be further kept during our will and pleasure only, and not otherwise.

And yet, nevertheless, we are contented and pleased, for the good and welfare of the said plantation, That the said Treasurer and Company shall, for the dispatch and finishing of the said lottery or lotteries, have six months warning, after the said year ended, before our will and pleasure shall, for and on that behalf, be construed, deemed, and adjudged to be in anywise altered and determined.

And our further will and pleasure is That the said lottery or lotteries shall and may be opened and held within our City of London, or in any other City or Cities, or elsewhere, within this our Realm of England, with such prizes, Articles, Conditions, and Limitations as to them, the said Treasurer and Company, in their discretions, shall seem convenient;

And that it shall and may be lawful to and for the said Treasurer and Company to elect and choose Receivers, Auditors, Surveyors, Commissioners, or any other officers whatsoever, at their will and pleasure, for the better marshaling and guiding and governing of the said lottery or lotteries; and that it shall be likewise lawful to and for the said Treasurer and any two of the said Council to administer unto all and every such persons, so elected and chosen for officers as aforesaid, one or more oaths for their good behaviour, just and true dealing, in and about the lottery or lotteries, to the intent and purpose that none of our loving subjects putting in their moneys, or otherwise adventuring in the said general lottery or lotteries, may be in anywise defrauded and deceived of their

said moneys, or evil and indirectly dealt withal in their said Adventures.

And we further grant, in manner and form aforesaid, That it shall and may be lawful to and for the said Treasurer and Company, under the seal of our Council for the plantation, to publish, or to cause and procure to be published, by proclamation or otherwise, the said proclamation to be made in their name, by virtue of these presents, the said lottery or lotteries in all Cities, Towns, Boroughs, Thoroughfares, and other places within our said Realm of England.

And we will and Command all Mayors, Justices of peace, Sheriffs, Bailiffs, Constables, and other our officers and loving subjects whatsoever, That in no wise they hinder or delay the progress and proceeding of the said lottery or lotteries, but be therein and touching the premises aiding and assisting by all honest, good, and lawful means and endeavours.

And further, our will and pleasure is that in all questions and doubts that shall arise upon any difficulty of Construction or interpretation of any thing contained in these or any other our former letters patents, the same shall be taken and interpreted in most ample and beneficial manner for the said Treasurer and Company, and their successors, and every member thereof.

And lastly, we do, by these presents, ratify and Confirm unto the said Treasurer and Company, and their successors, forever, all and all manner of privileges, franchises, liberties, Immunities, pre-eminences, profits, and Commodities whatsoever granted unto them in any our letters patents and not in these presents revoked, altered, changed, or abridged.

Although express mention, etc.

In witness whereof, etc. Witness, our self, at Westminster, the Twelfth day of March.

per breve de privato sigillo, etc.

[Transcribed from a photostatic copy of the enrollment of the charter on the patent roll. Manuscript in the British Public Record Office, London. Reference: C. 66/1911. Photostatic copy deposited in the State Department of Archives and History, Raleigh, North Carolina.]

Charter to Sir Robert Heath

October 30, 1629

INTRODUCTION

On October 30, 1629, King Charles I, who had ascended the throne about four years earlier, granted to his attorney general, Sir Robert Heath, the territory in America between thirty-one degrees and thirty-six degrees north latitude. This area, which extended from Albemarle Sound to about the northern boundary of modern Florida, and from the Atlantic to the Pacific Ocean, included most of present-day North Carolina. It was named Carolana.

Heath appears to have been associated with leaders of a group of French Huguenot refugees who wished to settle in North America. Existing records do not make clear the details of this association. There are also other questions regarding the Heath grant which the surviving records do not answer. For example, the terms of a private agreement between King Charles and Heath, referred to in the charter, are not known, for the document recording this agreement has been lost or destroyed.

The plans for a Huguenot settlement in "Carolana" failed to materialize, and Heath disposed of his interest, in the early 1630's, without having sent any colonists to America. Although Heath had no further official connection with colonization efforts, others continued to promote settlement of his province. Notable among these were Samuel Vassall and Henry Frederick Howard, Lord Maltravers, who had been assigned parts of Heath's interest. Apparently, neither established colonies in "Carolana."

The Heath charter was different in several respects from earlier grants of the North Carolina area. One provision, known as the bishop-of-Durham clause, conferred on Heath feudal powers that were almost kingly. Another provision authorized creation of a local nobility in "Carolana." A third new feature was a requirement that laws for the province be enacted "according to the wholesome directions of and with the counsel, assent, and approbation of the Freeholders of the same Province, or the Major part of them." Thus, the Heath charter set new precedents in grants of the North Carolina territory.

After some years had passed without colonies having been established in "Carolana," the crown presumed that the Heath charter had lapsed because of

failure to settle the area. On the basis of this presumption, King Charles II, in 1663, granted the Heath tract to eight of his own supporters; he renamed the tract Carolina and made the new grantees the lords and proprietors of the region. The authority of the crown to make this grant was disputed by those holding rights under the Heath charter, who immediately pressed their own claims to the region. To quiet these claims, the crown issued an order in council, on August 12, 1663, revoking all former grants of the territory, including that to Heath, and reaffirming the grant to the lords proprietors. Later, however, heirs to the Heath grant renewed their claims, maintaining that the order in council of August 12, 1663, did not constitute judicial action, and, therefore, was not a legal annulment of the charter. After many years of controversy, the rights of the Heath claimants were recognized. In 1768, more than a century after the dispute began, heirs to the Heath grant were awarded 100,000 acres of land in the interior of New York in settlement of their claims to "Carolana."

Although the Heath charter had little or no direct effect on the colonization of North Carolina, it did influence the history of the area, for it was used as a model when the 1663 charter was drafted. The chief provisions of the Heath grant reappeared in the lords proprietors' charters.

THE DOCUMENT

CHARLES, by the grace of God, of England, Scotland, France, and Ireland King, Defender of the Faith, etc. To all to whom these present letters shall come, greeting:

We have seen the enrollment of certain of our letters patents, under our great seal of England, made to Sir Robert Heath, Knight, our Attorney General, bearing date at Westminster the Thirtieth day of October in the fifth year of our reign, and enrolled in our Court of Chancery, and remaining upon Record among the Rolls of the said Court in these words:

The King, to all to whom these presents, etc., greeting:

Whereas, our beloved and faithful subject and servant, Sir Robert Heath, Knight, our Attorney General, kindled with a certain laudable and pious desire as well of enlarging the Christian religion as our Empire, and increasing the Trade and Commerce of this our Kingdom:

A certain Region or Territory, to be hereafter described, in our lands in the parts of America, betwixt one and thirty, and thirty-six degrees of Northern latitude, inclusively, placed, yet hitherto untilled, neither inhabited by ours or the Subjects of any other Christian King, Prince, or state, But in some parts of it inhabited by certain Barbarous men who have not any knowledge of the Divine Deity; He being about to lead thither a Colony of men, large and plentiful, professing the true religion, sedulously and industriously applying themselves to the culture of the said lands and to merchandising; to be performed by industry and at his own charges, and others by his example;

And in this his purpose in this affair, for our service and honour, he has given us full satisfaction; which purpose of his being so laudable, and manifestly tending to our honour and the profit of our Kingdom of England, We, with a Royal regard considering these things, do think meet to approve and prosecute them;

For which end the said Sir Robert Heath has humbly supplicated that all that Region, with the Isles thereunto belonging, with certain sorts of privileges and jurisdictions for the wholesome government of his Colony and Region aforesaid, and for the estate of the appurtenances, may be given, granted, and confirmed to Him, his heirs and Assigns, by our Royal Highness:

Know, therefore, that we, prosecuting with our Royal favour the pious and laudable purpose and desire of our aforesaid Attorney, of our Especial grace, certain knowledge, and mere motion, have Given,

Granted, and confirmed, and, by this our present charter, to the said Sir Robert Heath, Knight, his heirs and assigns, for ever, do give, Grant, and confirm: all that River or Rivulet of St. Mathew on the South side, and all that river or Rivulet of the Great Pass on the North side; and all the lands, Tenements, and Hereditaments lying, being, and extending within or between the said Rivers, by that draught or Tract, to the Ocean upon the East Side; and so to the west, and so far as the Continent there extends itself, with all and every their appurtenances; and also, all those our Islands of Veajus Bahama, and all other Isles and Islands lying Southerly there or near upon the foresaid continent; All which lie, inclusively, within the degrees of thirty-one and thirty-six of Northern latitude;

And all and singular the ports and stations of shipping, and the Creeks of the Sea belonging to the Rivers, Islands, and lands aforesaid; with the fishings of all sorts of fish, Whales, Sturgeons, and of other Royalties in the Sea or in the Rivers;

Moreover, all veins, Mines, or pits, either open or concealed, of Gold, Silver, Jewels, and precious stones; and all other things whatsoever, whether of stones or metals, or any other thing or matter found or to be found in the Region, Territory, Isles, or Limits aforesaid;

And furthermore, the Patronages and advowsons of all churches which shall happen to be built hereafter in the said Region, Territory, and Isles and limits by the increase of the religion and worship of Christ;

Together with all and singular these, and these so Amply: Rights, Jurisdictions, privileges, prerogatives, Royalties, liberties, and immunities, with Royal rights and franchises whatsoever, as well by Sea as by land, within that Region, Territory, Isles, and limits aforesaid;

To have, exercise, use, and enjoy, in like manner as any Bishop of Durham within the Bishopric, or County Palatine, of Durham, in our Kingdom of England, ever heretofore had, held, used, or enjoyed, or of right ought or could have, hold, use, or enjoy.

And, by these presents, we make, create, and constitute the same Sir Robert Heath, his Heirs and assigns, true and absolute Lords and Proprietors of the Region and Territory aforesaid, and all other the premises, for us, our heirs and successors;

Saving always, the faith and allegiance due to us, our heirs and Successors;

To have, hold, possess, and enjoy the said Region, Isles, Rivers, and the rest of the premises, to the said Sir Robert Heath, Knight, his Heirs and assigns, to the sole and proper Use and behoof of him, Sir Robert Heath, Knight, his heirs and assigns, for ever; with that meaning, that the

said Sir Robert Heath, his heirs and assigns, shall plant the premises according to certain instructions and directions of Ours, signed with our Royal hand, of the date of the presents, remaining with our principal Secretary, to our use, our heirs and successors;

To be held of Us, our Heirs and Successors, Kings of England, in chief, by Knight's service; and by paying for it, to us, our Heirs and successors, one Circle of Gold, formed in the fashion of a crown, of the weight of twenty Ounces, with this inscription engraved upon it, *DEUS CORONET OPUS SUUM,* whensoever, and as often as it shall happen, that we, Our Heirs or Successors, shall enter the said Region; and also, the fifth part of all the metal of Gold and Silver, which in English is called Gold and Silver Ore, which shall, from time to time, happen to be found within the foresaid limits; and such a proportion of the profits and commodities out of the premises as are fully contained in the instructions and declarations aforesaid.

But that the aforesaid Region or Territory, so granted and described, may be more illustrious by Us than all the other Regions of that Land, and may be adorned with more ample Titles:

Know, that we, of our free grace, certain knowledge, and mere motion, do think fit to erect the said Region, Territory, and Isles into a Province, and, by the fullness of our power and Kingly Authority, for Us, our Heirs and Successors, we do erect and incorporate them into a Province, and name the same CAROLANA, or the Province of Carolana, and the foresaid Isles the Carolarns Islands; and so we will that in all times hereafter they shall be named.

And because we herebefore have ordained and made the foresaid Sir Robert Heath, Knight, true Lord and proprietor of all the aforenamed Province:

Furthermore, know ye, that we, for our selves, our Heirs and Successors, do give Power to the said Sir Robert, of whose faith, prudence, industry, and provident circumspection we have great confidence, and to his Heirs and assigns, for the good and happy Government of the said Province, to form, make, and enact, and Publish under the Seal of the said Sir Robert, his Heirs and assigns, what Laws soever may concern the public state of the said province, or the private profit of all, according to the wholesome directions of and with the counsel, assent, and approbation of the Freeholders of the same Province, or the Major part of them; Who, when and as often as need shall require, shall, by the aforesaid Sir Robert Heath, his Heirs and Assigns, and in that form which to him or them shall seem best, be called together to make laws; and those to be for all

men within the said province and the bounds of it for the time being, or under his or their Government or power, either Sailing towards Carolana or returning from thence, either Outward to England or Outward to any other Dominion of Ours whatsoever; constituted by imposition of fines, imprisonment, or any other constraint whatsoever; and we grant to the said Sir Robert, his heirs and assigns, free, full, and all kind of power, by the Tenor of these presents, if the quality of the offence requires it, to punish by the loss of life or limb, by himself, his Heirs or assigns, or by their Deputies, Lieutenants, Judges, Justices, Magistrates, Officers, and Ministers, to be constituted and made according to the tenor and true intent of these presents, duly to be executed;

And also, to the said Sir Robert Heath, his Heirs and assigns, as to them shall seem most meet, power of constituting and ordaining Judges and Justices, Magistrates and officers whatsoever, for whatsoever causes and with what power soever, and in what form, by Sea or by Land;

Also, crimes and all excesses whatsoever against such laws, either before judgment received or after, power of remitting, releasing, pardoning, and abolishing; and all and singular complements of justice, courts, tribunals, forms of judgments, and manners of process belonging to them; although there be not mention made nor expression of them in these presents;

Which Laws, as aforesaid, to be proclaimed, and to be endowed with the most absolute firmness of right; we will, enjoin, command, and order that they be inviolably observed and kept by all men the Lieges and Subjects of Us, our Heirs and Successors, as far as it may concern them, and under the pains in them expressed and to be expressed;

Yet, so that the foresaid laws and ordinances be consonant to Reason, and not repugnant or contrary but, as conveniently as may be done, consonant to the Laws, Statutes, Customs, and rights of our Realm of England.

And because in the Government of so great a Province sudden chances many times happen to which it will be necessary to apply a remedy before that the Freeholders of the said province can be called together to make Laws; neither will it be convenient upon a continued title in an Emergent occasion to gather together so great a people:

Therefore, for the better Government of the said Province, we will and ordain, and, by these presents, for Us, our Heirs and Successors, do grant unto the said Sir Robert Heath, his Heirs and assigns, by himself or by magistrates and Officers duly constituted for that purpose, as before is said, shall and may have power from time to time to make and constitute

wholesome and convenient Ordinances within the Province aforesaid, to be kept and observed as well for the preserving the peace as for the better Government of the people there living; and to give public notice of them to all whom it does or may concern; which Ordinances we will that they be inviolably observed within the said province under the pains expressed in them;

So as the said Ordinances be consonant to Reason and not repugnant nor contrary, but, as conveniently as may be done, consonant, to the Laws, Statutes, and rights of our Realm of England, as is aforesaid;

So also, that the same Ordinances extend not themselves against the right or interest of any person or persons or to distrain, bind, or burden in or upon his freehold, Goods, or chattels, or to be received any where than in the same province or the Isles aforesaid.

Moreover, that New Carolana may happily increase by the multitude of people thronging thither, and also that they be firmly defended from the incursions of the Barbarous and of other piratical or plundering Enemies:

Therefore, we, for our selves, our Heirs and Successors, at the will and pleasure of the said Sir Robert Heath, his heirs and assigns, do give and grant, by these presents, to all men and our Subjects lieges, of our Heirs and Successors, both those in present and to come, unless it shall be in an especial manner forbidden, power, licence, and liberty to build and fortify themselves and their families in the said Province of Carolana, for the public safety of their seats there planted, tilled, and inhabited, with forts, castles, and other fortifications; with fitting ships, also, and convenient furniture for transportation; the statute of Fugitives or any other whatsoever contrary to these premises in any wise notwithstanding.

We will also, and, for Us, our Heirs and Successors, out of our great favour, we firmly command, constitute, ordain, and require that the said Province be in our Allegiance; and that all and every our Subjects and Lieges, and of our Heirs and Successors, brought or to be brought into the said Province, their children, either their already born or hereafter to be born, are and shall be Natural and Lieges to Us, our Heirs and Successors; and in all things shall be held, treated, reputed, and accounted as faithful Lieges of us, our heirs and Successors, born in our Kingdom of England;

And also, that they shall possess lands, Tenements, Rents, services, and Hereditaments whatsoever with our Kingdom of England and other our Dominions, to purchase, receive, take, have, hold, buy, and possess, and them to use and enjoy, and also, them to give, sell, alienate, and be-

queath; and also, all liberties, franchises, and privileges of this our Realm to have and possess freely, quietly, and peaceably; and that they may use and enjoy them as our lieges born or to be born within our Kingdom of England, without impediment, Molestation, or vexation, claim, or grievance, from us, our Heirs and successors, whatsoever; any statute, Act, Ordinance, or provision here upon to the contrary notwithstanding.

Furthermore, that our Subjects may be incited with a ready and cheerful mind to undertake this expedition with the hope of gain and the sweetness of privileges:

Know, that we, out of our especial favour, certain knowledge, and mere motion, do give licence and grant free power, as well to the said Sir Robert Heath, Knight, his Heirs and assigns, as to all others who shall go from time to time to inhabit in Carolana aforesaid, all and singular, all and singular their goods, as well movable as immovable, Wares, Merchandise, also Weapons and Warlike instruments, offensive and defensive, in any ports of Ours, our Heirs and Successors, to be laded in ships for to be transported into the province of Carolana, by Him, or his or their assigns; and this without molestation by us, our Heirs and Successors, or any officers of Us, our Heirs or Successors, or Taxminders to Us, our Heirs and Successors; paying, notwithstanding, to Us, our Heirs and Successors, all and all manner of impositions, Subsidies, Customs, and other Dues, for the said things, wares, and merchandises so exported, as are usual and accustomed; any Statute, Act, Ordinance, or other thing whatsoever to the contrary notwithstanding;

Always provided, that before the said Goods, things, and merchandises are carried to and loaded in the ships, that licence for them be desired and obtained from the High Treasurer of the Kingdom of England to Us, our Heirs and Successors, or the commissioners for our Treasury, or from Six or more of the Privy Council of Us, our Heirs and Successors, inscribed under their hands; To which Treasurer, Commissioners, and Privy Council of Us, our Heirs and Successors, or to any Six or more of them, we, for Our selves, our Heirs and Successors, have given and granted, as, by these presents, we do give and grant, power to grant licence in the form aforesaid.

And because in so remote a Region, Seated among so many barbarous nations, it is probable that the incursions as well of those Barbarous as of other enemies, Pirates, and Robbers may cause fear:

Therefore, we, for our selves, our Heirs and Successors, have given to the foresaid Sir Robert Heath, Knight, his heirs and assigns, by himself, his Captains, or other his officers, that all men, of whatever condition or

wheresoever born, being at that time in the province of Carolana, power to call to their Colours; to cause Musters, to make war, to pursue enemies and Robbers aforesaid, by Land and Sea, even beyond the bounds of his province, and them, with God's blessing, to overcome and to take, and, being taken by right of war, to slay, or, according to his pleasure, to preserve; and all and every thing which do appertain to the right and Office of a Captain General, or have been used to appertain, to be done; and, by these presents, do give full and free power as any Captain General ever had.

We will also, and, by this our charter, do give power, Liberty, and Authority to the foresaid Sir Robert Heath, Knight, his Heirs and assigns, That, in case of Rebellion, sudden tumult, or sedition, if any such shall chance to be, which God forbid, either upon the land within the Province aforesaid or upon the wide Ocean, either making a journey towards Carolana aforesaid or returning from thence, we, by these presents, for us, our heirs and Successors, do give and grant power and Authority most ample to himself, or by Captains, Deputies, or other their officers Authorized to this purpose, under their Seals, against all authors of innovations, seditions against the Government of him or them, withdrawing themselves, speakers evil of the militia, Renegades, deserters ——[1] or any others whatsoever offending against the matter, manner, and Discipline Military, shall, by them, be punished by law Military, so freely and in such ample manner and form as any Captain General, by the virtue of his office, may or could do.

Furthermore, lest the way to Honours and Dignities may seem to be shut and altogether barred up to men honestly born, and who are willing to undertake this present expedition, and are desirous, in so remote and far distant a Region, to deserve well of Us and of our Kingdoms, in peace and war; for that, do, for our selves, our heirs and Successors, Give full and free power to the foresaid Sir Robert Heath, Knight, his heirs and assigns, to confer favours, graces, and honours upon those well-deserving Citizens that inhabit within the foresaid province, and the same with whatever Titles and dignities, provided they be not the same as are now used in England, to adorn at his pleasure;

Also, to erect villages into Boroughs, and Boroughs into Cities, for the merits of the inhabitants and convenience of the places, with privileges and befitting immunities to be erected and incorporated; and to do all other and Singular upon the premises which shall seem most con-

---

[1] A blank in the manuscript is indicated thus: ——.

venient to him or them, although they be such which, of their own natures, do require mandates or warrant more especial than is expressed in these presents.

And because the beginnings of Colonies and all public goods and affairs do wont to labour under divers inconveniences and difficulties:

Therefore, we, favouring the beginnings of this present Colony, and that those that are molested in one thing may be relieved in another providing by our Kingly care, out of our especial grace, certain knowledge, and mere motion, by this our charter, do give and grant licence to the foresaid Sir Robert Heath, his heirs and assigns, and to all the Dwellers and inhabitants of Carolana aforesaid Whatsoever, both present and to come:

That whatsoever Wares or Merchandises out of the growth and increase of the said province, by land or Sea, freely to bring, by himself, or his factors or Assigns, into whatever port of us, our heirs and Successors, of our Kingdoms of England or Ireland; and them to unlade and otherwise thereof to dispose; or, if need be, continually to keep for a whole year the said merchandises from being unladed, or them again into the same or other ships to lade, and to export them into what Regions soever they please, whether Ours or Strangers';

Always provided, that so many and such Customs, impositions, subsidies, and Tolls, and other duties which they are bound to pay to us, our heirs and Successors, and only such and the like as our other Subjects for the time being are bound to pay, beyond what and which by no means we will that the inhabitants of the aforesaid Carolana be molested or Grieved.

And furthermore, of our more ample and special favour, and out of our certain knowledge and mere motion, we, for our selves, our heirs and successors, do grant to the foresaid Sir Robert Heath, Knight, his Heirs and assigns, full and absolute power and Authority of making, erecting, and constituting within the foresaid province of Carolana, and the Isles aforesaid, so many or such Sea ports, stations of ships, Creeks, and other places of lading for ships, boats, and other vessels, and in so many and in such like places, and with such rights, jurisdictions, liberties, and privileges belonging to the like ports, as to him or them shall seem most expedient; And that all and singular ships, boats, and other vessels whatsoever, for whatever cause of merchandising coming to or going from the said Province, shall be laded and unladed only at such ports as shall be erected and appointed so by the said Sir Robert Heath, his heirs or Assigns; any use or custom or any other thing notwithstanding;

Always saving and reserving, to all our subjects of our kingdom of

England, our heirs and Successors, liberty of fishing, as well in the Sea as in the Creeks of the foresaid province, and privilege to salt, harden, and dry fishes upon the shores of the said province, as it has been reasonably used and enjoyed heretofore, anything in these presents to the contrary notwithstanding; All which liberties and privileges the Subjects of us, our heirs and Successors, as is aforesaid, shall enjoy, yet without doing any notable hurt or injury in any way to the aforesaid Sir Robert Heath, his Heirs and assigns, or to the Dwellers or inhabitants on the ports, creeks, and shores aforesaid of the same province, and more especial in their Trees there growing; And if any one commits any such harm or injury, he shall undergo the peril and danger of the highest displeasure of Us, our heirs and Successors, and the due chastisement of the Law.

And if by chance hereafter some doubts and questions may be framed about the true sense and meaning of any word, clause, or sentence contained in this our present charter:

We will, enjoin, and command that always, and in all things, that interpretation be used, and shall be received in all our Courts, which shall be judged more benign, profitable, and favourable to the foresaid Sir Robert Heath, Knight, his heirs and assigns, and to the dwellers and inhabitants of the foresaid province; provided always, that no interpretation be made by which the religion of the Holy God, and true Christian, or the Allegiance due to Us, our heirs and Successors, may suffer in the least any lessening, prejudice, or loss.

Nevertheless, we will, and our trust in the aforesaid Sir Robert Heath, Knight, his heirs and assigns, is, and the aforesaid Sir Robert Heath, Knight, for himself, his Heirs, executors, and assigns, does agree and grant to and with us, our Heirs and Successors, that the said Sir Robert Heath, Knight, his heirs and assigns, in the Province and foresaid Isles to be planted and inhabited, shall so behave themselves in all things as we, by our instructions and directions signed with our Royal hand, as aforesaid, most especially to instruct and direct them, shall think most convenient and necessary for our honour and service;

Nevertheless, always provided, that if it shall happen the River or Rivulet or Isles aforesaid, or other the premises, or any part or parcel of the same, to be now granted to any person or persons, by Us or by our dear Father, King James, or is now actually possessed or inhabited by any of our subjects, or by the subjects of any other Christian Prince or State, that then these our letters patents, and all in them contained, so far as they contain so much of the premises so granted and which are now so

actually possessed and inhabited, as is aforesaid, shall be void and of no effect; These our letters Patents, or anything in them contained, to the contrary in any wise notwithstanding.

And that express mention, etc. In witness whereof, etc. Witness, the King, at Westminster, the Thirtieth Day of October. *Per breve de privato Sigillo.*

And we have thought fit, by these presents, to exemplify the Tenor and enrollment of our foresaid letters patents, at the request of the foresaid Sir Robert Heath, Knight.

In Testimony whereof we have caused these our letters to be made Patent.

Witness, our self, at Canterbury, the Fourth Day of August, in the Seventh Year of our Reign.

Examined by us: Rob. Rich et Jo. Mychell, clerks.

[Transcribed from a photostatic reproduction of a paper copy of an exemplification under the great seal, dated August 4, 1631. Manuscript in the British Public Record Office, London. Reference: P. R. O. 30/24/48. Photostatic copy deposited in the State Department of Archives and History, Raleigh, North Carolina.]

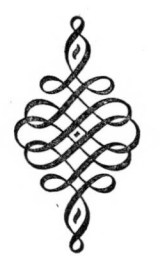

Charter to the Lords Proprietors of Carolina

March 24, 1663

INTRODUCTION

A charter granting the old Heath tract to eight prominent supporters of King Charles II passed the seals on March 24, 1663. The recipients of this charter had helped Charles regain the English throne after an exile following the execution of his father, Charles I. The territory granted, which had been called Carolana in the Heath charter, was now named Carolina, and the grantees were designated "the true and absolute Lords and Proprietaries" of the province.

All of the men to whom Carolina was granted had given King Charles substantial aid. Edward Hyde, Earl of Clarendon, had gone into exile with Charles and had been a leader in restoring the monarchy. George Monck, Duke of Albemarle, who had been commander of troops under Cromwell, had used his influence over the army to provide decisive assistance in effecting the restoration of the monarchy. William Craven, Earl of Craven, had contributed large sums of money to Charles' cause, and he had lost much property through confiscation by the Commonwealth. John Berkeley, Baron Berkeley of Stratton, had gone to London to plead openly for the life of Charles I; consequently, he had been forced to flee to Paris and live in exile until the restoration. Anthony Ashley Cooper, Baron Ashley of Wimborne St. Giles, had supported Cromwell for a time, but later he had opposed Cromwell in Parliament and had been influential in returning power to that body as the first step in restoring the monarchy. Sir George Carteret, governor of the Isle of Jersey, had provided hospitality to Charles and his retinue during the exile and had contributed substantial sums for arms and ammunition for the royalist forces. Sir William Berkeley, governor of Virginia, had kept that colony loyal to Charles and had aided Cavaliers who sought refuge in Virginia. Sir John Colleton had raised troops and had contributed money for King Charles' cause; he later had become a planter in Barbados. Colleton and William Berkeley, both of whom had first-hand knowledge of America, appear to have taken the initiative in obtaining the charter.

The 1663 charter provided the basis for the beginning of representative gov-

ernment in North Carolina. It required that, except in emergencies, laws promulgated by the proprietors be enacted "with the advice, assent, and approbation of the Freemen of the said Province, or of the greater part of them, or of their Delegates or Deputies," whom the proprietors were directed to assemble from time to time "in such manner and form as to them shall seem best." Although at times during the proprietary period the assembly was allowed little power, popular participation in the government of the colony was maintained in form throughout the period. Eventually, the assembly became an important governmental agency in the colony.

Another significant feature of the 1663 charter is a provision giving the proprietors feudal powers equal to those formerly possessed by the bishop of the county palatine of Durham. This provision became the legal basis for many features of the Fundamental Constitutions of Carolina, by means of which the proprietors sought to establish a feudal type of society in their province. Another provision of the charter authorized the proprietors to create a local nobility in Carolina. This provision had little effect, as few noblemen were created by the proprietors.

A third important feature of the proprietary charter is a provision authorizing religious tolerance in Carolina. Although the Church of England was to be the established church in the province, the proprietors were given "Licence, liberty, and Authority" to grant "Indulgencies and Dispensations" to those "Who really in their Judgments, and for Conscience sake" could not conform to the ritual and beliefs of the established church. Such a provision had not appeared in previous charters involving the North Carolina area. In conformity with the religious tolerance provision, the proprietors permitted all religious groups to follow their own forms of worship in Carolina.

By 1663, a few settlers from the Virginia colony already had moved into the area adjoining Albemarle Sound. Although this settlement was thought to be included in the grant to the proprietors, it was not. The mistake seems not to have been discovered for some time, as the proprietors established government, granted land, and exercised other privileges in the Albemarle region, despite its omission from their grant. Soon after the charter was issued, the proprietors in England authorized their fellow proprietor in America, Sir William Berkeley, who was governor of Virginia, to exercise governmental authority over the Albemarle settlement. A year later, in October, 1664, William Drummond was appointed governor of Albemarle. It was not until June, 1665, however, that the proprietors were given legal authority over the settlement, by issuance of a second charter adding the Albemarle area and other territory to Carolina.

THE DOCUMENT

CHARLES THE SECOND, BY THE grace of God, King of England, Scotland, France, and Ireland, defender of the Faith, etc. To ALL to whom these presents shall come, Greeting:

WHEREAS, our right trusty and right well-beloved Cousins and Counsellors: Edward, Earl of Clarendon, our High Chancellor of England; and George, Duke of Albemarle, Master of our Horse and Captain General of all our Forces; Our right trusty and well-beloved William, Lord Craven; John, Lord Berkley; Our right trusty and well-beloved Counsellor, Anthony, Lord Ashley, Chancellor of our Exchequer; Sir George Carterett, Knight and Baronet, Vice Chamberlain of our Household; And our trusty and well-beloved Sir William Berkley, Knight; and Sir John Colleton, Knight and Baronet, being excited with a laudable and pious zeal for the propagation of the Christian Faith and the enlargement of our Empire and Dominions, HAVE humbly besought leave of us, by their industry and Charge, to Transport and make an ample Colony of our Subjects, Natives of our Kingdom of England and elsewhere within our Dominions, unto a certain Country, hereafter described, in the parts of AMERICA not yet cultivated or planted, and only inhabited by some barbarous People who have no knowledge of Almighty God;

AND WHEREAS, the said Edward, Earl of Clarendon; George, Duke of Albemarle; William, Lord Craven; John, Lord Berkley; Anthony, Lord Ashley; Sir George Carterett; Sir William Berkley; and Sir John Colleton, have humbly besought us to give, grant, and Confirm unto them, and their heirs, the said Country, with Privileges and Jurisdictions requisite for the good Government and safety thereof:

KNOW YE, therefore, that We, favouring the pious and noble purpose of the said Edward, Earl of Clarendon; George, Duke of Albemarle; William, Lord Craven; John, Lord Berkley; Anthony, Lord Ashley; Sir George Carterett; Sir William Berkley; and Sir John Colleton, Of our especial grace, certain knowledge, and mere motion, HAVE given, granted, and Confirmed, AND, by this our present Charter, for us, our heirs and Successors, Do give, grant, and Confirm, unto the said Edward, Earl of Clarendon; George, Duke of Albemarle; William, Lord Craven; John, Lord Berkley; Anthony, Lord Ashley; Sir George Carterett; Sir William Berkley; and Sir John Colleton, their heirs and Assigns:

ALL that Territory or Tract of ground, situate, lying, and being within our Dominions in America, extending from the North end of the Island called Luck Island, which lies in the Southern Virginia Seas and

within six and Thirty Degrees of the Northern Latitude, and to the West as far as the South Seas; and so Southerly as far as the River Saint Mathias, which borders upon the Coast of Florida, and within one and Thirty Degrees of Northern Latitude; and West in a direct Line as far as the South Seas aforesaid; Together with all and singular Ports, Harbours, Bays, Rivers, Isles, and Islets belonging unto the Country aforesaid; And also, all the Soil, Lands, Fields, Woods, Mountains, Farms, Lakes, Rivers, Bays, and Islets situate or being within the Bounds or Limits aforesaid; with the Fishing of all sorts of Fish, Whales, Sturgeons, and all other Royal Fishes in the Sea, Bays, Islets, and Rivers within the premises, and the Fish therein taken;

AND moreover, all Veins, Mines, and Quarries, as well discovered as not discovered, of Gold, Silver, Gems, and precious Stones, and all other, whatsoever be it, of Stones, Metals, or any other thing whatsoever found or to be found within the Country, Isles, and Limits aforesaid;

AND FURTHERMORE, the Patronage and Advowsons of all the Churches and Chapels which, as Christian Religion shall increase within the Country, Isles, Islets, and Limits aforesaid, shall happen hereafter to be erected; Together with licence and power to Build and found Churches, Chapels, and Oratories in convenient and fit places within the said Bounds and Limits, and to cause them to be Dedicated and Consecrated according to the Ecclesiastical Laws of our Kingdom of England; Together with all and singular the like and as ample Rights, Jurisdictions, Privileges, Prerogatives, Royalties, Liberties, Immunities, and Franchises of what kind soever within the Country, Isles, Islets, and Limits aforesaid;

TO HAVE, use, exercise, and enjoy, and in as ample manner as any Bishop of Durham, in our Kingdom of England, ever heretofore have held, used, or enjoyed, or of right ought or could have, use, or enjoy.

AND them, the said Edward, Earl of Clarendon; George, Duke of Albemarle; William, Lord Craven; John, Lord Berkley; Anthony, Lord Ashley; Sir George Carterett; Sir William Berkley; and Sir John Colleton, their heirs and assigns, WE DO, by these presents, for us, our heirs and Successors, make, Create, and Constitute the true and absolute Lords and Proprietaries of the Country aforesaid, and of all other the premises;

SAVING always, the Faith, Allegiance, and Sovereign Dominion due to us, our heirs and Successors, for the same; and Saving also, the right, title, and interest of all and every our Subjects of the English Nation which are now Planted within the Limits and bounds aforesaid, if any be;

TO HAVE, HOLD, possess, and enjoy the said Country, Isles, Islets,

and all and singular other the premises; to them, the said Edward, Earl of Clarendon; George, Duke of Albemarle; William, Lord Craven; John, Lord Berkley; Anthony, Lord Ashley; Sir George Carterett; Sir William Berkley; and Sir John Colleton, their heirs and Assigns, forever;

To BE HELD of us, our heirs and Successors, as of our Manor of East Greenwich, in our County of Kent, in Free and Common Soccage, and not in Capite nor by knight's Service;

YIELDING AND PAYING yearly, to us, our heirs and Successors, for the same, the yearly Rent of Twenty Marks of Lawful money of England, at the Feast of All Saints, yearly, forever, The First payment thereof to begin and be made on the Feast of All Saints which shall be in the year of Our Lord One thousand six hundred Sixty and five; AND also, the fourth part of all Gold and Silver Ore which, within the limits aforesaid, shall, from time to time, happen to be found.

AND that the Country thus by us granted and described may be dignified with as large Titles and Privileges as any other parts of our Dominions and Territories in that Region:

KNOW YE, that We, of our further grace, certain knowledge, and mere motion, HAVE thought fit to Erect the same Tract of Ground, Country, and Island into a Province, and, out of the fullness of our Royal power and Prerogative, WE DO, for us, our heirs and Successors, Erect, Incorporate, and Ordain the same into a province, and do call it the Province of CAROLINA, and so from henceforth will have it called.

AND FORASMUCH AS we have hereby made and Ordained the aforesaid Edward, Earl of Clarendon; George, Duke of Albemarle; William, Lord Craven; John, Lord Berkley; Anthony, Lord Ashley; Sir George Carterett; Sir William Berkley; and Sir John Colleton, their heirs and Assigns, the true Lords and Proprietors of all the Province aforesaid:

KNOW YE, therefore, moreover, that We, reposing especial Trust and Confidence in their fidelity, Wisdom, Justice, and provident circumspection, for us, our heirs and Successors, Do Grant full and absolute power, by virtue of these presents, to them, the said Edward, Earl of Clarendon; George, Duke of Albemarle; William, Lord Craven; John, Lord Berkley; Anthony, Lord Ashley; Sir George Carterett; Sir William Berkley; and Sir John Colleton, and their heirs, for the good and happy Government of the said Province:

To ORDAIN, make, Enact, and under their Seals to publish any Laws whatsoever, either appertaining to the public State of the said Province or to the private utility of particular Persons, according to their best discretion, of and with the advice, assent, and approbation of the Freemen

of the said Province, or of the greater part of them, or of their Delegates or Deputies; whom, for enacting of the said Laws, when and as often as need shall require, WE WILL that the said Edward, Earl of Clarendon; George, Duke of Albemarle; William, Lord Craven; John, Lord Berkley; Anthony, Lord Ashley; Sir George Carterett; Sir William Berkley; and Sir John Colleton, and their heirs, shall, from time to time, assemble, in such manner and form as to them shall seem best;

AND the same Laws duly to execute upon all people within the said Province and Limits thereof for the time being, or which shall be Constituted under the power and Government of them, or any of them, either Sailing towards the said Province of CAROLINA or returning from thence towards England, or any other of our or foreign Dominions; by Imposition of penalties, Imprisonment, or any other punishment, YEA, if it shall be needful and the quality of the Offence require it, by taking away member and life, either by them, the said Edward, Earl of Clarindon; George, Duke of Albemarle; William, Lord Craven; John, Lord Berkley; Anthony, Lord Ashley; Sir George Carterett; Sir William Berkley; and Sir John Colleton, and their heirs, or by them or their Deputies, Lieutenants, Judges, Justices, Magistrates, Officers, and Ministers, to be Ordained or appointed according to the tenor and true intention of these presents;

AND LIKEWISE, to appoint and establish any Judges or Justices, Magistrates or Officers whatsoever within the said Province, at Sea or land, in such manner and form as unto the said Edward, Earl of Clarindon; George, Duke of Albemarle; William, Lord Craven; John, Lord Berkley; Anthony, Lord Ashley; Sir George Carterett; Sir William Berkley; and Sir John Colleton, or their heirs, shall seem most convenient;

ALSO, to remit, release, Pardon, and abolish, whether before Judgment or after, all Crimes and Offences whatsoever against the said Laws; and to do all and every other thing and things which unto the Complete establishment of Justice, unto Courts, Sessions, and forms of Judicature, and manners of proceeding therein, do belong, although in these presents express mention be not made thereof;

AND by Judges, by him or them delegated, to award Process, hold Pleas, and determine, in all the said Courts and Places of Judicature, all Actions, Suits, and Causes whatsoever, as well Criminal as Civil, real, mixt, personal, or of any other kind or nature whatsoever;

WHICH LAWS, so as aforesaid, to be published OUR PLEASURE IS, and We do enjoin, require, and Command shall be absolute, firm, and available in law; And that all the liege People of us, our heirs and Successors,

within the said Province of CAROLINA, do observe and keep the same inviolably in those parts, so far as they concern them, under the pains and penalties therein expressed or to be expressed;

PROVIDED, nevertheless, that the said laws be consonant to reason and, as near as may be conveniently, agreeable to the laws and Customs of this our Kingdom of England.

AND because such assemblies of Freeholders cannot be so suddenly called as there may be occasion to require the same:

WE DO, therefore, by these presents, give and Grant unto the said Earl of Clarendon; George, Duke of Albemarle; William, Lord Craven; John, Lord Berkley; Anthony, Lord Ashley; Sir George Carterett; Sir William Berkley; and Sir John Colleton, their heirs and Assigns, by themselves or their Magistrates in that behalf lawfully authorized, full power and authority, from time to time, to make and Ordain fit and wholesome Orders and Ordinances within the Province aforesaid, to be kept and observed, as well for the keeping of the Peace as for the better Government of the People there abiding; and to publish the same to all to whom it may concern;

WHICH Ordinances We do, by these presents, straightly Charge and Command to be inviolably observed within the said Province, under the penalties therein expressed; So as such Ordinances be reasonable, and not repugnant or contrary, but as near as may be agreeable, to the laws and Statutes of this our Kingdom of England; And so as the same Ordinances do not extend to the binding, charging, or taking away of the right or interest of any Person or Persons in their freehold, goods, or Chattels whatsoever.

AND to the end the said Province may be the more happily increased by the multitude of People resorting thither, and may likewise be the more strongly defended from the incursions of Savages and other Enemies, Pirates, and robbers:

THEREFORE, We, for us, our heirs and Successors, Do give and Grant, by these presents, Power, licence, and liberty unto all the liege people of us, our heirs and Successors, in our Kingdom of England or elsewhere within any other our Dominions, Islands, Colonies, or Plantations, Excepting those who shall be especially forbidden, to transport themselves and Families unto the said Province, with convenient Shipping and fitting Provisions, and there to settle themselves, dwell, and inhabit; any law, Act, Statute, Ordinance, or other thing to the contrary in any wise notwithstanding.

AND WE WILL also, and, of our more especial grace, for us, our heirs

and Successors, do straightly enjoin, Ordain, Constitute, and Command, that the said Province of Carolina shall be of our Allegiance; And that all and singular the Subjects and liege people of us, our heirs and Successors, transported or to be transported into the said Province, and the Children of them and of such as shall descend from them there, born or hereafter to be born, be and shall be Denizens and lieges of us, our heirs and Successors, of this our Kingdom of England; and be in all things held, treated, and reputed as the liege, faithful people of us, our heirs and Successors, born within this our said Kingdom or any other of our Dominions; and may inherit or otherwise Purchase and receive, take, have, hold, buy, and possess any lands, Tenements, or hereditaments within the same Places, and them may Occupy and enjoy, give, sell, alien, and bequeath; as likewise, all liberties, Franchises, and Privileges of this our Kingdom of England, and of other our Dominions aforesaid, may freely and quietly have, possess, and enjoy as our liege people born within the same, without the let, molestation, vexation, trouble, or grievance of us, our heirs and Successors; any Statute, Act, Ordinance, or Provision to the contrary notwithstanding.

And furthermore, that our Subjects, of this our said Kingdom of England and other our Dominions, may be the rather encouraged to undertake this Expedition with ready and cheerful minds:

Know Ye, that We, of our especial grace, certain knowledge, and mere motion, Do give and Grant, by virtue of these presents, as well to the said Edward, Earl of Clarendon; George, Duke of Albemarle; William, Lord Craven; John, Lord Berkley; Anthony, Lord Ashley; Sir George Carterett; Sir William Berkley; and Sir John Colleton, and their heirs, as unto all others as shall, from time to time, repair unto the said Province with a purpose to inhabit there or to trade with the Natives of the said Province, full liberty and Licence to lade and freight in any Ports whatsoever of us, our heirs and Successors;

And into the said Province of Carolina, by them, their Servants and Assigns, to Transport all and singular their goods, Wares, and Merchandises; as likewise, all sorts of grain whatsoever, and any other things whatsoever necessary for the food and Clothing, not prohibited by the laws and Statutes of our Kingdoms and Dominions; to be Carried out of the same without any let or molestation of us, our heirs and Successors, or of any other our Officers and Ministers whatsoever; Saving also, to us, our heirs and Successors, the Customs and other duties and payments due for the said Wares and Merchandises, according to the several rates of the Places from whence the same shall be transported.

We Will also, and, by these presents, for us, our heirs and Successors, Do give and Grant Licence, by this our Charter, unto the said Edward, Earl of Clarendon; George, Duke of Albemarle; William, Lord Craven; John, Lord Berkley; Anthony, Lord Ashley; Sir George Carterett; Sir William Berkley; and Sir John Colleton, their heirs and Assigns, and to all the Inhabitants and Dwellers in the Province aforesaid, both present and to come, full power and absolute authority to Import or unlade, by themselves or their Servants, Factors, or Assigns, all Merchandises and goods whatsoever that shall arise of the fruits and Commodities of the said Province, either by land or Sea, into any the Ports of us, our heirs and Successors, in our Kingdom of England, Scotland, or Ireland, Or otherwise to dispose of the said goods in the said Ports; and, if need be, within one year next after the unlading, to lade the said Merchandises and goods again into the same or other Ships, and to Export the same into any other Countries, either of our Dominions or foreign, being in Amity with us, our heirs and Successors; So as they pay such Customs, Subsidies, and other duties for the same, to us, our heirs and Successors, as the rest of our Subjects of this our Kingdom for the time being shall be bound to pay, beyond which We will not that the inhabitants of the said Province of Carolina shall be any way Charged.

Provided, nevertheless, and our Will and pleasure is, and We have further, for the Considerations aforesaid, of our more especial grace, certain knowledge, and mere motion, given and Granted, and, by these presents, for us, our heirs and Successors, Do give and grant, unto the said Edward, Earl of Clarindon; George, Duke of Albemarle; William, Lord Craven; John, Lord Berkley; Anthony, Lord Ashley; Sir George Carterett; Sir William Berkley; and Sir John Colleton, their heirs and Assigns, full and free licence, liberty, and authority, at any time or times from and after the Feast of Saint Michaell The Archangel which shall be in the year of our Lord Christ One thousand six hundred Sixty and Seven, as well to Import and bring into any of our Dominions from the said Province of Carolina, or any part thereof, the several goods and Commodities hereinafter mentioned: That is to say, Silks, Wines, Currants, Raisins, Capers, Wax, Almonds, Oil, and Olives; without paying or Answering to us, our heirs or Successors, any Custom, Impost, or other duty for or in respect thereof, for and during the term and space of Seven years, to commence and be accounted from and after the First Importation of four Tons of any the said goods in any one Bottom, Ship, or Vessel from the said Province into any of our Dominions; as also, to export and carry out of any of our Dominions into the said Province of Carolina, Custom

free, all sorts of Tools which shall be useful or necessary for the Planters there in the accommodation and Improvement of the premises; any thing before in these presents contained, or any Law, Act, Statute, Prohibition, or other matter or thing heretofore had, made, Enacted, or provided, or hereafter to be had, made, Enacted, or Provided, to the contrary in any wise notwithstanding.

And furthermore, of our more ample and especial grace, certain knowledge, and mere motion, We do, for us, our heirs and Successors, Grant unto the said Edward, Earl of Clarendon; George, Duke of Albemarle; William, Lord Craven; John, Lord Berkley; Anthony, Lord Ashley; Sir George Carterett; Sir William Berkley; and Sir John Colleton, their heirs and Assigns, full and absolute power and authority to Make, Erect, and Constitute within the said Province of Carolina, and the Isles and Islets aforesaid, such and so many Seaports, harbours, Creeks, and other Places for discharge and unlading of goods and Merchandises out of Ships, Boats, and other Vessels, and for lading of them, in such and so many Places, and with such Jurisdictions, Privileges, Jurisdictions,[1] and Franchises unto the said Ports belonging, as to them shall seem most expedient;

And that all and singular the Ships, Boats, and other Vessels which shall come for Merchandise and Trade into the said Province, or shall depart out of the same, shall be laden and unladen at such Ports only as shall be erected and Constituted by the said Edward, Earl of Clarendon; George, Duke of Albemarle; William, Lord Craven; John, Lord Berkley; Anthony, Lord Ashley; Sir George Carterett; Sir William Berkley; and Sir John Colleton, their heirs and Assigns, and not elsewhere; any use, Custom, or any thing to the contrary in any wise notwithstanding.

And We do, furthermore, Will, appoint, and Ordain, and, by these presents, for us, our heirs and Successors, do Grant unto the said Edward, Earl of Clarendon; George, Duke of Albemarle; William, Lord Craven; John, Lord Berkley; Anthony, Lord Ashley; Sir George Carterett; Sir William Berkley; and Sir John Colleton, their heirs and Assigns, That they, the said Edward, Earl of Clarendon; George, Duke of Albemarle; William, Lord Craven; John, Lord Berkley; Anthony, Lord Ashley; Sir George Carterett; Sir William Berkley; and Sir John Colleton, their heirs and Assigns, may, from time to time, forever, have and enjoy the Customs and Subsidies, in the Ports, Harbours, Creeks, and other Places within the Province aforesaid, payable for goods, Merchandises, and

[1] Repetition in the manuscript.

Wares there laded or to be laded or unladed; the said Customs to be reasonably Assessed upon any occasion by themselves, and by and with the Consent of the free people there, or the greater part of them, as aforesaid; to whom We give power, by these presents, for us, our heirs and Successors, upon just Cause and in a due proportion, to Assess and Impose the same.

AND FURTHER, of our especial grace, certain knowledge, and mere motion, WE HAVE given, Granted, and Confirmed, and, by these presents, for us, our heirs and Successors, Do give, Grant, and Confirm, unto the said Edward, Earl of Clarendon; George, Duke of Albemarle; William, Lord Craven; John, Lord Berkley; Anthony, Lord Ashley; Sir George Carterett; Sir William Berkley; and Sir John Colleton, their heirs and Assigns, full and absolute licence, power, and authority that the said Edward, Earl of Clarendon; George, Duke of Albemarle; William, Lord Craven; John, Lord Berkley; Anthony, Lord Ashley; Sir George Carterett; Sir William Berkley; and Sir John Colleton, their heirs and Assigns, from time to time hereafter, forever, at his and their will and pleasure, may Assign, Alien, Grant, Demise, or enfeoff the premises, or any part or parcels thereof, to him or them that shall be willing to purchase the same, and to such Person or Persons as they shall think fit;

TO HAVE AND TO HOLD to them the said Person or Persons, their heirs and Assigns, in Fee simple or Fee tail, or for term of life or lives or years; to be held of them, the said Edward, Earl of Clarendon; George, Duke of Albemarle; William, Lord Craven; John, Lord Berkley; Anthony, Lord Ashley; Sir George Carterett; Sir William Berkley; and Sir John Colleton, their heirs and Assigns, by such Rents, Services, and Customs as shall seem meet to the said Edward, Earl of Clarendon; George, Duke of Albemarle; William, Lord Craven; John, Lord Berkley; Anthony, Lord Ashley; Sir George Carterett; Sir William Berkley; and Sir John Colleton, their heirs and Assigns, and not immediately of us, our heirs and Successors.

AND to the same Person or Persons, and to all and every of them, WE DO give and Grant, by these presents, for us, our heirs and Successors, Licence, authority, and power That such Person or Persons may have or take the premises, or any parcel thereof, of the said Edward, Earl of Clarendon; George, Duke of Albemarle; William, Lord Craven; John, Lord Berkley; Anthony, Lord Ashley; Sir George Carterett; Sir William Berkley; and Sir John Colleton, their heirs and Assigns; and the same to hold to themselves, their heirs or Assigns, in what estate of Inheritance soever, in Fee simple or Fee tail or otherwise, as to them and the said Earl

of Clarendon; George, Duke of Albemarle; William, Lord Craven; John, Lord Berkley; Anthony, Lord Ashley; Sir George Carterett; Sir William Berkley; and Sir John Colleton, their heirs and Assigns, shall seem expedient; The Statute made in the Parliament of Edward, Son of King Henry, heretofore King of England, our Predecessor, commonly called the Statute of *Quia Emptores Terrarum*, or any other Statute, Act, Ordinance, use, Law, Custom, or any other matter, Cause, or thing heretofore published or provided to the contrary in any wise notwithstanding.

And because many Persons born or inhabiting in the said Province, for their deserts and Services, may expect, and be capable of, Marks of Honour and favour, which, in respect of the great distance, cannot conveniently be Conferred by us:

Our Will and Pleasure, therefore, is, and We do, by these presents, Give and Grant unto the said Edward, Earl of Clarendon; George, Duke of Albemarle; William, Lord Craven; John, Lord Berkley; Anthony, Lord Ashley; Sir George Carterett; Sir William Berkley; and Sir John Colleton, their Heirs and Assigns, full Power and Authority to give and Confer, unto and upon such of the Inhabitants of the said Province as they shall think do or shall merit the same, such marks of favour and Titles of honour as they shall think fit; so as those Titles or honours be not the same as are enjoyed by or Conferred upon any the Subjects of this our Kingdom of England.

And further, also, We do, by these presents, for us, our heirs and Successors, give and grant Licence to them, the said Edward, Earl of Clarendon; George, Duke of Albemarle; William, Lord Craven; John, Lord Berkley; Anthony, Lord Ashley; Sir George Carterett; Sir William Berkley; and Sir John Colleton, their heirs and Assigns, full power, liberty, and licence to Erect, raise, and build, within the said Province and Places aforesaid, or any part or parts thereof, such and so many Forts, Fortresses, Castles, Cities, Boroughs, Towns, Villages, and other Fortifications whatsoever, And the same, or any of them, to Fortify and furnish with Ordnance, Powder, Shot, Armour, and all other Weapons, Ammunition, and habiliments of War, both offensive and defensive, as shall be thought fit and convenient, for the safety and welfare of the said Province and Places, or any part thereof; And the same, or any of them, from time to time, as occasion shall require, to dismantle, disfurnish, demolish, and pull down; and Also, to place, Constitute, and appoint, in or over all or any of the said Castles, Forts, Fortifications, Cities, Towns, and Places aforesaid, Governors, Deputy Governors, Magistrates, Sher-

iffs, and other Officers, Civil and Military, as to them shall seem meet;

AND to the said Cities, Boroughs, Town, Villages, or any other Place or Places within the said Province, to grant Letters or Charters of Incorporation, with all Liberties, Franchises, and Privileges requisite and usual, or to or within any Corporations within this our Kingdom of England granted or belonging; And in the same Cities, Boroughs, Towns, and other Places, to Constitute, Erect, and appoint such and so many Markets, Marts, and Fairs as shall in that behalf be thought fit and necessary;

AND further, also, to Erect and make in the Province aforesaid, or any part thereof, so many Manors as to them shall seem meet and convenient; and in every of the same Manors to have and to hold a Court Baron, with all things whatsoever which to a Court Baron do belong; And to have and to hold Views of Frankpledge and Courts Leet, for the Conservation of the Peace and better Government of those parts, within such Limits, Jurisdiction, and Precincts as by the said Edward, Earl of Clarendon; George, Duke of Albemarle; William, Lord Craven; John, Lord Berkley; Anthony, Lord Ashley; Sir George Carterett; Sir William Berkley; and Sir John Colleton, or their heirs, shall be appointed for that purpose, with all things whatsoever which to a Court Leet or View of Frankpledge do belong; the same Courts to be held by Stewards, to be Deputed and authorized by the said Edward, Earl of Clarendon; George, Duke of Albemarle; William, Lord Craven; John, Lord Berkley; Anthony, Lord Ashley; Sir George Carterett; Sir William Berkley; and Sir John Colleton, or their heirs, or by the Lords of other Manors and Leets for the time being, when the same shall be Erected.

AND because that, in so remote a Country and situate among so many barbarous Nations, the Invasions as well of Savages as other Enemies, Pirates, and Robbers may probably be feared:

THEREFORE, WE HAVE given, and, for us, our heirs and Successors, Do give, power, by these presents, unto the said Edward, Earl of Clarendon; George, Duke of Albemarle; William, Lord Craven; John, Lord Berkley; Anthony, Lord Ashley; Sir George Carterett; Sir William Berkley; and Sir John Colleton, their heirs and Assigns, by themselves or their Captains or other their Officers, to Levy, Muster, and Train all sorts of men, of what Condition or wheresoever born, in the said Province for the time being; and to make War and pursue the Enemies aforesaid, as well by Sea as by land, yea, even without the limits of the said Province; and, by God's assistance, to vanquish and take them, and, being

taken, to put them to death, by the law of war, or to save them, at their pleasure; and to do all and every other thing which unto the Charge And Office of a Captain General of an Army belongs, or has accustomed to belong, as fully and freely as any Captain General of an Army has ever had the same.

ALSO, our Will and pleasure is, and, by this our Charter, WE DO give unto the said Edward, Earl of Clarendon; George, Duke of Albemarle; William, Lord Craven; John, Lord Berkley; Anthony, Lord Ashley; Sir George Carterett; Sir William Berkley; and Sir John Colleton, their heirs and Assigns, full power, liberty, and authority, in case of rebellion, tumult, or Sedition, if any should happen, which God forbid, either upon the land within the Province aforesaid or upon the main Sea in making a Voyage thither or returning from thence, by him and themselves, their Captains, Deputies, or Officers, to be authorized under his or their Seals for that purpose, to whom also, for us, our heirs and Successors, WE DO give and Grant, by these presents, full power and authority, to exercise Martial Law against mutinous and seditious Persons of those parts, such as shall refuse to submit themselves to their Government, or shall refuse to serve in the Wars, or shall fly to the Enemy, or forsake their Colors or Ensigns, or be loiterers or Stragglers, or otherwise howsoever offending against Law, Custom, or Discipline Military; as freely and in as ample manner and form as any Captain General of an Army, by virtue of his Office, might, or has accustomed to, use the same.

AND Our further pleasure is, and, by these presents, for us, our heirs and Successors, WE DO Grant unto the said Edward, Earl of Clarendon; George, Duke of Albemarle; William, Lord Craven; John, Lord Berkley; Anthony, Lord Ashley; Sir George Carterett; Sir William Berkley; and Sir John Colleton, their heirs and Assigns, and to the Tenants and Inhabitants of the said Province of Carolina, both present and to come, and to every of them, that the said Province, and the Tenants and Inhabitants thereof, shall not from henceforth be held or reputed a Member or part of any Colony whatsoever, in America or elsewhere, now transported or made, or hereafter to be transported or made; nor shall be depending on, or subject to, their Government in any thing, but be absolutely separated and divided from the same;

AND OUR pleasure is, by these presents, that they be separated, and that they be subject immediately to our Crown of England, as depending thereof, forever; And that the Inhabitants of the said Province, nor any

or [2] them, shall, at any time hereafter, be compelled or compellable, or be any ways subject or liable, to appear or Answer to any matter, Suit, Cause, or Plaint whatsoever, out of the Province aforesaid, in any other of our Islands, Colonies, or Dominions, in America or elsewhere, other than in our Realm of England and Dominion of Wales.

And because it may happen that some of the People and Inhabitants of the said Province cannot in their private opinions Conform to the Public Exercise of Religion according to the Liturgy, forms, and Ceremonies of the Church of England, or take or subscribe the Oaths and Articles made and established in that behalf; And for that the same, by reason of the remote distances of those Places, Will, as We hope, be no breach of the unity and uniformity established in this Nation:

Our Will and pleasure, therefore, is, And We do, by these presents, for us, our heirs and Successors, Give and Grant unto the said Edward, Earl of Clarendon; George, Duke of Albemarle; William, Lord Craven; John, Lord Berkley; Anthony, Lord Ashley; Sir George Carterett; Sir William Berkley; and Sir John Colleton, their heirs and Assigns, full and free Licence, liberty, and Authority, by such legal ways and means as they shall think fit, to give and grant unto such Person and Persons inhabiting and being within the said Province, or any part thereof, Who really in their Judgments, and for Conscience sake, cannot or shall not Conform to the said Liturgy and Ceremonies, and take and Subscribe the Oaths and Articles aforesaid, or any of them, such Indulgencies and Dispensations in that Behalf, for and during such time and times, and with such limitations and restrictions, as they, the said Edward, Earl of Clarendon; George, Duke of Albemarle; William, Lord Craven; John, Lord Berkley; Anthony, Lord Ashley; Sir George Carterett; Sir William Berkley; and Sir John Colleton, their heirs or Assigns, shall, in their discretions, think fit and reasonable;

And with this express Proviso and Limitation also, that such Person and Persons to whom such Indulgencies or Dispensations shall be granted, as aforesaid, do and shall, from time to time, Declare and continue all fidelity, Loyalty, and Obedience to us, our heirs and Successors; and be subject and obedient to all other the Laws, Ordinances, and Constitutions of the said Province, in all matters whatsoever, as well Ecclesiastical as Civil; And do not in any wise disturb the Peace and safety thereof, or scandalize or reproach the said Liturgy, forms, and Ceremonies, or any thing relating thereunto, or any Person or Persons what-

[2] Thus in the manuscript.

soever for, or in respect of, his or their use or exercise thereof, or his or their obedience or Conformity thereunto.

AND in Case it shall happen that any doubts or questions should arise concerning the true Sense and understanding of any word, Clause, or Sentence contained in this our present Charter:

WE WILL, Ordain, and Command that, at all times and in all things, such interpretation be made thereof, and allowed in all and every of our Courts whatsoever, as lawfully may be Adjudged most advantageous and favourable to the said Edward, Earl of Clarendon; George, Duke of Albemarle; William, Lord Craven; John, Lord Berkley; Anthony, Lord Ashley; Sir George Carterett; Sir William Berkley; and Sir John Colleton, their heirs and Assigns.

ALTHOUGH EXPRESS MENTION be not made in these presents of the true yearly value and certainty of the premises, or any part thereof, or of any other gifts and grants made by us, our Ancestors or Predecessors, to them, the said Edward, Earl of Clarendon; George, Duke of Albemarle; William, Lord Craven; John, Lord Berkley; Anthony, Lord Ashley; Sir George Carterett; Sir William Berkley; and Sir John Colleton, or any other Person or Persons whatsoever, Or any Statute, Act, Ordinance, Provision, Proclamation, or restraint heretofore had, made, published, ordained, or Provided, or any other thing, Cause, or matter whatsoever to the contrary thereof in any wise notwithstanding.

IN WITNESS whereof We have caused these our Letters to be made Patent.

WITNESS, our Self, at Westminster, the Four and Twentieth day of March, in the Fifteenth year of our Reign.

By the King
HOWARD

[Transcribed from the original charter, which is in the State Department of Archives and History, Raleigh, North Carolina.]

Charter to the Lords Proprietors of Carolina

June 30, 1665

INTRODUCTION

On June 30, 1665, a second charter was issued to the "Lords and Proprietaries" of Carolina. The new grant ostensibly was intended to enlarge the territory of the province, but it may have been intended also to remove a possible defect in the proprietors' title, arising from the fact that the 1663 charter had been issued prior to the order in council declaring the Heath grant void. Under the new charter, the northern boundary of the province was located in the vicinity of the present Virginia–North Carolina line; it extended westward to the Pacific Ocean. The southern boundary, which also extended from ocean to ocean, was placed about one hundred miles south of the present Georgia–Florida line.

The proprietors were authorized by their second charter to divide Carolina into "several counties, baronies, and colonies" and to enact laws for individual subdivisions as well as for the whole province. There also were changes in the wording of provisions regarding religious tolerance. Otherwise, the provisions of the new charter were practically the same as those of the first one.

The lords proprietors were never successful in their attempts to govern Carolina. Confusion and governmental instability were almost constant, and economic progress was slow. Before the end of the seventeenth century, crown officials had become dissatisfied with conditions in the province and had begun to advocate nullification of the proprietors' charter. In the early 1700's, crown officials undertook to institute legal proceedings against the charter, but they failed, for several of the proprietors were members of the House of Lords, and parliamentary privilege protected them against such action. In 1719, the South Carolina inhabitants revolted against the proprietary government, and the crown took over the government of that colony. In North Carolina, the proprietors continued to govern until 1729, when all but one sold their interests in Carolina to the crown. The Earl of Granville, who refused to sell his interest, retained his property rights, but he was forced to relinquish governmental authority. Thus, in 1729, government under the proprietors' charters ended in North Carolina.

THE DOCUMENT

CHARLES THE SECOND, by the grace of God, etc.

Whereas, by our letters Patent, bearing date the Four and twentieth day of March in the fifteenth year of Our reign, we were graciously pleased to grant to our right trusty and right well-beloved Cousin and Counsellor, Edward, Earl of Clarendon, our High Chancellor of England; our right trusty and right entirely beloved Cousin and Counsellor, George, Duke of Albemarle, Master of our Horse; our right trusty and well-beloved William, now Earl of Craven; our right trusty and well-beloved Counsellor, John, Lord Berkeley; our right trusty and well-beloved Counsellor, Anthony, Lord Ashley, Chancellor of Our Exchequer; Our right trusty and well-beloved Counsellor, Sir George Carterett, Knight and Baronet, Vice Chamberlain of Our Household; Our right trusty and well-beloved Sir John Colleton, Knight and Baronet; and Sir William Berkeley, Knight:

All that Province, Territory, or Tract of Ground called Carolina, situate, lying, and being within our Dominions of America, extending from the North end of the Island called Luke Island,[1] which lies in the Southern Virginia Seas and within six and thirty degrees of the Northern latitude, and to the West as far as the South Seas; and so respectively as far as the River of Mathias, which borders upon the Coast of Florida, and within one and thirty degrees of the Northern Latitude; and so West in a direct line as Far as the South Seas aforesaid:

Now Know ye, that we, at the humble request of the said Grantees in the aforesaid Letters Patents named, and as a further Mark of our especial favour toward them, We are graciously pleased to enlarge our said Grant unto them, according to the bounds and limits hereafter specified, and in favour to the pious and noble purpose of the said Edward, Earl of Clarendon; George, Duke of Albemarle; William, Earl of Craven; John, Lord Berkeley; Anthony, Lord Ashley; Sir George Carterett; Sir John Colleton; and Sir William Berkeley, their heirs and Assigns:

All that Province, Territory, or Tract of ground, situate, lying, and being within our Dominions of America aforesaid, extending North and Eastward as far as the North end of Carahtuke River or Gullet; upon a straight westerly line to Wyonoake Creek, which lies within or about the degrees of thirty six and thirty Minutes, Northern latitude, and so West

[1] *Luck Island* in the charter of 1663.

in a direct line as far as the South Seas; and South and Westward as far as the degrees of twenty nine, inclusive, northern latitude; and so West in a direct line as far as the south Seas; together with all and singular Ports, Harbours, Bays, Rivers, and Islets belonging unto the Province or Territory aforesaid;

And also, all the Soil, Lands, Fields, Woods, Mountains, farms, Lakes, Rivers, Bays, and Islets situate or being within the bounds or limits last before mentioned; with the Fishing of all sorts of Fish, Whales, Sturgeons, and all other Royal Fishes in the Sea, Bays, Islets, and Rivers within the premises, and the Fish therein taken, together with the Royalty of the Sea upon the Coast within the limits aforesaid;

And moreover, all veins, Mines, and Quarries, as well discovered as not discovered, of Gold, Silver, Gems, and precious Stones, and all other, whatsoever be it, of Stones, Metals, or any other things found or to be found within the Province, Territory, Islets, and limits aforesaid;

And furthermore, the Patronages and Advowsons of all the Churches and Chapels which, as Christian Religion shall increase within the Province, Territory, Isles, and Limits aforesaid, shall happen hereafter to be erected; together with licence and power to build and found Churches, Chapels, and Oratories in convenient and fit places within the said bounds and limits, And to cause them to be dedicated and consecrated according to the Ecclesiastical laws of our Kingdom of England; together with all and singular the like and as ample Rights, Jurisdictions, privileges, prerogatives, Royalties, liberties, Immunities, and Franchises of what kind soever within the Territory, Isles, Islets, and limits aforesaid;

To have, hold, use, exercise, and enjoy the same as amply and fully, and in as ample manner, as any Bishop of Durham, in our Kingdom of England, ever heretofore had, held, used, or enjoyed, or of right ought or could have, use, or enjoy.

And them, the said Edward, Earl of Clarendon; George, Duke of Albemarle; William, Earl of Craven; John, Lord Berkeley; Anthony, Lord Ashley; Sir George Carterett; Sir John Colleton; and Sir William Berkeley, their heirs and Assigns, we do, by these presents, for us, our heirs and successors, make, Create, and Constitute the true and absolute Lords and Proprietaries of the said Province or Territory, and of all other the premises;

Saving always, the faith, Allegiance, and sovereign dominion due to us, our heirs and successors, for the same;

To have, hold, possess, and enjoy the said Province, Territory, Is-

lets, and all and singular other the premises; to them, the said Edward, Earl of Clarendon; George, Duke of Albemarle; William, Earl of Craven; John, Lord Berkeley; Anthony, Lord Ashley; Sir George Carterett; Sir John Colleton; and Sir William Berkeley, their heirs and Assigns, forever;

To be held of us, our heirs and Successors, as of our Manor of East Greenwich, in Kent, in Free and Common Soccage, and not in capite or by knight service;

Yielding and paying yearly, to us, our heirs and successors, for the same, the fourth part of all Goods [2] and Silver Ore which, within the limits hereby granted, shall, from time to time, happen to be found, over and besides the yearly rent of twenty Marks and the fourth part of Gold and Silver Ore in and by the said recited letters Patents reserved and payable.

And that the Province or Territory hereby granted and described may be dignified with as large titles and privileges as any other parts of our Dominions and Territories in that Region:

Know ye, that we, of our further grace, certain knowledge, and mere motion, have thought fit to annex the same tract of Ground and Territory unto the same Province of Carolina, and, out of the fullness of our Royal power and prerogative, we do, for us, our heirs and successors, annex and unite the same to the Province of Carolina.

And Forasmuch as we have made and Ordained the aforesaid Edward, Earl of Clarendon; George, Duke of Albemarle; William, Earl of Craven; John, Lord Berkeley; Anthony, Lord Ashley; Sir George Carterett; Sir John Colleton; and Sir William Berkeley, their heirs and Assigns, the true Lords and Proprietors of all the Province or Territory aforesaid:

Know ye, therefore, moreover, that we, reposing special trust and confidence in their fidelity, wisdom, Justice, and provident circumspection, for us, our heirs and Successors, do grant full and absolute power, by virtue of these presents, to them, the said Edward, Earl of Clarendon; George, Duke of Albemarle; William, Earl of Craven; John, Lord Berkeley; Anthony, Lord Ashley; Sir George Carterett; Sir John Colleton; and Sir William Berkeley, and their heirs and Assigns, for the good and happy Government of the said whole Province or Territory, full power and authority to erect, Constitute, and make several Counties, Baronies, and Colonies of and within the said Provinces, Territories,

---

[2] Thus in the manuscript.

lands, and hereditaments, in and by the said recited Letters Patents and these presents granted or mentioned to be granted, as aforesaid, with several and distinct Jurisdictions, powers, liberties, and privileges;

And also, to Ordain, make, and Enact, and under their Seals to Publish, any laws and Constitutions whatsoever, either appertaining to the Public State of the said whole Province or Territory, or of any distinct or particular County, Barony, or Colony of or within the same, or to the private utility of particular Persons, according to their best discretion, by and with the advice, assent, and approbation of the Freemen of the said Province or Territory, or of the Freemen of the County, Barony, or Colony For which such law or Constitution shall be made, or the greater part of them, or of their Delegates or Deputies; Whom, for Enacting of the said laws, when and as often as need shall require, We Will, that the said Edward, Earl of Clarendon; George, Duke of Albemarle; William, Earl of Craven; John, Lord Berkeley; Anthony, Lord Ashley; Sir George Carterett; Sir John Colleton; and Sir William Berkeley, and their heirs or Assigns, shall, from time to time, Assemble, in such manner and form as to them shall seem best;

And the same laws duly to execute upon all People within the said Province or Territory, County, Barony, or Colony, and the limits thereof for the time being, [or] which shall be Constituted under the power and Government of them, or any of them, either sailing towards the said Province or Territory of Carolina or returning from thence towards England, or any others of ours or Foreign Dominions; by Imposition of penalties, Imprisonments, or any other punishment, yea, if it shall be needful and the quality of the Offence require it, by taking away member and life, either by them, the said Edward, Earl of Clarendon; George, Duke of Albemarle; William, Earl of Craven; John, Lord Berkeley; Anthonie, Lord Ashley; Sir George Carterett; Sir John Colleton; and Sir William Berkeley, and their heirs, or by them or their Deputies, Lieutenants, Judges, Justices, Magistrates, or Officers whatsoever, as well within the said Province as at Sea, in such manner and form as unto the said Edward, Earl of Clarendon; George, Duke of Albemarle; William, Earl of Craven; John, Lord Berkeley; Anthony, Lord Ashley; Sir George Carterett; Sir John Colleton; and Sir William Berkeley, or their heirs, shall seem most convenient;

Also, to remit, release, pardon, and abolish, whether before Judgement or after, all Crimes and Offences whatsoever against the said laws; and to do all and every other thing and things which unto the complete establishment of Justice, unto Courts, Sessions, and forms of Judicature,

and manners of proceeding therein, do belong, Although in these presents express mention is not made thereof;

And by Judges, to him or them delegated, to award process, hold Pleas, and determine, in all the said Courts and Places of Judicature, All Actions, Suits, and Causes whatsoever, as well criminal as civil, real, mixt, personal, or of any other kind or nature whatsoever;

Which laws, so as aforesaid, to be published Our pleasure is, and we do enjoin, require, and Command shall be absolute, firm, and available in law; And that all the Liege people of us, our heirs and successors, within the said Province or Territory, do observe and keep the same inviolably in those parts, so far as they concern them, under the pains and penalties therein expressed or to be expressed;

Provided, Nevertheless, that the said laws be consonant to reason and, as near as may be conveniently, agreeable to the laws and Customs of this our Realm of England.

And because such Assemblies of Freeholders cannot be so suddenly called as there may be occasion to require the same:

We do, therefore, by these presents, give and Grant unto the said Edward, Earl of Clarendon; George, Duke of Albemarle; William, Earl of Craven; John, Lord Berkeley; Anthony, Lord Ashley; Sir George Carterett; Sir John Colleton; and Sir William Berkeley, their heirs and Assigns, by themselves or their Magistrates in that behalf lawfully authorized, full power and authority, from time to time, to make and Ordain fit and wholesome Orders and Ordinances, within the Province or Territory aforesaid, or any County, Barony, or Province of or within the same; to be kept and observed, as well for the keeping of the Peace as for the better Government of the People there abiding; and to publish the same to all to whom it may concern;

Which Ordinances we do, by these presents, straightly Charge and Command to be inviolably observed within the same Province, Territory, Counties, Baronies, and Provinces, under the Penalties therein expressed; so as such Ordinances be reasonable, and not repugnant or contrary, but as near as may be agreeable, to the laws and Statutes of this Our Kingdom of England; And so as the same Ordinances do not extend to the binding, charging, or taking away of the right or Interest of any person or persons in their Freehold, Goods, or Chattels whatsoever.

And to the end the said Province or Territory may be the more happily increased by the multitude of people resorting thither, and may likewise be the more strongly defended from the Incursions of Savages and other Enemies, Pirates, and Robbers:

Therefore, we, for us, our heirs and successors, do give and grant, by these presents, power, licence, and liberty unto all the liege people of us, our heirs and successors, in our Kingdom of England or elsewhere within any other our Dominions, Islands, Colonies, or Plantations, Excepting those who shall be specially forbidden, to transport themselves and Families into the said Province or Territory, with convenient shipping and fitting provisions, and there to settle themselves, dwell, and Inhabit; Any Law, Act, Statute, Ordinance, or other thing to the contrary in any wise notwithstanding.

And we will also, and, of our especial grace, for us, our heirs and successors, do straightly enjoin, Ordain, Constitute, and Command, that the said Province or Territory shall be of our allegiance; And that all and singular the Subjects and Liege people of us, our heirs and successors, transported or to be transported into the said Province, and the Children of them and such as shall descend from them there, born or hereafter to be born, be and shall be Denizens and Lieges of us, our heirs and successors, of this our Kingdom of England; and be in all things held, treated, and reputed as the liege, faithful People of us, our heirs and successors, born within this our said Kingdom or any other of Our Dominions; and may inherit or otherwise purchase and receive, take, hold, buy, and possess any lands, tenements, or hereditaments within the said places, and them may occupy and enjoy, sell, alien, and bequeath; as likewise, all liberties, Franchises, and privileges of this our Kingdom, and of other our Dominions aforesaid, may freely and quietly have, possess, and enjoy as our liege People born within the same, without the molestation, vexation, trouble, or grievance of us, our heirs and successors; Any Act, Statute, Ordinance, provision to the contrary notwithstanding.

And furthermore, that Our Subjects, of this our said Kingdom of England and other our Dominions, may be the rather encouraged to undertake this expedition with ready and cheerful miens:

Know ye, that we, of our especial grace, certain knowledge, and mere motion, do give and grant, by virtue of these presents, as well to the said Edward, Earl of Clarendon; George, Duke of Albemarle; William, Earl of Craven; John, Lord Berkeley; Anthony, Lord Ashley; Sir George Carterett; Sir John Colleton; and Sir William Berkeley, and their heirs, as unto all others as shall, from time to time, repair unto the said Province or Territory with a purpose to inhabit there or to trade with the Natives thereof, full liberty and licence to lade and Freight in any Ports whatsoever of us, our heirs and successors;

And into the said Province of Carolina, by them, their Servants and

Assigns, to transport all and singular their Goods, Wares, and Merchandises; as likewise, all sorts of Grain whatsoever, and any other things whatsoever necessary for their food and Clothing, not prohibited by the laws and Statutes of our Kingdom and Dominions; to be carried out of the same without any Let or molestation of us, our heirs and successors, or of any other our Officers and Ministers whatsoever; saving also, to us, our heirs and successors, the Customs and other duties and payments due for the said Wares and Merchandises, according to the several rates of the places from whence the same shall be transported.

We will also, and, by these presents, for us, our heirs and successors, do give and grant licence, by this our Charter, unto the said Edward, Earl of Clarendon; George, Duke of Albemarle; William, Earl of Craven; John, Lord Berkeley; Anthony, Lord Ashley; Sir George Carterett; Sir John Colleton; and Sir William Berkeley, their heirs and Assigns, and to all the Inhabitants and dwellers in the Province or Territory aforesaid, both present and to come, full power and absolute authority to import or unlade, by themselves or their servants, Factors, or Assigns, all Merchandises and Goods whatsoever that shall arise of the fruits and commodities of the said Province or Territory, either by land or Sea, into any the Ports of us, our heirs and successors, in our Kingdom of England, Scotland, or Ireland, or otherwise to dispose of the said Goods in the said Ports; and, if need be, within one year next after the unlading, to lade the said Merchandises and Goods again into the same or other Ships, And to export the same into any other Countries, either of our Dominions or Foreign, being in Amity with us, our heirs and Successors; so as they pay such Customs, subsidies, and other duties for the same, to us, our heirs and successors, as the rest of Our Subjects of this our Kingdom for the time being shall be bound to pay, beyond which we will not that the Inhabitants of the said Province or Territory shall be any way charged.

Provided, Nevertheless, and our will and pleasure is, and we have further, for the considerations aforesaid, of our especial grace, certain knowledge, and mere motion, given and Granted, And, by these presents, for us, our heirs and successors, do give and Grant, unto the said Edward, Earl of Clarendon; George, Duke of Albemarle; William, Earl of Craven; John, Lord Berkeley; Anthony, Lord Ashley; Sir George Carterett; Sir John Colleton; and Sir William Berkeley, their heirs and Assigns, full and free licence, liberty, power, and authority, at any time or times from and after the Feast of St. Michaell the Archangel which shall be in the year of Our Lord Christ One thousand six hundred sixty

and seven, as well to import and bring into any our Dominions from the said Province of Carolina, or any part thereof, the several Goods and Commodities hereinafter mentioned: that is to say, Silks, Wines, Currants, Raisins, Capers, Wax, Almonds, Oil, and Olives; without paying or answering to us, our heirs or Successors, Any Custom, Impost, or other duty for or in respect thereof, for and during the term and space of seven years, to commence and be accounted from and after the first Importation of Four Tons of any the said Goods in any one Bottom, Ship, or vessel from the said Province or Territory into any of Our Dominions; as also, to export and carry out of any of our Dominions into the said Province or Territory, Custom free, for all sorts of Tools which shall be useful and necessary for the Planters there in the accommodation and Improvement of the premises; Any thing before in these presents contained, or any law, Act, Statute, prohibition, or other matter or thing heretofore had, made, enacted, or provided, or hereafter to be had, made, Enacted, or provided, or hereafter to be had, made, enacted, or provided,[3] in any wise notwithstanding.

And furthermore, of our more ample and especial grace, certain knowledge, and mere motion, we do, for us, our heirs and successors, grant unto the said Edward, Earl of Clarendon; George, Duke of Albemarle; William, Earl of Craven; John, Lord Berkeley; Anthony, Lord Ashley; Sir George Carterett; Sir John Colleton; and Sir William Berkeley, their heirs and Assigns, full and absolute power and authority to make, erect, and Constitute within the said Province or Territory, and the Isles and Islets aforesaid, such and so many Sea Ports, harbours, Creeks, and other places for discharge and unlading of Goods and Merchandises out of Ships, Boats, and other vessels, and for lading of them, in such and so many places, as with such Jurisdictions, privileges, and Franchises unto the said Ports belonging, as to them shall seem most expedient;

And that all and singular the Ships, Boats, and other vessels which shall come for Merchandise and Trade into the said Province or Territory, or shall depart out of the same, shall be laden and unladen at such ports only as shall be erected and constituted by the said Edward, Earl of Clarendon; George, Duke of Albemarle; William, Earl of Craven; John, Lord Berkeley; Anthony, Lord Ashley; Sir George Carterett; Sir John Colleton; and Sir William Berkeley, their heirs and Assigns, and not else-

[3] Repetition in the manuscript.

where; Any use, Custom, or any thing to the contrary in any wise notwithstanding.

And we do, furthermore, will, appoint, and Ordain, and, by these presents, for us, our heirs and Successors, do grant unto the said Edward, Earl of Clarendon; George, Duke of Albemarle; William, Earl of Craven; John, Lord Berkeley; Anthony, Lord Ashley; Sir George Carterett; Sir John Colleton; and Sir William Berkeley, their heirs and Assigns, that they, the said Edward, Earl of Clarendon; George, Duke of Albemarle; William, Earl of Craven; John, Lord Berkeley; Anthony, Lord Ashley; Sir George Carterett; Sir John Colleton; and Sir William Berkeley, their heirs and Assigns, may, from time to time, forever, have and enjoy the Customs and Subsidies, in the Ports, harbours, Creeks, and other places within the Province aforesaid, payable for the Goods, Merchandises, and Wares there laded or to be laded or unladed; the said Customs to be reasonably assessed upon any occasion by themselves, and by and with the consent of the Free people, or the greater part of them, as aforesaid; To whom we give power, by these presents, for us, our heirs and successors, upon just cause and in a due proportion, to Assess and Impose the same.

And further, of our especial grace, certain knowledge, and mere motion, we have given, granted, and Confirmed, And, by these presents, for us, our heirs and successors, do give, grant, and Confirm, unto the said Edward, Earl of Clarendon; George, Duke of Albemarle; William, Earl of Craven; John, Lord Berkeley; Anthony, Lord Ashley; Sir George Carterett; Sir John Colleton; and Sir William Berkeley, their heirs and Assigns, full and absolute power, licence, and authority that they, the said Edward, Earl of Clarendon; George, Duke of Albemarle; William, Earl of Craven; John, Lord Berkeley; Anthony, Lord Ashley; Sir George Carterett; Sir John Colleton; and Sir William Berkeley, their heirs and Assigns, from time to time hereafter, forever, at his and their will and pleasure, may Assign, alien, Grant, demise, or enfeoff the premises, or any part or parcel thereof, to him or them that shall be willing to purchase the same, and to such person and persons as they shall think fit;

To have and to hold to them the said person or persons, their heirs and Assigns, in Fee simple or in Fee Tail, or for the term of life or lives or years; To be held of them, the said Edward, Earl of Clarendon; George, Duke of Albemarle; William, Earl of Craven; John, Lord Berkeley; Anthony, Lord Ashley; Sir George Carterett; Sir John Colleton;

and Sir William Berkeley, their heirs and Assigns, by such Rents, Services, and Customs as shall seem fit to them, the said Edward, Earl of Clarendon; George, Duke of Albemarle; William, Earl of Craven; Anthony, Lord Ashley; Sir George Carterett; Sir John Colleton; and Sir William Berkeley, their heirs and Assigns, and not of us, our heirs and successors.

And to the same Person and Persons, and to all and every of them, we do give and grant, by these presents, for us, our heirs and successors, Licence, authority, and power that such person or persons may have and take the premises, or any parcel thereof, of the said Earl of Clarendon; George, Duke of Albemarle; William, Earl of Craven; Anthony, Lord Ashley; John, Lord Berkeley; Sir George Carterett; Sir John Colleton; and Sir William Berkeley, their heirs and Assigns; And the same to hold to themselves, their heirs or Assigns, in what Estate of Inheritance soever, in Fee simple or in Fee Tail or otherwise, as to them, the said Earl of Clarendon; George, Duke of Albemarle; William, Earl of Craven; John, Lord Berkeley; Anthony, Lord Ashley; Sir George Carterett; Sir John Colleton; and Sir William Berkeley, their heirs and Assigns, shall seem expedient; The Statute in the Parliament of Edward, Son of King Henry, heretofore King of England, Our Predecessor, commonly called the Statute of *Quia Emptores Terrarum,* or any other Statute, Act, Ordinance, use, law, Custom, or any other matter, cause, or thing heretofore published or provided to the Contrary in any wise notwithstanding.

And because many persons born and inhabiting in the said Province, for their deserts and services, may expect, and be capable of, Marks of honour and favour, which, in respect of the great distance, cannot conveniently be conferred by us:

Our will and pleasure, therefore, is, And we do, by these presents, give and grant unto the said Edward, Earl of Clarendon; George, Duke of Albemarle; William, Earl of Craven; John, Lord Berkeley; Anthony, Lord Ashley; Sir George Carterett; Sir John Colleton; and Sir William Berkeley, their heirs and Assigns, full power and authority to give and Confer, unto and upon such of the Inhabitants of the said Province or Territory as they shall think do or shall merit the same, such Marks of favour and titles of honour as they shall think fit; so as these titles or honours be not the same as are enjoyed by or conferred upon any of the Subjects of this our Kingdom of England.

And further, also, we do, by these presents, for us, our heirs and Successors, give and grant licence to them, the said Edward, Earl of

Clarendon; George, Duke of Albemarle; William, Earl of Craven; John, Lord Berkeley; Anthony, Lord Ashly; Sir George Carterett; Sir John Colleton; and Sir William Berkeley, their heirs and Assigns, full power, liberty, and licence to erect, raise, and build, within the said Province and Places aforesaid, or any part or parts thereof, such and so many Forts, Fortresses, Castles, Cities, Boroughs, Towns, villages, and other Fortification whatsoever, And the same, or any of them, to fortify and furnish with Ordnance, Powder, Shot, Armour, and all other weapons, Ammunition, and habiliments of war, both defensive and offensive, as shall be thought fit and convenient, for the safety and welfare of the said Province and Places, or any part thereof; And the same, or any of them, from time to time, as occasion shall require, to dismantle, disfurnish, demolish, and pull down; And also, to place, constitute, and appoint, in or over all or any of the said Castles, Forts, Fortifications, Castles,[4] Towns, and Places aforesaid, Governors, Deputy Governors, Magistrates, Sheriffs, and other Officers, civil and Military, as to them shall seem meet;

And to the said Cities, Boroughs, Towns, villages, or any other place or places within the said Province or Territory, to grant letters or Charters of Incorporation, with all liberties, Franchises, and privileges requisite or usual, or to or within this our Kingdom of England granted or belonging; And in the same Cities, Boroughs, Towns, and other places, to Constitute, erect, and appoint such and so many Markets, Marts, and Fairs as shall in that behalf be thought fit and necessary;

And further, also, to erect and make in the Province or Territory aforesaid, or any part thereof, so many Manors, with such Seigniories, as to them shall seem meet and convenient; And in every of the said Manors to have and to hold a Court Baron, with all things whatsoever which to a Court Baron do belong; And to have and to hold views of Frankpledge and Courts Leet, for the conservation of the Peace and better Government of those parts, with such Limits, Jurisdiction, and precincts as by the said Edward, Earl of Clarendon; George, Duke of Albemarle; William, Earl of Craven; John, Lord Berkeley; Anthony, Lord Ashley; Sir George Carterett; Sir John Colleton; and Sir William Berkeley, or their heirs, shall be appointed for that purpose, with all things whatsoever which to a Court Leet or view of Frankpledge do belong; the same Courts to be held by Stewards, to be deputed and authorized by the said Edward, Earl of Clarendon; George, Duke of Albe-

[4] Repetition in the manuscript.

marle; William, Earl of Craven; John, Lord Berkeley; Anthony, Lord Ashley; Sir George Carterett; Sir John Colleton; and Sir William Berkeley, or their heirs, [or] by the Lords of the Manors and Leets for the time being, when the same shall be erected.

And because that, in so remote a Country and situate amongst so many barbarous Nations, the Invasions as well of Savages as other Enemies, Pirates, and Robbers may probably be feared:

Therefore, we have given, and, for us, our heirs and Successors, do give, power, by these presents, unto the said Edward, Earl of Clarendon; George, Duke of Albemarle; William, Earl of Craven; John, Lord Berkeley; Anthony, Lord Ashley; Sir George Carterett; Sir John Colleton; and Sir William Berkeley, their heirs or Assigns, by themselves or their Captains or other Officers, to levy, muster, and train all sorts of Men, of what Condition soever or wheresoever born, whether in the said Province or elsewhere, for the time being; and to make war and pursue the Enemies aforesaid, as well by Sea as by land, yea, even without the limits of the said Province; And, by God's assistance, to vanquish and take them, And, being taken, to put them to death, by the law of war, And to save them, at their pleasure; And to do all and every other things which to the Charge and Office of a Captain General of an Army belongs, or has accustomed to belong, as fully and freely as any Captain General of an Army has had the same.

Also, our will and Pleasure is, and, by this our Charter, we do give and Grant unto the said Edward, Earl of Clarendon; George, Duke of Albemarle; William, Earl of Craven; John, Lord Berkeley; Anthony, Lord Ashley; Sir George Carterett; Sir John Colleton; and Sir William Berkeley, their heirs and Assigns, full power, liberty, and authority, in case of Rebellion, tumult, or sedition, if any should happen, which God forbid, either upon the land within the Province aforesaid or upon the Main Sea in making a voyage thither or returning from thence, by him and themselves, their Captains, Deputies, or Officers, to be authorized under his or their Seals for that purpose, to whom also, for us, our heirs and successors, we do give and grant, by these presents, full power and authority, to exercise Martial law against mutinous and seditious persons of those parts, such as shall refuse to submit themselves to their Government, or shall refuse to serve in the wars, or shall fly to the Enemy, or forsake their Colours or Ensigns, or be loiterers or Stragglers, or otherwise howsoever offending against law, Custom, or military discipline; as freely and in as ample manner and form as any Captain General

of an Army, by virtue of his Office, might, or has accustomed to, use the same.

And our further pleasure is, And, by these presents, for us, our heirs and Successors, we do grant unto the said Edward, Earl of Clarendon; George, Duke of Albemarle; William, Earl of Craven; John, Lord Berkeley; Anthony, Lord Ashley; Sir George Carterett; Sir John Colleton; and Sir William Berkeley, their heirs and Assigns, and to the Tenants and Inhabitants of the said Province or Territory, both present and to come, and to every of them, that the said Province or Territory, and the Tenants and Inhabitants thereof, shall not from henceforth be held or reputed any member or part of any Colony whatsoever, in America or elsewhere, now transported or made, or hereafter to be transported or made; nor shall be depending on, or subject to, their Government in any thing, but be absolutely separated and divided from the same;

And our pleasure is, by these presents, that they be separated, and that they be subject immediately to our Crown of England, as depending thereof, forever; And that the Inhabitants of the said Province or Territory, nor any of them, shall, at any time hereafter, be compelled or compellable, or by any ways subject or liable, to appear or answer to any matter, suit, Cause, or Plaint whatsoever, out of the Province or Territory aforesaid, in any other of our Islands, Colonies, or Dominions, in America or elsewhere, other than in our Realm of England and Dominion of Wales.

And because it may happen that some of the People and Inhabitants of the said Province cannot in their private opinions conform to the public exercise of Religion according to the liturgy, forms, and Ceremonies of the Church of England, or take or subscribe the Oath and Articles made and established in that behalf; And for that the same, by reason of the remote distances of those Places, will, as we hope, be no breach of the unity and Conformity established in this Nation:

Our will and pleasure, therefore, is, And we do, by these presents, for us, our heirs and successors, give and grant unto the said Edward, Earl of Clarendon; George, Duke of Albemarle; William, Earl of Craven; John, Lord Berkeley; Anthony, Lord Ashley; Sir George Carterett; Sir John Colleton; and Sir William Berkeley, their heirs and Assigns, full and free licence, liberty, and authority, by such ways and means as they shall think fit, to give and grant unto such Person and Persons inhabiting and being within the said Province or Territory, hereby or by the said recited letters Patents mentioned to be granted, as afore-

said, or any part thereof, such Indulgencies and dispensations in that behalf, for and during such time and times, and with such limitations and restrictions, as they, the said Edward, Earl of Clarendon; George, Duke of Albemarle; William, Earl of Craven; John, Lord Berkley; Anthony, Lord Ashley; Sir George Carterett; Sir John Colleton; and Sir William Berkeley, their heirs or Assigns, shall, in their discretion, think fit and reasonable;

And that no person or persons unto whom such liberty shall be given shall be any way molested, punished, disquieted, or called in question for any differences in opinion or practice in matters of Religious concernment, who do not actually disturb the Civil Peace of the Province, County, or Colony that they shall make their abode in; but all and every such Person and Persons may, from time to time, and at all times, freely and quietly have and enjoy his and their Judgements and Consciences in matters of Religion throughout all the said Province or Colony, they behaving themselves peaceably and [not] using this liberty to licentiousness, nor to the civil Injury or outward disturbance of others; Any law, Statute, or Clause, contained or to be contained, usage or Custom of Our Realm of England to the contrary hereof in any wise notwithstanding.

And in case it shall happen that any doubts or questions should arise concerning the true sense and understanding of any word, Clause, or sentence contained in this our present Charter:

We will, Ordain, and Command that, at all times and in all things, such Interpretations be made thereof, and allowed in all and every of Our Courts whatsoever, as lawfully may be adjudged most advantageous and favourable to the said Edward, Earl of Clarendon; George, Duke of Albemarle; William, Earl of Craven; John, Lord Berkeley; Anthony, Lord Ashley; Sir George Carterett; Sir John Colleton; and Sir William Berkeley, their heirs and Assigns.

Although express mention, etc.

In witness, etc.

Witness, our self, At Westminster, the thirtieth day of June.

per ipsum Regem

[Transcribed from a photostatic copy of the enrollment of the charter on the patent roll. Manuscript in the British Public Record Office, London. Reference: C. 66/3076 No. 6. Photostatic copy deposited in the State Department of Archives and History, Raleigh, North Carolina.]

CONSTITUTIONS

Concessions and Agreement between the Lords Proprietors and Major William Yeamans and Others

January 7, 1665

INTRODUCTION

Six months after receiving their first charter, the lords proprietors of Carolina authorized one of their number, Sir William Berkeley, governor of Virginia, to exercise governmental powers in Albemarle, the only settled area in Carolina. They also authorized Berkeley to select a governor and council for the settlement. In October, 1664, William Drummond was appointed governor, and a legislative assembly was convened by the following spring.

For nearly two years, government in Carolina was based on the proprietors' temporary authorizations and instructions. In January, 1665, the proprietors adopted a more formal plan of government for the province and incorporated it in an agreement made with a group from Barbados and elsewhere who proposed to settle in the Cape Fear region. This document, known as the Concessions and Agreement of 1665, is the first constitution, or over-all plan of government, put into effect in Carolina. An earlier plan, contained in a document called A Declaration and Proposals to All That Will Plant in Carolina, approved by the proprietors in 1663, was never put into effect, for it was applicable only to new colonies, and none were established under its terms. The plan provided in the Concessions and Agreement likewise was designed primarily for new settlements, but, unlike the earlier plan, it also applied to the existing settlement in Albemarle.

The Concessions and Agreement provided that Carolina be divided into large subdivisions, called counties, in each of which was to be established a governor, an assembly, and other agencies. Each county was to be divided into districts, which were to be administrative and judicial units. The present-day counties in North Carolina bear more likeness to the old districts, or precincts, than to the old counties, which eventually were abolished.

The known records do not show when the plan of government provided in the Concessions and Agreement was put into effect in Albemarle. Apparently, the

plan was in force by October, 1667, when Samuel Stephens was appointed to succeed Drummond as governor, for the proprietors' instructions to Stephens conformed to the provisions of the Concessions and Agreement. There is also question as to when government under the Concessions and Agreement ended. Although a different plan, the Fundamental Constitutions of Carolina, was sent to Albemarle in January, 1670, it appears that the old plan was continued for some time, perhaps until early in 1672. Thus, the system provided in the Concessions and Agreement may have been used five years or longer.

A significant feature of the Concessions and Agreement was the extensive power allowed the popular assembly, which was far greater than that required by the proprietors' charter. Consequently, the assembly was a major governmental agency in the early years of the Albemarle colony. Later, under the Fundamental Constitutions, the assembly lost most of its power, and many years passed before it regained its former status.

THE DOCUMENT

ARTICLES of Agreement had and made between Edward, Earl of Clarendon, Lord High Chancellor of England; George, Duke of Albemarle, Master of his Majesty's Horse and Captain General of all his Forces; William, Lord Craven; John, Lord Berkeley; Anthony, Lord Ashley, Chancellor of his Majesty's Exchequer; Sir George Cartrett, Knight and Baronet, Vice Chamberlain of his Majesty's Household; Sir John Colleton, Knight and Baronet; and Sir William Bekeley, Knight, the Lords Proprietors of the Province of Carolina of the one part, And Major William Yeamans of Barbados, for and on the behalf of Sir John Yeamans, Baronet, his Father; Colonel Edmund Reade; Symon Lambert; Niccolas Edwards; Robert Gibbs; Samuell Tidcombe; Henry Milles; Thomas Lake; Thomas Maycoke; John Somerhayes; Bartholomew Rees; John Gibbs; Basill Gibbs; John Dickenson; Thomas Gibbs; Benjamine Rees; Miles Scottow; Nathaniell Mearericke; Bartholomew Rees, Junior; John Arthur; Samuell Smith; Thomas Partrige; John Walice; John Brent; John Godfrey; George Thompson; Robert Williams; Lawrence Halsted; William Burges; John Tothill; James Thorpe; Robert Tothill; William Forster; Thomas Merricke; John Merricke; George Phillips; Edward Jacobs; Robert Hackett; Benjamine Waddon; Robert Johnston; Thomas Dickes; Thomas Clutterbooke; John Forster; William Sharpe; John Ham; John Start; Mathew Grey; John Kerie; Richard Baily; Edward Thorneburgh; Thomas Liston; Anthony Long; Thomas Norvill; Giles Hall; James Norvill; William Woodehouse; Jacob Scantlebury; Samuell Lambart; John Forster; William Byrdall; Richard Barrett; Edward Yeamans; John Killicott; Isaac Lovell; Thomas Clarke; John Woods; John Bellomy; John Greenesmith; Robert Brevitir; Thomas Dowden; Niccolas Browne; John Wilson; Robert Sinckler; Thomas Perkins; James Thorpe; Robert Richards; Benjamine Hadlut; Christopher Goupher; James Walter; James Haydensen; William Birdall; Mordecai Bouden, Junior; George Nore; Humphery Waterman; and himself, Adventurers to and Settlers of some part of the Province aforesaid, And of all others that shall Adventure, Settle, and plant in the said Province, of the other part, as follows:

WHEREAS, the said Major William Yeamans is Employed to the said Lords Proprietors by the persons above mentioned, and by them declared, under their hands, to be their Agent and Representative, and that they have given him full power to treat, propose, and conclude with the said Lords about all matters relating to that which they have already

done, as also to what shall be necessary and convenient to be done, obliging themselves, and their posterities, to accept of, stand to, and abide by whatsoever the said Major William Yeamans shall conclude of, and Agree upon, in relation to the Settlement of Carolina, or any part thereof; Now, in pursuance of the powers, etc., given to the said Major William Yeamans by the parties above mentioned, These present Articles do witness, And it is covenanted, Granted, and agreed by and between the said parties, as Follows:

Imprimis, The said Lords for their parts, their heirs, Executors, and Administrators, do covenant and promise to perform, fulfill, and keep all the Concessions and particulars that are to be by them performed and kept, mentioned in the Concessions and agreements hereunto annexed, containing the manner of Government, with several Immunities and privileges granted to all such persons as shall go or send to plant, or as are already planted, in the respective Counties or Colonies in the said Province of Carolina.

Item, The Lords do further covenant and promise that they will Cause to be shipped, before the first day of February next, Twelve pieces of Ordnance, with Carriages, Saddles, Sponges, and Shot convenient and Necessary, and Twenty barrels of powder, one hundred Firelocks, and one hundred Matchlocks, with Lead and Bullets fitting, as also two hundred pair of Bandoleers, for the Arming and Providing of a Fort, to be Erected and built near Port Royall, or near some other harbour, River, or creek whose mouth or Entrance is Southward or Westward of Cape Romania, in the Province aforesaid, by the Respective Adventurers before mentioned, or by any others Under their Authority.

Item, The Lords do further covenant that every one of the Adventurers of the Island of Barbados, and their associates of England, New England, the Leward Islands, and Barmothos, that have Subscribed and paid, or shall subscribe and pay within Forty days after notice of this in the Barbados and the other places, unto the Treasurer or Treasurers, appointed or to be appointed by the committee chosen or to be chosen by the adventurers, that are or shall be to receive the same, for the defraying the Charge of carrying people that cannot pay for the transportation of themselves to Port Royall, or some Harbour, River, or creek whose mouth or Entrance is to the Southward or Westward of Cape Romania, and for the making of some Fortification there for and towards a Settlement of those and other people in that place, and for other Necessary

charges concerning the Settlement aforesaid, And shall send such proportions of men, Armed and provided, as their own committee shall agree upon, in the first ship or ships that shall be set forth, to begin a Settlement there, Shall have Granted to them, and their heirs, forever, for every Thousand Pound of Sugar so Subscribed and Paid, five hundred acres of Land, and so in Proportion for a greater or Lesser sum Subscribed and Paid as aforesaid; to be taken up within five years after the date hereof, and settled as other Lands are to be settled, viz., with an able man, Armed with a good Firelock, bore Twelve Bullets to the Pound, Ten pounds of powder, and Twenty pounds of Bullets, with Six Months' provision, within one year after the taking up of the said land; which land shall be taken up to the South or westward of Cape Romania, and by Lots, as is proposed and Prescribed in the General Concessions and Agreements Concerning the Settlement of the Respective Counties in the said Province; And shall pay one half penny sterling for every acre, English measure, yearly, in manner as in the Concessions hereunto annexed.

ITEM, The Lords do further Covenant and promise That whoever shall go or send in the first Fleet with Colonel John Yeamans, he failing, with the first Governor or Deputy Governor, shall have for his own head one hundred and Fifty acres of Land, to him and his heirs, forever, English measure; And for every able man servant he or she shall carry or send, Armed and provided as aforesaid, one hundred and fifty acres of land, like measure; And to every such Servant, after the expiration of his or their time, Seventy five acres of Land, to be taken up by Lots as aforesaid, in the place before mentioned; And to every other Servant that shall there go after the first fleet, such quantities as in the General Declaration is expressed; upon which hundred and fifty acres of Land he shall be obliged to keep one able man, and no more, and in failure thereof, to Forfeit the same, as in the General Concessions and agreement is expressed; for which Land there shall be reserved yearly to the Lords, their heirs and assigns, one half penny per acre, English Measure, to be paid in manner as for other lands in the Concessions mentioned.

IN CONSIDERATION WHEREOF:

THE said Major William Yeamans does covenant as well, on the behalf of his Father, Sir John Yeamans, Baron, and of Colonel Edmund Reade, and of all the adventurers, Settlers, and planters before expressed, and of all others that shall adventure, settle, and plant, as of himself, that

they shall, for their part, perform, fulfill, and keep all the particulars that are to be by them performed, mentioned in the Concessions and Agreement hereunto annexed. And that there shall be provided, before the last day of September next, two ships, of one hundred and twenty tons each of them at least, with Ordnance Convenient in each ship, and with powder, shot, and provisions necessary for the transportation of such persons as cannot pay for the passage of themselves to the Southward of Cape Romania; there to Settle and plant and to erect a fort, and in it to plant the Artillery sent by the Lords aforesaid, for the retreat and preservation of the first Settlers and of those that shall follow. In witness of truth the said Major William Yeamans has hereunto set his hand and Seal, this Seventh day of January, In the Sixteenth year of his Majesty's reign, Anno Domini 1664.[1]

THE CONCESSIONS and Agreement of the Lords Proprietors of the Province of Carolina to and with the adventurers of the Island of Barbados, and their Associates of England, New England, the Caribbia Islands, and Barmothos, to the Province of Carolina, and all that shall plant there, In order to the Settling and Planting of the County of Clarendine, The County of Albemarle, and the County ——,[2] which latter is to be to the Southward or westward of Cape Romania, all within the Province aforesaid:

1. IMPRIMIS, We do Consent and agree That the Governor of each County have power, by the advice of his Council, to depute one in his place and Authority in case of death or removal, to Continue until our further order, unless we have commissionated one before.

2. ITEM, That he have likewise power to make choice of and to take to him Six Councillors at least, or Twelve at most, or any even Number between Six and Twelve; with whose advice and consent, or with at least three of the Six, or four of a greater Number, all being Summoned, he is to govern according to the Limitations and Instructions following, during our pleasure.

3. ITEM, That the chief Registers or Secretaries which we have Chosen or shall Choose, we failing, that he shall Choose, shall keep exact entries in fair books of all public affairs of the said Counties and, to avoid

[1] In present-day reckoning, 1665. From the twelfth century until September, 1752, England used the Julian calendar, according to which the new year began on March 25. The period from January 1 through March 24, therefore, was included in the year preceding that to which it belongs in the Gregorian calendar.

[2] A blank in the manuscript is indicated thus: ——.

deceits and Lawsuits, shall record and enter all Grants of Land from the Lords to the planter, and all conveyances of Land, house, or houses from man to man; As also, all Leases for land, house, or houses made or to be made by the Landlord to any tenant for more than one year; which Conveyance or Lease shall be first acknowledged by the Grantor or Lessor, or proved by the oath of two witnesses to the conveyance or Lease, before the Governor or some Chief Judge of a Court for the time being; who shall, Under his hand, Upon the backside of the said deed or Lease, Attest the acknowledgement or proof, as aforesaid, which shall be warrant for the Registers to record the same; which Conveyance or Lease so recorded shall be good and effectual in Law, notwithstanding any other Conveyance, deed, or Lease for the said Land, house, or houses, or for any part there, although dated before the Conveyance, deed, or Lease so recorded as aforesaid. And the said registers shall do all other thing or things that we, by our Instructions, shall direct, and the Governor, Council, and Assembly shall ordain, for the good and welfare of the said Counties.

4. ITEM, That the Surveyor General that we have Chosen or shall Choose, we failing, that the Governor shall Choose, shall have power, by himself or Deputy, to Survey, lay out, and bound all such lands as shall be granted from the Lords to the Planters, and all other Lands within the said Counties, etc., which may concern particular men, as he shall be desired to do; And a particular thereof certify to the Registers, to be recorded as aforesaid; Provided, That if the said Registers and Surveyors, or either of them, shall so misbehave themselves As that the Governor and Council, or Deputy Governor and Council, or the Major part of them, shall find it reasonable to suspend their Actings in their respective Employments, it shall be Lawful for them so to do, Until further order from Us.

5. ITEM, That all choice of Officers made by the Governor shall be for no Longer time than during our pleasure.

6. ITEM, That the Governors, Councillors, Assemblymen, Secretaries, surveyors, and all other officers of trust shall swear or subscribe, in a book to be provided for that purpose, that they will bear true allegiance to the King of England, his heirs and Successors; and that they will be faithful to the Interest of the Lords Proprietors of the said Province, and their heirs, executors, and assigns, and endeavor the peace and welfare of the said Province; and that they will truly and faithfully

discharge their respective trusts in their respective Offices, and do equal Justice to all men according to their best skill and Judgement, without corruption, favor, or affection; and the names of all that have sworn or Subscribed to be entered in a Book. And whosoever shall subscribe and not swear, and shall Violate his promise in that Subscription, shall be liable to the same punishment That the persons are or may be that have sworn and broken their Oaths.

7. ITEM, That all persons that are or shall become subjects to the King of England, and swear or subscribe Allegiance to the King and faithfulness to the Lords as above, shall be admitted to plant and become freemen of the province, and enjoy the Freedoms and Immunities hereafter expressed, Until some stop or Contradiction be made by Us, the Lords, or else by the Governor, Council, and Assembly; which shall be in force until the Lords see Cause to the contrary; provided, that such stop shall not any ways prejudice the right or Continuance of any person that has been received before such stop or order come from the Lords or General Assembly.

8. ITEM, That no person or persons, qualified as aforesaid, within the province, or all or any of the Counties before expressed, at any time shall be any ways molested, punished, disquieted, or called in question for any differences in opinion or practice in matters of religious Concernment, who do not actually disturb the Civil peace of the said Province or Counties; but that all and every such person and persons may, from time to time, and at all times, freely and fully have and enjoy his and their Judgements and Consciences in matters of religion throughout all the said province, they behaving themselves peaceably and quietly and not Using this Liberty to Licentiousness, nor to the Civil Injury or outward disturbance of others; any Law, statute, or Clause, Contained or to be Contained, usage or Custom of this realm of England to the Contrary hereof in anywise notwithstanding.

9. ITEM, That no pretence may be taken by Us, our heirs or assigns, for or by reason of our right of patronage and power of advowson, granted Unto Us by his Majesty's Letters Patents aforesaid, to infringe thereby the General clause of Liberty of Conscience aforementioned: We do hereby grant unto the General assemblies of the several Counties power, by act, to constitute and appoint such and so many Ministers or Preachers as they shall think fit, and to establish their maintenance; Giving Liberty besides to any person or persons to keep and maintain what preachers or Ministers they please.

10. ITEM, That the Inhabitants being freemen, or Chief agents to others, of the Counties aforesaid do, as soon as this our Commission shall arrive, by Virtue of a writ in our Names, by the Governor to be, for the present, Until our seal comes, Sealed and signed, make Choice of twelve Deputies or representatives from amongst themselves, who, being Chosen, are to Join with him, the said Governor, and Council, for the making of such Laws, Ordinances, and Constitutions as shall be necessary for the present good and welfare of the Several Counties aforesaid; but as soon as Parishes, divisions, tribes, or districts of the said Counties are made, that then, the Inhabitants or Freeholders of the Several and respective Parishes, Tribes, divisions, or districts of the Counties aforesaid do, by our writs, under our Seal, which we Engage shall be in due time issued, Annually meet on the first day of January and Choose freeholders for each respective division, Tribe, or parish, to be the deputies or representatives of the same; which body of Representatives, or the Major part of them, shall, with the Governor and Council aforesaid, be the General Assembly of the County for which they shall be Chosen, the Governor, or his Deputy, being present, Unless they shall wilfully refuse; in which Case, they may appoint themselves a president during the absence of the Governor, or his Deputy Governor.

WHICH ASSEMBLIES ARE TO HAVE POWER:

1. ITEM, To appoint their own times of meeting and to adjourn their Sessions from time to time to such times and places as they shall think Convenient; as also, to ascertain the Number of their Quorum; Provided, that such numbers be not less than the third part of the whole, in whom or more shall be the full power of the General Assembly, Viz.:

2. ITEM, To Enact and make all such Laws, Acts, and constitutions as shall be necessary for the well Government of the County for which they shall be Chosen, and them to repeal; Provided, that the same be consonant to reason and, as near as may be Conveniently, agreeable to the Laws and Customs of his Majesty's Kingdom of England; Provided also, that they be not against the Interest of Us, the Lords Proprietors, our heirs or assigns, nor any of these our present Concessions, Especially that they be not against the Article for Liberty of Conscience above mentioned; which Laws, etc., so made, shall receive publication from the Governor and Council, but as the Laws of Us and our General Assembly, and be in force for the space of one year and a half, and no more, Unless Contradicted by the Lords Proprietors, within which time

they are to be presented to Us, our heirs, etc., for our Ratification; and being confirmed by Us, they shall be in Continual force till expired by their own Limitation, or by Act of Repeal, in like manner, as aforesaid, to be passed and Confirmed.

3. ITEM, By act, as aforesaid, to Constitute all Courts for their respective Counties, together with the Limits, powers, and Jurisdictions of the said Courts; as also, the Several Offices and Number of officers belonging to each of the said respective Courts, Together with their Several and respective Salaries, fees, and perquisites, Their appellations and dignities, with the penalties that shall be due to them for breach of their Several and respective duties and Trusts.

4. ITEM, By act, as aforesaid, to lay equal taxes and Assessments, equally to raise monies or goods, Upon all Lands (excepting the Lands of Us, the Lords Proprietors, before Settling) or persons within the Several precincts, Hundreds, Parishes, Manors, or whatsoever other divisions shall hereafter be made and Established in the said Counties, as oft as necessity shall require, and in such manner as to them shall seem most equal and easy for the said Inhabitants, in order to the better supporting of the public Charge of the said Government, and for the mutual safety, defence, and Security of the said Counties.

5. ITEM, By act, as aforesaid, to erect within the said Counties such and so many Baronies and Manors, with their necessary Courts, Jurisdictions, freedoms, and privileges, as to them shall seem Convenient; as also, to divide the said Counties into Hundreds, parishes, Tribes, or such other divisions and districts as they shall think fit; and the said Divisions to distinguish by what Names we shall order or direct, and in default thereof, by such Names as they please; As also, within any part of the said Counties to create and appoint such and so many ports, harbours, Creeks, and other places for the convenient Lading and Unlading of goods and Merchandise out of ships, boats, and other vessels as they shall see expedient, with such Jurisdictions, privileges, and franchises to such Ports, etc., belonging as they shall Judge most Conducing to the General good of the said plantation or Counties.

6. ITEM, By their enacting, to be Confirmed as aforesaid, to erect, raise, and build within the said Counties, or any part thereof, such and so many Forts, Fortresses, Castles, Cities, Corporations, Boroughs, towns, Villages, and other places of strength and defence, and them, or any of them, to Incorporate, with such Charters and privileges as to them

shall seem good and our Charter will permit; and the same, or any of them, to fortify and furnish with such Proportions of ordnance, powder, shot, Armor, and all other weapons, Ammunition, and Habiliments of war, both offensive and defensive, as shall be thought Necessary and Convenient for the Safety and welfare of the said Counties; but they may not at any time demolish, dismantle, or disfurnish the same without the Consent of the Governor and the Major part of the Council of that County where such forts, Fortresses, etc., shall be erected and built.

7. Item, By act, as aforesaid, to Constitute trained bands and Companies with the Number of Soldiers for the Safety, strength, and defence of the said Counties and province, and of the Forts, Castles, Cities, etc.; to suppress all Mutinies and Rebellions; To make war, offensive and defensive, with all Indians, strangers, and Foreigners as they shall see cause; And to pursue an Enemy, by Sea as well as by land, if need be, out of the Limits and Jurisdictions of the said County, with the particular Consent of the Governor and under the Conduct of Our Lieutenant General, or Commander in Chief, or whom he shall appoint.

8. Item, By Act, as aforesaid, to give Unto all strangers as to them shall seem meet a Naturalization, and all such freedoms and privileges within the said Counties as to his Majesty's Subjects do of right belong, they swearing or Subscribing as aforesaid; which said strangers, so Naturalized and privileged, shall also have the same Immunities from Customs as is granted by the King to Us, and by Us to the said Counties, and shall not be liable to any other Customs than the rest of his Majesty's Subjects in the said Counties are, but be in all respects accounted in the Province and Counties aforesaid as the King's Natural Subjects.

9. Item, By act, as aforesaid, to prescribe the quantities of Land which shall be, from time to time, allotted to every head, free or Servant, male or female; And to make and ordain Rules for the Casting of Lots for land, and laying out of the same; Provided, that they do not [in] their said prescriptions exceed the Several proportions which are hereby granted by Us to all persons Arriving in the said Counties or adventuring thither.

10. Item, The General Assembly, by Act, as aforesaid, shall make provision for the Maintenance and Support of the Governor and for the defraying of all Necessary Charges of the Government; As also, that the Constables of the respective Counties shall Collect the half penny per acre payable to the Lords in their Counties, and pay the same to the re-

ceiver that the Lords shall appoint to receive the same, unless the said General Assembly shall prescribe some other way whereby the Lords may have their rents duly Collected without Charge or trouble to them.

11. Lastly, To enact, constitute, and Ordain all such other Laws, acts, and constitutions as shall or may be necessary for the good prosperity and Settlement of the said Counties, excepting what by these presents are excepted, and Conforming to Limitations herein expressed.

The Governors are, with their Council, before Expressed:

1. Item, To see that all Courts established by the Laws of the General Assembly and all ministers and officers, civil or Military, do and execute their several duties and offices respectively, according to the Laws in force, and to punish them from swerving from the Laws, or acting Contrary to their trust, as the nature of their offence shall require.

2. Item, According to the Constitutions of the General Assembly, to Nominate and Commissionate the several Judges, Members, and officers of Courts, whether Magisterial or Ministerial, and all other Civil officers, as Justices, Coroners, etc., and their Commissions and powers and Authorities to revoke at pleasure; Provided, that they appoint none but such as are freeholders in the Counties aforesaid, unless the General Assembly consent.

3. Item, According to the Constitutions of the General Assembly, to appoint Courts and officers in cases criminal, and to empower them to inflict penalties upon offenders against any of the Laws in force in the said Counties as the said Laws shall ordain, whether by fine, Imprisonment, Banishment, Corporal punishment, or to the taking away of Member or life itself, if there be cause for it.

4. Item, To place officers and Soldiers for the safety, strength, and defence of the Forts, Castles, Cities, etc., according to the Number appointed by the General Assembly; to Nominate, place, and Commissionate all military officers Under the Dignity of the Lieutenant General, who is commissionated by Us, over the Several trained bands and Companies Constituted by the General Assembly, as Colonels, Captains, etc., and their Commissions to revoke at pleasure; the Lieutenant General, with the advice of his Council, unless some present danger will not permit him to advise, to muster and train all the Soldiers within the said County or Counties, to prosecute war, pursue an Enemy, Suppress rebel-

lions and mutinies, as well by Sea as Land; And to exercise the whole Militia as fully as by our Letters patents from the King we can empower him or them to do; Provided, that they appoint no Military officers but what are freeholders in the said Counties, unless the General Assembly shall Consent.

5. ITEM, Where they see cause, after Condemnation, to reprieve Until the Case may be presented, with a Copy of the whole trial Proceedings and proofs, to the Lords, who will accordingly either pardon or Command Execution of the Sentence on the offender, who is, in the mean time, to be kept in safe Custody till the pleasure of the Lords be known.

6. ITEM, In case of death or other removal of any of the representatives within the year, to Issue Summons by writ to the respective division or divisions for which he or they were Chosen, Commanding the Freeholders of the same to choose others in their stead.

7. ITEM, To make warrants and to Seal Grants of Lands, according to these our Concessions and the prescriptions by the advice of the General Assembly, in such form as shall be at large set down in our Instructions to the Governor, in his Commission, and which are hereafter expressed.

8. ITEM, To act and do all other thing or things that may Conduce to the safety, peace, and well Government of the said Counties, as they shall see fit; so as they be not Contrary to the Laws of the Counties aforesaid.

FOR THE BETTER SECURITY OF THE PROPRIETIES OF ALL THE INHABITANTS:

1. ITEM, They are not to impose nor suffer to be imposed any tax, Custom, Subsidy, Tallage, Assessment, or any other duty whatsoever, upon any Color or pretence, upon the said County or Counties, and the Inhabitants thereof, other than what shall be Imposed by the Authority and consent of the General Assembly, and then only in manner as aforesaid.

2. ITEM, They are to take care that Land quietly held, planted, and possessed Seven years after its being first duly Surveyed by the Surveyor General, or his order, shall not be subject to any review, resurvey, or alteration of bounds, on what pretence soever, by any of us, or any officers or Ministers Under Us.

3. Item, They are to take care that no man, if his cattle stray, range, or graze on any ground within the said Counties not actually appropriated or set out to particular persons, shall be liable to pay any trespass for the same to Us, our heirs, etc.; Provided, that Custom of Commons be not thereby pretended to, nor any person hindered from taking Up and appropriating any Lands so grazed Upon, and that no person purposely do suffer his cattle to graze on such lands.

4. Item, It is our will and desire that the Inhabitants of the said Counties and adventurers thither shall enjoy all the same Immunities from customs for exporting Certain goods from these Realms of England, etc., thither as the King has been graciously pleased to grant to Us; as also, for the Encouragement of the Manufacturers of wine, Silk, oil, Olives, fruit, Almonds, etc., mentioned in the patent, have privilege for bringing them Custom free into any of his Majesty's dominions, for the same time and Upon the same terms as we ourselves may, by our patent.

And that the planting of the Counties aforesaid may be the more speedily promoted:

1. Item, The Governors are to take notice That we do hereby grant unto all persons who have already adventured to Carolina, or shall transport themselves or Servants before the first day of January which shall be in the year of our Lord one thousand Six hundred sixty five, these following proportions of Land: Viz., If to the County of Clarendon, one hundred acres, English measure, to every freeman, and as much to his wife if he have one, And to every freewoman that already is or shall arrive into the said County, with a Servant or Servants, to plant within the time aforesaid; one hundred acres, Like measure, To a master or Mistress for every able man Servant he or she has brought or sent, or shall bring or send as aforesaid, being each of them Armed with a good firelock or Matchlock, bore Twelve bullets to the pound, Ten pounds of powder, and Twenty pounds of bullets, with Match proportionable, and Victualled for Six months; fifty acres, of like measure, for every weaker Servant he or she has brought or sent, or shall bring or send as aforesaid, as women, Children, and Slaves above the age of fourteen years; And fifty acres, like measure, for every Christian Servant that is brought or sent within the said time, to his or her proper use and behoof, when their time of Servitude is expired.

2. ITEM, To every freeman and freewoman that shall arrive in the said County, Armed and provided as aforesaid, within the second year, from the first day of January, one thousand Six hundred Sixty five, to the first of January, one thousand Six hundred Sixty Six, with an intention to plant, Seventy five acres of Land; and Seventy [8] acres for every able man Servant that he or they shall Carry or send, armed and provided as aforesaid.

3. ITEM, For every weaker servant or slave, aged as aforesaid, that shall be carried or sent thither within the Second years as aforesaid, forty acres of Land; To every Christian Servant that shall arrive the second year, forty acres of land, of like measure, after the expiration of his Servitude.

4. ITEM, To every freeman or freewoman, armed and provided as aforesaid, that shall go and arrive, with an intention to plant, within the third year, from January, one Thousand Six hundred Sixty Six, to January, one thousand Six hundred Sixty Seven, fifty acres of Land, like measure; and for every able man Servant that he or they shall carry or send within the said time, armed and provided as aforesaid, the like quantity of Land; and for every weaker Servant or slave, aged as aforesaid, that he or they shall Carry or send within the third year, Twenty five acres of Land; and to every Christian Servant so carried or sent in the third year, Twenty five acres of Land, of like measure, after the expiration of his or their time of Service.

5. ITEM, We do hereby grant unto all persons who have already adventured to Carolina, or shall transport themselves or Servants before the first day of January which shall be in the year of our Lord one thousand Six hundred Sixty five, these following proportions of Land: If to the County of Albemarle, Eighty Acres, English measure, to every freeman, and as much to his wife, if he have one; And to every freewoman that already is or shall arrive into the said County, with a Servant or Servants, to plant, within the time aforesaid, Eighty Acres, like measure; To a master or Mistress, for every able man Servant he or she has brought or sent, or shall bring or send as aforesaid, being each of them armed with a good firelock or Matchlock, bore twelve bullets to the pound, Ten pounds of powder, and Twenty pounds of bullets, with match proportionable, and Victualled for Six Months, Eighty acres, of like measure; and for every weaker Servant he or she has brought or

[8] Thus in the manuscript.

sent, or shall bring or send as aforesaid, as women, Children, and Slaves above the age of Fourteen years, Forty acres, like measure; And for every Christian Servant that is brought or sent within the said time, to his or her proper use and behoof, when their time of Servitude is expired, Forty acres, of like measure;

6. ITEM, To every freeman and freewoman that shall arrive in the said County, armed and provided as aforesaid, within the Second year, from the first day of January, one thousand Six hundred Sixty five, to the first day of January, one thousand Six hundred Sixty six, with an intention to plant, Sixty Acres; and Sixty acres for every able man Servant that he or they shall carry or send, Armed and provided as aforesaid.

7. ITEM, For every weaker Servant or slave, aged as aforesaid, that shall be Carried or sent thither within the Second year, as aforesaid, Thirty acres, Like measure; To every Christian Servant that shall arrive the second year, Thirty acres of Land, of like measure, after the expiration of his or their time of Servitude.

8. ITEM, To every freeman and freewoman, armed and provided as aforesaid, that shall go and arrive, with an Intention to plant, within the Third year, from January, one thousand Six hundred Sixty Six, to January, one thousand Six hundred Sixty Seven, Forty acres of Land, like measure; and for every able man Servant that he or they shall carry or send within the said time, armed and provided as aforesaid, the like quantity of land; And for every weaker Servant or Slave, aged as aforesaid, that he or they shall carry or send within the Third year, Twenty acres of Land, like measure; And to every Christian Servant so Carried or sent within the Third year, Twenty acres of Land, of like measure, after the expiration of his or their time of Service.

9. ITEM, We do hereby grant unto all persons who have already adventured to Carolina, or shall transport themselves or Servants before the first day of January which shall be in the year of our Lord one thousand Six hundred Sixty five, these following proportions: Viz., To every freeman that shall go with the first Governor from the port where he Embarks, or shall meet him at the Rendezvous he appoints, and from thence go with him to the Southward or westward of Cape Romania, within the Province aforesaid, for the Settling of a Plantation there, which we Name to be the County of ——, Armed with a good Musket, bore Twelve bullets to the pound, with Ten pounds of powder and Twenty pounds of Bullets, with Bandoleers and match convenient, and

with Six months' provision for his own person, arriving there, one hundred and fifty acres of Land, English measure; And for every able man Servant that he shall Carry with him, Armed and provided as aforesaid, and Arriving there, the like quantity of one hundred and fifty acres; and whoever shall send Servants at that time shall have for every able man Servant he or she so sends, Armed and provided as aforesaid, and arriving there, the like quantity of one hundred and fifty acres; And for every weaker Servant or Slave, male or female, exceeding the age of Fourteen years, which any one shall send or Carry, Arriving there, Seventy five acres of Land; and to every Christian Servant exceeding the age aforesaid, after the expiration of their time of Service, Seventy five acres of Land, for their own Use.

10. ITEM, To every Master or Mistress that shall go before the first day of January which shall be in the year of our Lord one Thousand Six hundred Sixty five, one hundred and Twenty acres of Land; and for every able man Servant that he or she shall carry or send, armed and provided as aforesaid, and arriving within the time aforesaid, the like quantity of one hundred and Twenty acres of Land; and for every weaker Servant or slave, male or female, exceeding the age of Fourteen years, arriving there, Sixty acres of land; and to every Christian Servant, to their own use and behoof, Sixty acres of Land.

11. ITEM, To every freeman and freewoman that shall arrive in the said County, armed and provided as aforesaid, within the Second year, from the first of January, one thousand Six hundred Sixty five, to the first of January, one thousand Six hundred Sixty Six, with an Intention to plant, Ninety acres of Land, English measure; and for every able man Servant that he or she shall Carry or send, Armed and provided as aforesaid, Ninety acres of Land, of Like measure.

12. ITEM, And for every weaker Servant or slave, aged as aforesaid, that shall be so Carried or sent thither within the second year as aforesaid, Forty five acres of Land, of like measure; and to every Christian Servant that shall arrive the Second year, Forty five acres of Land, of like measure, after the expiration of his or their time of Service, for their own use and behoof; all which Lands so granted in the 9, 10, 11, and 12 articles preceding, and the 13th following, are meant and intended to be taken up and given in the County of ——, and not elsewhere.

13. ITEM, To every freeman and freewoman, Armed and provided as aforesaid, that shall go and arrive, with intention to plant, within the

Third year, from January, one thousand Six hundred Sixty Six, to January, one thousand Six hundred Sixty Seven, armed and provided as aforesaid, Sixty acres of Land, like measure; and for every able man Servant that he or they shall Carry or send within the said time, Armed and provided as aforesaid, the like quantity of Sixty acres of Land; And for every weaker Servant or Slave, aged as aforesaid, that he or they shall carry or send within the Third year, Thirty acres of Land; And to every Christian Servant so Carried or sent in the third year, Thirty acres of land, of like measure, after the expiration of his or their time of Service; ALL which land, and all other that shall be possessed in said Counties, are to be held on the same terms and Conditions as is before mentioned, and as hereafter, in the following Paragraphs, is more at Large expressed; PROVIDED, That all the before mentioned Land, and all other whatsoever that shall be taken up and so settled in the said Province, shall afterwards, from time to time, for the space of Thirteen years from the date hereof, be held upon the Condition aforesaid of Continuing one able man Servant, or two such weaker Servants as aforesaid, on every hundred Acres a Master or Mistress shall possess besides what was granted for his or her own person; In failure of which, upon Notification to the present Occupant, or his assigns, there shall be three years given to such for their Completing the said Number of persons, or for their sale or other disposure of such part of their Lands as are not so peopled; within which time of three years, if any person holding any Lands shall fail, by himself, his Agents, executors, or Assigns, or some other way, to provide such Number of persons, Unless the General Assembly shall, without respect to poverty, Judge that it was impossible for the party so failing to keep or procure his or her Number of Servants to be provided as aforesaid, In such Case, we, the Lords, to have power of disposing of so much of such Land as shall not be planted with its due Number of persons, as aforesaid, to some other that will plant the same; PROVIDED always, that any person who has a stock of Cattle, Sheep, or such like on his hands shall, for every greater sort of Cattle which he has at the time of such forfeiture, as horses, Kine, etc., retain two acres, and for every lesser sort, as sheep, hogs, etc., one acre; Provided also, that no persons arriving into the said Counties with purpose to settle, they being Subjects or Naturalized as aforesaid, be denied a grant of such proportions of Land as at the time of their arrival are due to themselves or Servants by Concession from Us, as aforesaid, but have full Licence to take Up and settle the same in such order and manner as is granted or prescribed; all Lands, notwithstanding the powers in the Assembly aforesaid, shall

be taken up by warrant from the Governor, and Confirmed by the Governor and Council, Under a Seal to be provided for that purpose, in such order and method as shall be set down in this declaration, and more at Large in the Instructions to the Governor and Council.

And that the lands may be the more Regularly laid out and all persons the better ascertained of their titles and possessions:

1. Item, In the bounding of the County of Clarendon, the Governor and Council, and Assembly if any be, are to make Choice of, and Confine themselves and planters to, one side of the main river near Cape Faire, on which some of the adventurers are already settled, or Intend to settle, and the Islands in or near the said River next the side they settle on, Unless they have already settled some Island near the other side, which, if they have, they may Continue thereon.

2. Item, The Governor of the County of ——, with the advice of his Council, is to bound the said County as he shall see fit, not exceeding Forty miles square or Sixteen hundred Square miles.

3. Item, They are to take Care and direct that all Lands be divided by General Lots, none less than two thousand two hundred Acres nor more than two and Twenty thousand Acres in each Lot, excepting Cities, towns, etc., and the near Lots of townships; and that the same be Undecimally divided, one Eleventh part by Lot to Us, our heirs and Assigns, the Remainder to persons as they come to plant the same, in such proportions as is allowed.

4. Item, That the Governor of each County, or whom he shall depute, in Case of death or absence, if some one be not before commissionated by us, as aforesaid, do give to every person to whom land is due a warrant, Signed and Sealed by himself and the Major part of his Council, and directed to the Surveyor General, or his Deputy, Commanding him to lay out, Limit, and bound —— Acres of Land, as his due proportion is for such a person in such allotment; according to which warrant, the Register having first recorded the same and attested the record upon the warrant, the Surveyor General, or his Deputy, shall proceed, and Certify to the Chief Secretary or Register the Name of the person for whom he has laid out land, by virtue of what authority, the date of the Authority or warrant, the Number of Acres, the bounds, and on what point of the Compass the Several Limits thereof lie; which Certificate the Register is likewise to enter in a book to be prepared for that purpose, with an Alphabetical table referring to the book, That so

the Certificate may be the easier found, and then to file the Certificates, and the same to keep Safely; The Certificate being entered, a warrant Comprehending all the particulars of Land mentioned in the Certificate aforesaid is to be signed and Sealed by him and his Council, or the Major part of them as aforesaid, they having seen the entry, and directed to the Register or Chief Secretary for his preparing a Grant of the Land to the party for whom it is laid out; which Grant shall be in the form following, Viz.:

THE LORDS PROPRIETORS of the Province of Carolina do hereby grant unto A. B., of the County of Clarendon (or in what County the same shall be), in the province aforesaid, a plantation in the said County, containing ____ Acres, English measure, and Bounding as in the said Certificates; To hold to him (or her), his (or her) heirs and Assigns, for ever; Yielding and paying yearly to the said Lords Proprietors, their heirs or assigns, every Twenty fifth day of March, according to the English Account, one half penny of Lawful English money for every of the said Acres; To be held [as] of the manor of ____, in free and Common Soccage; the first payment of which rent to begin the Twenty fifth day of March which shall be in the year of our Lord One thousand Six hundred and Seventy, According to the English Account; Given Under the Seal of the County of Clarendon the ____ day of ____ in the year of our Lord ____.

To which Instrument the Governor, or his Deputy, has hereby full Authority to put the Seal of the said County and to Subscribe his Name, As also, the Council, or the Major part of them, are to Subscribe their Names; and then the Instrument or Grant is to be, by the Register, Recorded in a book of Records for that purpose; all which being done according to these Instructions, we hereby declare that the same shall be effectual in Law for the Enjoyment of the said plantation, and all the benefits and profits of and in the Same, Except the half part of Mines of Gold and Silver, paying the rent as aforesaid; Provided, that if any plantation so granted shall, by the space of three years, be neglected to be planted with a Sufficient Number of Servants, as is before mentioned, that then it shall be Lawful for us otherwise to dispose thereof, in whole or in part, This grant notwithstanding.

5. ITEM, We do also grant Convenient proportions of Land for highways and for streets, not exceeding one hundred foot in breadth, in Cities, towns, villages, etc., for Churches, Forts, wharfs, Quays, Har-

bours, and for public houses; and to each parish, for the use of their Ministers, one hundred Acres, in such [places] as the General Assembly shall appoint.

6. ITEM, The Governors are to take notice that all such Lands laid out for the uses and purposes in the next preceding Article shall be free and exempt from all rents, Taxes, and other Charges or duties whatsoever payable to Us, our heirs or assigns.

7. ITEM, That in laying out Lands for Cities, Towns, Villages, Boroughs, or other Hamlets, the said lands be undecimally divided, one Eleventh part to be by lot laid out for Us, and the rest divided to such as shall be willing to build thereon, they paying after the rate of one half penny per Acre yearly, to us, As for their other Lands, as aforesaid; which said Lands, in Cities, towns, etc., is to be Assured to each possessor by the same way and Instrument as is before mentioned.

8. ITEM, That all Rules Relating to building of each street or quantity of ground to be allotted to each house within the said Respective Cities, Boroughs, and towns be wholly left, by act as aforesaid, to the wisdom and direction of the General Assembly.

9. ITEM, That the Inhabitants of the said County have free passage through or by any Seas, bounds, Creeks, Rivers, Rivulets, etc., in the said Province of Carolina through or by which they must necessarily pass to come from the Main Ocean to the Counties aforesaid, or any part of the Province aforesaid.

10. LASTLY, It shall be Lawful for the Representatives of the Freeholders to make any address to the Lords touching the Governor and Council, or any of them, or Concerning any Grievances whatsoever, or for anything they shall desire, without the Consent of the Governor and Council, or any of them.

[Transcribed from a photostatic copy of a manuscript in the British Public Record Office, London. Reference: P. R. O. 30/24/48. Photostatic copy deposited in the State Department of Archives and History, Raleigh, North Carolina.]

The Fundamental Constitutions of Carolina

INTRODUCTION

In 1669, the lords proprietors of Carolina adopted for their province a new plan of government, officially called the Fundamental Constitutions of Carolina, but often referred to as the "Grand Model." This plan was quite different from that provided in the Concessions and Agreement, which, having been intended to attract settlers, allowed the colonists a large degree of control over their government. The new plan gave the people little part in government, for it was intended primarily to promote the interests of the proprietors and to "avoid erecting a numerous Democracy."

The Fundamental Constitutions have been attributed to the philosopher John Locke, and they are included in collections of his writings. Among historians, however, there is question as to what extent, if any, Locke contributed to the composition of the "Grand Model." Although an early copy is in Locke's handwriting, this may not be significant, as Locke was secretary to the proprietary board, a position that normally would have required preparation of such a copy. Locke also was secretary to Lord Ashley, who, like Locke, has been suggested as author of the Fundamental Constitutions. There is reason also to think that other proprietors had part in formulating the "Grand Model." Several were associated with James Harrington, who, in 1656, published *The Commonwealth of Oceana*, which contains ideas similar to those expressed in the Fundamental Constitutions. As the same ideas also are incorporated in the proprietors' charters, it seems obvious that the proprietors had in mind such a plan long before the Constitutions were drafted. Locke was not associated with the proprietors when the charters were issued and, therefore, could not have suggested to them those features of the Fundamental Constitutions which are provided for in the charters. Although he could have drafted the "Grand Model," and may have originated some of its provisions, it is also possible that Locke merely recorded and put into appropriate form decisions reached by the proprietors. Some of the errors in the copy of the Constitutions that is said to be in Locke's handwriting indicate that the latter is true. In that copy, from which the 1669 version of the Constitutions was transcribed for this volume, *preservation* was written for *persuasion*, *narrative* for *maritime*, *pass* for *possess*, *recorded* for *reckoned*, *counsellors* for *chancellors*, and *marshalls* for *masters*. These and other errors in the manuscript appear more likely

to have been made by a person recording what was said by others than by one setting forth his own ideas.

The Fundamental Constitutions were intended to provide a governmental structure which would enable the proprietors to exercise the feudal powers granted in their charters. Such powers were conferred in several provisions, such as that authorizing creation of a local nobility, the clause exempting Carolina from the statute of *quia emptores terrarum* (which forbade further subinfeudation), the provision authorizing creation of manors and manorial courts, and the bishop-of-Durham clause. The last of these provisions was the most comprehensive in the authority conferred, for it granted powers and privileges as great as any which the bishop of Durham ever "held, used, or enjoyed, or of right ought or could have, use, or enjoy." At the height of his power, which was in the fourteenth century, the bishop had possessed almost regal authority in Durham; he had enacted laws, levied taxes, raised troops, impressed ships, made truce with enemies, and exercised other such powers. Similar powers were specifically granted in the proprietors' charters, reinforcing the broad grant in the bishop-of-Durham clause.

The "Grand Model" provided not only a governmental system for Carolina but also a social and economic system. As in all feudal societies, control over land was to be the basis of governmental power and of legal and social status. The Constitutions placed ultimate governmental control in the hands of the proprietors, who had right to all of the land in the province. Next to them in power and status were the local nobility, of which there were to be two ranks, *landgrave* and *cacique*. Titles of nobility, to be conferred by the proprietors, would carry with them grants of large tracts of land and special privileges, such as membership in parliament and the right to be tried in a proprietors' court instead of lower courts. Beneath the nobility were to be the *freemen*, who could own land, have a limited part in government, and enjoy certain legal rights, such as appeal from lower courts. Below the freemen were to be *leet-men*, who were to be tenants of the noblemen and lords of manors; they would be bound to the land on which they lived and have status similar to that of serfs in medieval Europe. Leet-men were given no voice in government, and they were to be tried in manorial courts, without right of appeal. Still lower on the scale were slaves, who would be subject to their masters in all respects except religion. Land granted to noblemen and freemen would be subject to rents, paid to the proprietors; leet-men would owe rents to the lords of the land on which they lived.

The Constitutions provided that the province of Carolina was to be divided into *counties*. One fifth of each county would be divided into eight *seigniories*, to be assigned to the proprietors. Another fifth would be divided into eight *baronies*, to be granted to the local nobility; four baronies were to go to one man, entitled *landgrave*, and the other four would be divided between two *caciques*. The remainder of the county was to be divided into four *precincts*, each to be subdivided into *colonies;* land in the colonies was to be granted to freemen.

The supreme governmental agency provided in the Fundamental Constitutions was the *palatine's court*, composed of the eight proprietors, the eldest of whom would hold the office of *palatine*. Beneath this agency, seven other courts were provided, each consisting of a proprietor and six *councillors*, selected by a

complicated procedure which assured that at least half the councillors in each court would be members of the local nobility, sons of proprietors, or sons of local noblemen. Executive, administrative, and judicial functions were assigned to the proprietors' courts. The Fundamental Constitutions also provided for an agency called the *grand council,* which was assigned executive, judicial, and legislative powers. Another agency, called the *parliament,* was to be the assembly for the province. The grand council was to be composed of the eight proprietors and the forty-two councillors of the proprietors' courts. Among its powers was that of deciding what matters might go before the parliament, which was prohibited from considering any matter that had not first passed the grand council and been proposed by it. The parliament was to consist of the proprietors or their deputies, all of the landgraves and caciques of the province, and one freeholder from each precinct, who was to be elected by the freeholders of his precinct. All actions by the parliament would require ratification by the palatine and three other proprietors. Any action of the grand council and parliament could be nullified by the palatine's court. All of these agencies—the eight proprietors' courts, the grand council, and the parliament—were to have jurisdiction over the entire province.

In addition to agencies for the whole province, the Fundamental Constitutions provided for local courts and officials, including municipal officers. They also guaranteed to freemen certain individual rights, such as trial by jury and protection against double jeopardy, and they provided that all inhabitants, including slaves, should be permitted to belong to whatever religious groups they chose. Provision also was made for such governmental activities as the exercise of eminent domain and the keeping of legal records and vital statistics.

The "Grand Model" was intended to last forever, and it was designed for a society which the proprietors expected to develop in Carolina, not for conditions existing in the province when the instrument was drafted. After adoption of the Constitutions, therefore, the proprietors instructed officials in Albemarle to make effective only those features which were considered practicable under existing conditions. Even limited implementation, however, required significant changes in the government that had been established in Albemarle under the Concessions and Agreement. The assembly was deprived of power to initiate legislation, and the governor lost much of his authority and prestige. Some of the powers lost by the assembly and the governor were assigned to the council, which thereby acquired greater prestige as well as increased authority.

Although the proprietors expected eventually to make the Fundamental Constitutions fully effective, they never succeeded in doing this. Like the early instructions to the governor at Albemarle, later instructions to governors were, in effect, modifications of the "Grand Model." From time to time, the proprietors formally revised "The Sacred and Unalterable Form and Rule of Government," of which they sent at least five versions to Carolina.

The Fundamental Constitutions, adopted July 21, 1669, were first sent to Albemarle in January, 1670. A copy already had been given to a colony which sailed for Port Royal, in modern South Carolina, in August, 1669. Although the proprietors soon appointed deputies in Albemarle and took other steps to conform to the "Grand Model," these changes appear to have been nominal and to have

had little practical effect. On March 1, 1670, the proprietors adopted a new version of the Fundamental Constitutions, which they claimed was the official form, asserting that the earlier version was only a draft sent for temporary use. Apparently, the Albemarle government was not reorganized until after receipt of the 1670 version. The proprietors formally revised the "Grand Model" twice in 1682, in January and in August, to meet objections raised by groups proposing to settle in Carolina. As actual government of the colonies was conducted under modifications of the Constitutions, contained in the proprietors' instructions to governors, alterations in the official version had little real effect. Settlers in Albemarle, however, expressed dissatisfaction with certain features of the "Grand Model," and protests against alteration of the original form were made by inhabitants of South Carolina. There were frequent disorders in both colonies, and, in 1693, the proprietors officially suspended the Fundamental Constitutions. Five years later, the Constitutions were revived, after drastic revision. Although the 1698 version was more practicable than the earlier ones, its full enforcement was never attempted. After 1700, the proprietors gradually ceased referring to the "Grand Model."

It is difficult to determine what effect the Fundamental Constitutions had on the development of North Carolina, for few records of the colony in its early years have survived. On the surface, it would appear that they had little influence, for they were never fully implemented. A landed nobility never developed in North Carolina, nor did serfdom develop. The palatine's court was the only proprietors' court organized, and the grand council and parliament were never constituted as provided in the Constitutions. Nevertheless, the governmental agencies that were established in the colony bore the imprint of the "Grand Model," and the policies of the proprietors were directed toward full implementation of the Constitutions. These agencies and policies necessarily had important effects on the colony. For example, the assembly in North Carolina had little power for many years, and it did not regain its former right to initiate legislation until the Constitutions were suspended, in the 1690's. Violence and confusion were frequent in the colony as long as the Fundamental Constitutions were the official "Form and Rule." These disorders may have been due in large part to the form of government, which provided settlers with no legitimate channels for initiating change.

THE DOCUMENTS

Version of July 21, 1669 [1]

OUR Sovereign Lord the King having, out of his royal grace and bounty, granted unto us the Province of Carolina, with all the royalties, Proprieties, Jurisdictions, and privileges of a County Palatine, as large and ample as the County Palatine of Durham, with other great privileges; for the better settlement of the Government of the said Place, and establishing the interest of the Lords Proprietors with Equality, and without confusion; and that the Government of this Province may be made most agreeable unto the Monarchy under which we live, and of which this province is a part; and that we may avoid erecting a numerous Democracy: We, the true and absolute Lords and Proprietors of the Province aforesaid, have agreed to this following form of Government, to be perpetually established amongst us, unto which we do oblige ourselves, our heirs and successors, in the most binding ways that can be devised.

2. Out of the eight Proprietors there shall be chosen, by themselves, a Palatine, who shall continue during life, whose son shall not be capable of immediately succeeding him after his death; but the eldest in Age of the other Proprietors shall succeed, to prevent the making the office in this little government Hereditary and to avoid the mischief of factions in Elections.

3. There shall be Seven other chief offices erected, viz., the chief Justice's, Chancellor's, Constable's, High Steward's, Treasurer's, Chamberlain's, Admiral's; which places shall be enjoyed by none but the Lords Proprietors, to be assigned at first by lot; and upon the vacancy of any one [2] of the seven great Offices by death, or otherwise, the Eldest proprietor <shall> have his choice of the said place.

---

[1] The manuscript from which this transcription was made consists of an apparently complete copy of a version of the Fundamental Constitutions and, in addition, notes showing numerous alterations. Various features of the manuscript indicate that some changes were merely corrections of errors but that others were made in the course of a comprehensive revision. This transcription gives the original text insofar as it can be distinguished. Words in angle brackets are interlinear or marginal insertions judged by the editor to be part of the original text. Other minor changes which appear contemporary with the original text are indicated in footnotes. Words in square brackets were taken from notes showing revisions; these have been used where the original text is illegible.

A transcription of revised and added articles, incorporating the indicated revisions, follows this transcription.

[2] Originally *other*, but changed to *one*.

4. Each Province shall be divided into Counties; each County shall consist of eight Seigniories, eight Baronies, and four precincts; each Precinct shall consist of Six Colonies.

5. Each Colony, Seigniory, and Barony shall consist of twelve thousand Acres, the eight Seigniories being the share of the eight Proprietors, and the eight Baronies of the Nobility; both which shares, being each of them a fifth part of the whole, are to be perpetually annexed, the one to the Proprietors, the other to the Hereditary Nobility, Leaving the Colonies, being three fifths, amongst the people; that so, in the Setting out and planting the lands, the Balance of Government may be preserved.

6. At any time before the year 1701, any of the <Lords> Proprietors shall have power to relinquish, Alienate, and dispose, to any other person, his Proprietorship, and all the Seigniories, powers, and Interest thereunto belonging, wholly and entirely together, and not otherwise. But after the year 1700, those who are then <Lords> Proprietors shall not have power to Alienate or make over their proprietorship, with Seigniories and privileges thereunto belonging, or any part thereof, to any person whatsoever, otherwise than as in article 18,[3] but it shall descend unto their heirs male; and for want of heirs male, it shall descend on that Landgrave or Cacique of Carolina who is descended of the next heir female of the said Proprietor; and for want of Such heirs, it shall descend on the next heir general; and for want of Such heirs, the remaining Seven proprietors shall, upon the Vacancy, choose a Landgrave to succeed the deceased proprietor, who being chosen by the majority of the Seven Surviving proprietors, he and his heirs Successively shall be proprietors as fully, to all intents and purposes, as any of the rest.

7. And that the number of eight Proprietors may be constantly kept, if, upon the vacancy of any Proprietorship, the Surviving Seven Proprietors shall not choose a Landgrave <or Cacique> as a proprietor before the Second session of Parliament after the vacancy, then the Parliament, at the next Session but one after Such vacancy, shall have power to choose any Landgrave <or Cacique> to be Proprietor; but whosoever after the year 1700, either by inheritance or choice, shall Succeed any Proprietor in his proprietorship, and Seigniories thereunto belonging, shall be obliged to take the name and Arms of that proprietor whom he Succeeds, which from thenceforth shall be the name and Arms of his Family and their posterity.

[3] Originally *16*, but changed to *18*.

8. Whatsoever Landgrave <or Cacique> shall be chosen into a proprietorship [4] shall take the Seigniories annexed to the said proprietorship, but shall relinquish all the Baronies belonging to his Landgraveship <or Caciqueship> to be disposed of by the proprietors as in the following Articles.

9. To every County there shall be three as the hereditary Nobility of this Palatinate, who shall be called the one a Landgrave and the other two Caciques, and shall have place in the Parliament there; the Landgrave shall have four Baronies, and the two Caciques, each of them, two apiece, hereditary,[5] and unalterably annexed to and settled upon the said Dignity.

10. The first Landgrave and Caciques of every County shall be nominated, not by the Joint election of the Proprietors all together, but the eight Proprietors shall, each of them separately, nominate and choose one Landgrave and two Caciques for the eight first Counties to be planted; and when the said eight Counties shall be planted, the proprietors shall, in the same manner, nominate and Choose eight more Landgraves and sixteen Caciques for the eight next Counties to be planted; and so proceed, in the same manner, till the whole province of Carolina be set out and planted according to the [proportions] in these fundamental Constitutions.

11. Any Landgrave or Cacique, at any time before the year 1701, shall have power to alienate, sell, or make over, to any other person, his dignity, with the Baronies thereunto belonging, all entirely together; but after the year 1700, no Landgrave or Cacique shall have power to alienate, Sell, make over, or let the hereditary Baronies of his dignity, or any part thereof, otherwise than as in Article 18; [6] but they shall all entirely, with the dignity thereunto belonging, descend unto his heirs Male; and for want of Such heirs Male, all entirely and undivided, to the next heir general; and for want of Such heirs, shall devolve into the hands of the Proprietors.

12. That the due number of landgraves and [7] Caciques may be always kept up, if, upon the devolution of any Landgraveship or Caciqueship, the Proprietors shall not settle the devolved dignity, with the Baro-

[4] This passage was changed to read: *Whatsoever Landgrave or Cacique shall, by inheritance or choice, come to be a Proprietor . . .* See Revisions for subsequent changes.

[5] *Hereditary* was changed to *hereditarily*.

[6] Originally *16*, but changed to *18*.

[7] Originally *or*, but changed to *and*.

nies thereunto annexed, before the second Session of Parliament after Such devolution, the Parliament, at the next <Biennial> Session but one after Such devolution, shall have power to make any one Landgrave or Cacique in the Room of him, who dying with out heirs, his dignity and Baronies devolved.

13. No one person shall have more than one dignity, with the Seigniories or Baronies thereunto belonging; but whensoever it shall happen that any one who is already Proprietor, Landgrave, or Cacique shall have any of those dignities descend to him by inheritance, it shall be at his choice to keep one of the two dignities, with the Lands annexed, he shall like best, but shall leave the other, with the lands annexed, to be enjoyed by him who, not being his heir apparent, and certain successor to his present dignity, is next afterward.

14. Whosoever, by right of Inheritance, shall come to be Landgrave or Cacique shall take the name and Arms of his predecessor in that dignity, to be from thenceforth the Name and Arms of his Family and their posterity.

15. Since the dignity of Proprietor, of [8] Landgrave, or Cacique cannot be divided, and the Seigniories or Baronies thereunto annexed must for ever, all entirely, descend with and accompany that dignity, when ever, for want of heirs Male, it shall descend upon the Issue Female, the Eldest Daughter and her heirs shall be preferred; and in the Inheritance of those dignities, and in the Seigniories or Baronies annexed, there shall be no Coheirs.

16. After the year 1700, whatsoever Landgrave or Cacique shall, without leave from the Palatine's Court, be out of Carolina during two successive biennial Parliaments shall, at the end of the second biennial Parliament after such his absence, be summoned by Proclamation; and if he come not into Carolina before the next biennial Parliament after Such Summons, then it shall be lawful for the grand Council, at a price set by the said Council and approved by the Parliament, to sell the Baronies, with the Dignities thereunto belonging, of the said absent Landgrave or Cacique, all together, to any one to whom the said Council shall think fit; but the price so paid for said Dignity or Baronies shall be deposited in the Treasury, for the sole use and behoof of the former owner, or his <heirs or> assigns.

---

[8] *Of* was struck out.

17. In every Seigniory, Barony, and Manor, the Lord shall have power, in his own name, to hold Court there, for trying of all causes, both Civil and Criminal; but where it shall concern any other person being no Inhabitant, Vassal, or Leet man of the said Barony or Seigniory <or manor>, he, upon paying down of forty shillings unto the Proprietors' use, shall have an appeal from thence unto the County Court; and if the Lord be cast, the said Lord shall pay unto the appellant the said forty shillings, with other charges.

18. The Lords of Seigniories and Baronies shall have power only of granting Estates, not exceeding three lives or one and thirty years, in two thirds of the said Seigniories or Baronies; and the remaining third shall be always Demesne.

19. Every Manor shall consist of not less than three thousand Acres and not above twelve thousand Acres in one entire piece; but any three thousand acres or more in one piece and the possession of one Man shall not be a manor unless it be constituted a manor by the grant of the Lords Proprietors.

20. Every Lord of a manor, within his manor, shall have all the powers, Jurisdictions, and Privileges which a Landgrave or Cacique has in his Baronies.

21. Any Lord of a manor may Alienate, sell, or dispose, to any other person, and his heirs, for ever, <his manor>, all entirely together, with all the privileges and Leet men thereunto belonging, so far forth as any other Colony Lands; but no grant of any part thereof, either in fee or for any longer term than three lives or twenty one years, shall be good against the next heir; neither shall a manor, for want of Issue Male, be divided amongst Coheirs; but the manor, if there be but one, shall all entirely descend to the Eldest Daughter and <her> heirs; if there be more manors than one in the possession of the deceased, the Eldest Sister shall have her choice, the Second next, and so on, beginning <again> at the Eldest, till all the manors be taken up; that So, the privileges which belong to manors being indivisible, the lands of the manor to which they are annexed may be Kept entire, and the manor not lose those privileges, which upon parcelling out to Several owners must necessarily cease.

22. In every Seigniory, Barony, and manor, all the tenants or Leet men shall be under the Jurisdiction of the Lord of the said Seigniory,

Barony, or Manor, without appeal from him unless as in the Article 26;[9] nor shall any Leet man or Leet woman have liberty to go off from the Land of his particular Lord and live any where else without Licences obtained from his Said Lord, under hand and Seal.

23. All the Children of Leet men shall be Leet men, and so to all generations.

24. No man shall be capable of having a Court Leet or Leet men but a Proprietor, Landgrave, or Cacique, or Lord of a Manor.

25. Whoever is Lord of Leet men shall, upon the marriage of a Leet man or Leet woman of his, give them ten Acres of Land for their lives, they paying to him therefor one eighth of all the yearly increase and growth of the said acres.

26. In case the Lord of any Seigniory, Barony, or manor shall have made a Contract or agreement with his Tenants, which agreement, by consent, is Registered in the next <precinct> Registry,[10] then, in Such case, the said Tenant may appeal unto, or bring his Complaint originally in, the County Court for the performance of Such agreements, and not other wise.

27. There shall be eight Courts or Councils for the dispatch of all affairs, the first, Called the Palatine's Court, to consist of the Palatine and the other Seven Proprietors. The other seven courts of the other seven great Officers shall consist, each of them, of a Proprietor and Six Councillors added to him; under each of these latter seven <Courts> shall be a College of twelve assistants. The twelve assistants <out> of the Several Colleges shall be Chosen: two out of the Landgraves, by the Landgraves' Chamber during the Session of Parliament; two out of the Caciques, by the Caciques' Chamber during the Session of Parliament; two out of the Landgraves, Caciques, or Eldest sons of the Proprietors, by the Palatine's Court; four more of the twelve shall be chosen by the Commons' Chamber, during the Session of Parliament, out of such as have been or are members of Parliament, Sheriffs, or Justices of the County Court; the other two shall be Chosen by the Palatine's Court out of the aforesaid members of Parliament, or Sheriffs, or Justices of the County Court, or

---

[9] Originally *24*, but changed to *26*.

[10] *Next precinct* was struck out, and *of the County Court* was inserted after *Registry*. This change appears to be contemporary with the original writing. Later, the entire article was struck out. See Revisions.

the Eldest sons of Landgraves or Caciques, or younger Sons of Proprietors.

28. Out of these Colleges shall be Chosen Six Councillors to be joined with each Proprietor in his Court; of which six, one shall be of those who were Chosen into any of the Colleges by the Palatine's Court out of the Landgraves, Caciques, or Eldest Sons of Proprietors; one out of those who were Chosen into any of the Colleges by the Landgraves' Chamber; and one <out of> those who were Chosen into any one of the Colleges by the Caciques' Chamber; two out of those who were Chosen into any one of the Colleges by the Commons' Chamber; and one out of those who were Chosen by the Palatine's Court into any of the Colleges out of the Proprietors' younger Sons, or Eldest Sons of Landgraves or Caciques, or Commons Qualified as aforesaid.

29. When it shall happen that any Councillor dies, and thereby there is a vacancy, the grand council shall have power to remove any Councillor that is willing to be removed out of any other of the Proprietors' Courts to fill up this vacancy, provided they take a man of the Same degree and choice the other was <of> whose vacant place <is> to be filled; but if no Councillor consent to be removed, or upon Such remove, the last remaining vacant place in any of the Proprietors' Courts shall be filled up by the choice of the grand Council, who shall have power to remove out of any of the Colleges any Assistant who is of the same degree and choice that Councillor was <of> into whose vacant place he is to succeed; the grand Council, also, shall have power to remove any Assistant that is willing out of one College into another, provided he be of the same degree and choice; but the last remaining vacant place in any College shall be filled up by the same choice and out of the same degree of persons the Assistant was of who is dead or removed. No Place shall be vacant in any Proprietors' Court above six Months; no place shall be vacant in any College longer than the next session of Parliament.

30. No man being a member of the grand Council or of any of the seven Colleges shall be turned out but For misdemeanor, of which the grand Council shall be Judge; and the vacancy of the person so put out shall be filled, not by the Election of the grand Council, but by those who first chose him, and out of the same degree he was <of> who is expelled.

31. All Elections in the Parliament, in the Several Chambers of the Parliament, and in the grand Council shall be passed by balloting.

32. The Palatine's Court shall consist of the Palatine and Seven Proprietors, wherein nothing shall be acted without the presence and consent of the Palatine, or his Deputy, and three others of the Proprietors, or their Deputies. <This Court> shall have power to call Parliaments, to pardon all Offences, to make Elections of all Officers in the Proprietors' dispose; and also, they shall have power, by their Order to the Treasurer, to dispose of all public Treasure, excepting money granted by the Parliament and by them directed to Some <particular> public use; and also, they shall have a Negative upon all Acts, Orders, Votes, and Judgments of the grand Council and the Parliament; and shall have all the powers granted to the Proprietors by their patent, except in such things as are limited by these fundamental constitutions and form of government.

33. The Palatine him self, when he in person shall be either in the Army or in any of the Proprietors' Courts, shall then have the power of General or of that Proprietor in whose Court he is then present; and the Proprietor in whose Court the Palatine then presides shall, during his presence there, be but as one of the Council.

34. The Chancellor's [11] Court, consisting of one of the Proprietors and his six Councillors, who shall be called vice-chancellors, shall have the Custody of the Seal of the Palatinate, under which all charters, of Lands or otherwise, Commissions, and grants of the Palatine's Court shall pass, etc. To this Court, also, belongs all state matters, dispatches, and treaties, with the Neighbour Indians or any other, so far forth as is permitted by our Charter from our Sovereign Lord the King. To this office, also, belongs all Innovations of the Law of Liberty of conscience, and all disturbances of the public peace upon pretence of Religion, as also, the Licence of printing. The twelve assistants belonging to this Court shall be called Recorders.

35. The Chancellor, or his Deputy, shall be always Speaker in Parliament and President of the grand council, and in his and his Deputy's absence, one of his Vice-Chancellors.

The Chief Justice's Court, consisting of one of the proprietors and his six Councillors, who shall be called Justices of the Bench, shall

[11] Originally *Councillor's*, but changed to *Chancellor's*.

Judge all appeals, both in cases Civil and Criminal, except all Such cases as shall be under the Jurisdiction and Cognizance of any other of the Proprietors' Courts, which shall be tried in those Courts respectively. The Government and regulations of the Registries of writings and contracts shall belong to the Jurisdiction of this Court. The twelve assistants of this Court shall be called Masters.[12]

36. The High Constable's Court, consisting of one of the Proprietors and his six Councillors, who shall be called Marshals, shall order and determine of all Military affairs by land, and all land forces, Arms, Ammunition, Artillery, Garrisons, and Forts, etc., and whatever belongs unto war. His twelve assistants shall be called Lieutenant Generals. In time of actual war, The High Constable, whilst he is in the Army, shall be General of the Army, and the six Councillors, or such of them as the Palatine's Court shall for that time <and service> appoint, shall be the immediate great Officers under him, and the Lieutenant Generals next to them.

37. The Admiral's Court, consisting of one of the Proprietors and his Six Councillors, called Consuls, shall have the care and inspection over all ports, Moles,[13] and Navigable Rivers so far as the Tide flows; and also, all the public Shipping of Carolina, and stores thereunto belonging, and all maritime [14] affairs. This Court, also, shall have the power of the Court of Admiralty; and also, to hear and try by Law-Merchant all cases in Matters of Trade between the Merchants of Carolina amongst them selves, arising without the limits of Carolina; as also, all controversies in Merchandising that shall happen between Denizens of Carolina and foreigners. The twelve Assistants belonging to this court shall be called proconsuls.

38. The Treasurer's Court, consisting of one proprietor and his Six Councillors, called under-Treasurers, shall take care of all matters that [15] concerns the public revenue and Treasury. The twelve assistants shall be called Auditors.

39. The High Steward's court, consisting of a proprietor and his six Councillors, who shall be called Comptrollers, shall have the care of all foreign and domestic Trade, Manufactures, public buildings and

[12] Originally *Marshals,* but changed to *Masters.*
[13] Originally *Marts,* but changed to *Moles.*
[14] Originally *narrative,* but changed to *maritime.*
[15] Originally *of,* but changed to *that.*

work-houses, high ways, passages by water above the flood of the Tide, drains, sewers and Banks against inundations, Bridges, Posts, Carriers, Fairs, Markets, and all things in order to Travel and commerce, and anything that may corrupt, deprave, or Infect the common Air or water, and all other things wherein the Public <trade>, commerce, or health is concerned; and also, the setting out and surveying of lands; and also, the setting out and appointing <places> for towns to be built on in the Precincts, and the prescribing and determining the Figure and bigness of the said Towns according to such Models as the said court shall order, contrary or differing from which Models it shall not be lawful for any one to build in any Town.

40. This Court shall have power, also, to make any public building or any new high way, or enlarge any old high way, upon any Man's Land whatsoever; as also, to make cuts, Channels, Banks, locks, and Bridges, for making Rivers Navigable, for draining of Fens, or any other public uses; the damage the owner of such land, on or through where any such public thing shall be made, shall receive thereby shall be valued by a Jury of twelve men of the Precinct in which any such thing is done, and satisfaction shall be made accordingly by a Tax, either on the County or that particular precinct, as the grand Council shall think fit to order in that particular case. The twelve assistants belonging to this Court shall be called Surveyors.

41. The Chamberlain's Court, consisting of a proprietor and his six Councillors, called Vice-Chamberlains, shall have the power to convocate the grand Council; shall have the care of all Ceremonies, Precedency, Heraldry, reception of public Messengers, and pedigrees; the Registries of all Births, Burials, and Marriages; legitimation and all cases concerning Matrimony or arising from it; and shall, also, have power to Regulate all Fashions, Habits, Badges, Games, and Sports. The twelve assistants belonging to this Court shall be called Provosts.

42. All causes belonging to, or under the Jurisdiction of, any of the Proprietors' Courts shall in them respectively be tried and ultimately determined, without any further appeal.

43. The proprietors' Courts shall have a power to mitigate all fines and suspend all executions, either before or after sentence, in any of the other respective Inferior Courts.

44. In all debates, hearings, or Trials in any of the Proprietors' Courts, the twelve assistants belonging to the Said Court respectively

shall have Liberty to be present, but shall not interpose unless their opinions be required, nor have any Vote at all; but their <business shall> be, by direction of the respective courts, to prepare Such business as shall be committed to them; as also, to bear Such Offices and dispatch Such affairs, either where the Court is kept or else where, as the Court shall think fit.

45. In all the Proprietors' Courts <any> three shall make a Quorum.

46. The grand Council shall consist of the Palatine, and Seven Proprietors, and the forty two Councillors of the Several Proprietors' Courts; who shall have power to determine any Controversies that may arise between any of the Proprietors' Courts about their respective Jurisdictions; to make peace and war, Leagues, Treaties, etc., with any of the Neighbour Indians; To issue out their General Orders to the Constable's and Admiral's Court for the Raising, disposing, or disbanding the Forces, by land or by Sea; to prepare all matters to be proposed in Parliament; nor shall any Tax or law or other matters whatsoever be proposed, debated, or Voted in Parliament but what has first passed the grand Council and, in form of a bill to be passed, is by them presented to the Parliament; nor shall any bill So prepared <and presented by the grand Council to the Parliament to be enacted, whether it be an antiquated Law or otherwise, be voted or passed into an Act of Parliament>,[16] or be at all Obligatory, unless it be three Several days read openly in the Parliament, and then, afterwards, by Majority of Votes, Enacted, during the same session wherein it was thrice read, and also confirmed by the Palatine and three of the Proprietors as is above said.

47. The grand Council shall always be Judges of all Causes and appeals that concerns the Palatine, or any of the proprietors, or any councillor of any Proprietors' Court in any Case which other wise should have been Tried in that Court in which the said Councillor is Judge him self.

48. The Grand Council, by their warrants to the Treasurer's Court, shall dispose of all the money given by the Parliament and by them directed to any particular public use.

---

[16] The passage in angle brackets was taken from a marginal note rewording the original passage, which reads as follows: *to be enacted, whether it an* ——— [blank] *law or otherwise, or passed into an Act of Parliament.*

49. The Quorum of the grand Council shall be thirteen, whereof a Proprietor, or his Deputy, shall be always one.

50. The Palatine, or any of the Proprietors, shall have power, under hand and seal, to be Registered in the grand Council, to make a Deputy; who shall have the same power, to all intents and purposes, that he himself who [17] deputes him, except in confirming Acts of Parliament, as in Article <70>; all Such deputation shall cease and determine of them selves at the end of four years, and at any time shall be revocable at the pleasure of the Deputator.

51. No Deputy of any Proprietor shall have any power whilst the deputator is in any part of Carolina, except the Proprietor whose deputy he is be a Minor.

52. During the minority of any Proprietor, his Guardian shall have power to constitute and appoint his deputy.[18]

53. The Eldest of the Proprietors who shall be personally in Carolina shall of Course be the Palatine's Deputy; and if no Proprietor be in Carolina, he shall choose his deputy out of the heirs apparent of any of the Proprietors, if any such be there; and if there be no heir apparent of any of the Proprietors, above twenty one years old, in Carolina, then he shall choose for Deputy any one of the Landgraves of the grand Council; and till he have, by deputation, under hand and Seal, Chosen any one of the forementioned heirs apparent or Landgrave to be his deputy, the Eldest Man of the Landgraves, and for want of Landgraves, the Eldest Man of the Caciques, who shall be personally in Carolina shall of course be his deputy.

54. The Proprietors' deputy shall be always one of their own Six Councillors respectively.

55. In every County there shall be a Court, consisting of a Sheriff and four Justices of the County, being Inhabitants and having, each of them, at least five hundred Acres of Freehold within the said County, to be chosen and Commissionated from time to time by the Palatine's court; who shall try and Judge all appeals from any of the precinct Courts.

---

[17] Originally *that*, but changed to *who*.
[18] Article 52 is opposite article 53, instead of preceding it.

56. For any personal causes Exceeding the value of two hundred pounds, or in Title of Lands, or in any Criminal Cause, either party, upon paying twenty pounds to the Proprietors' use, shall have Liberty of Appeal from the County Court unto the respective Proprietors' Court.

57. In every Precinct there shall be a Court, consisting of a Steward and four Justices of the Precinct, being Inhabitants and having three hundred Acres of Freehold within the said Precinct; who shall Judge all Criminal causes, except for Treason, Murder, and any other offences punished with death; and all civil causes whatsoever, and in all personal actions not exceeding fifty pounds without appeal; but where the Cause shall exceed that Value, or concern a Title of land, and in all Criminal causes, there, either party, upon paying five pounds to the Proprietors' use, shall have Liberty of appeal unto the County Court.

58. No cause shall be twice tried in any one Court, upon any reason or pretence whatsoever.

59. For Treason, Murder, and all other offences punishable with death, there shall be a Commission, twice a year at least, granted unto one or more members of the <Grand> Council or Colleges, who shall come as Itinerant Judges to the Several Counties, and, with the Sheriff and four Justices, shall hold assizes, and Judge all Such causes. But upon paying of fifty pounds to the proprietors' use, there shall be Liberty of appeal to the respective Proprietors' Court.

60. The grand Juries at the Several assizes shall have, upon their Oaths, and, under their hands and Seals, deliver in to the Itinerant Judges a presentment of Such grievances, Misdemeanors, exigencies, or defects which they shall think necessary for the Public good of the Country; which presentment shall, by the Itinerant Judges, at the End of their circuit, be delivered in to the grand Council at their next Sitting; and whatsoever therein concerns the Execution of Laws already made, the Several Proprietors' Courts, in the matters belonging to each of them respectively, shall take Cognizance of <it>, and <give> such order about it as shall be Effectual for the due Execution of the laws; but whatever concerns the making of any new laws shall be referred to the Several respective Courts to which that matter belongs, and by them prepared and brought to the grand Council.

61. For Terms, there shall be quarterly Such a certain number of days, not exceeding twenty one at any one time, as the Several respective

Courts shall appoint; the time for the beginning of the Term in the precinct Court shall be the first Monday in January, April, July, and October; and in the County Court, the first Monday of February, May, August, November; and in the Proprietors' <Courts>, the first Monday of March, June, September, and December.

62. For Juries [19] in the Precinct Court, no Man shall be a Jury Man under fifty Acres of Freehold. In the County Court, or at the assizes, no man shall be a Jury Man under two hundred acres of Freehold. No man shall be a Grand Jury Man under three hundred acres of freehold; and in the Proprietors' Courts, no Man shall be a Jury Man under five hundred acres of Freehold.

63. Every Jury shall consist of twelve Men; and <it> shall <not> be necessary they should all agree, but the Verdict shall be according to the consent of the Majority.

64. It shall be a base and vile thing to Plead for money or Reward; nor shall any one, except he be a Near Kinsman, not farther off than Cousin German to the party concerned, be admitted to plead another man's cause till, before the Judge in open Court, he has taken an Oath that he does <not> plead for money or reward, nor has nor will receive, nor directly nor indirectly bargained with the party, whose cause he is going to Plead, for any money or other reward for Pleading his Cause.

65. There shall be a Parliament, consisting of the Proprietors, or their deputies, the Landgraves and Caciques, and one Freeholder out of every Precinct, to be Chosen by the Freeholders of the said Precinct respectively. They shall sit all together in one Room, and have every member one Vote.

66. No man shall be Chosen a member of Parliament who has less than five hundred Acres of Freehold within the Precinct for which he is Chosen; nor shall any have a vote in choosing the said member that has less than fifty acres of Freehold within the said precinct.

67. A new Parliament shall be assembled the first Monday of the Month of November every second year, and shall meet and Sit in the Town they last Sat in, without any Summons, unless by the Palatine, or his Deputy, together with any three of the Proprietors, or their Deputies, they be Summoned to meet at any other place; and if there shall be any occasion of a Parliament in these Intervals, it shall be in the power

[19] *For Juries* was struck out.

of the Palatine, with any three of the Proprietors, to assemble them on forty days' notice, at such time and place as they shall think fit; and the Palatine, or his Deputy, with the advice and consent of any three of the Proprietors, or their Deputies, shall have power to dissolve the Said Parliament when they shall think fit.

68. At the opening of every Parliament, the first thing that shall be done shall be the reading of these fundamental constitutions, which the Palatine, and Proprietors, and the rest of the members then present shall Subscribe. Nor shall any Person whatsoever Sit or Vote in the Parliament till he has, that Sessions, Subscribed these fundamental constitutions in a book kept for that purpose by the Clerk of the Parliament.

69. And [20] in order to the due Election of members for this Biennial Parliament, it shall be lawful for the Freeholders of the respective precincts to meet the first Tuesday in September every two years, in the Same Town or place that they last met in, to choose Parliament men, and there choose those members that are to Sit the next November following, unless the Steward of the Precinct shall, by Sufficient notice Thirty days before, appoint some other place for their meeting in order to the Election.

70. No act or Order of Parliament shall be of any force unless it be Ratified in open Parliament, during the same Session, by the Palatine, or his Deputy, and three more of the Proprietors, or their deputies; and then not to continue longer in force but until the End of the next Biennial Parliament, unless in the mean time it be Ratified under the hand and seal of the Palatine him self and three more of the Proprietors them selves, and, by their Order, published at the next Biennial Parliament.

71. Any Proprietor, or his Deputy, may enter his Protestation against any act of the Parliament, before the Palatine or his deputy's consent be given as aforesaid, if he shall conceive the said act to be contrary to this Establishment or any of these Fundamental Constitutions of the Government; and in Such case, after a full and free debate, the several Estates shall retire into four several Chambers, the Palatine and Proprietors into one, the Landgraves into another, and the Caciques into another, and those Chosen by the Precincts into a fourth; and if the major part of any four of these Estates [21] shall Vote that the law is not agreeable to this Establishment and fundamental constitution

---

[20] *And* was struck out.

[21] Thus in the manuscript. See Revisions.

of the Government, then it shall pass no further, but be as if it had never been proposed.

72. To avoid multiplicity of laws, which by degrees always change the Right foundations of the Original Government, all acts of Parliament whatsoever, in what form soever passed or enacted, shall, at the end of Sixty years after their enacting, respectively Cease and determine of them selves, and, without any repeal, become Null and void, as if no such acts or laws had ever been made.

73. Since multiplicity of Comments, as well as of laws, have great inconveniences, and Serve only to obscure and perplex, all manner of comments and expositions on any part of these fundamental constitutions, or on any part of the Common or Statute law of Carolina, are absolutely prohibited.

74. There shall be a Registry in every precinct, wherein shall be enrolled all deeds, Leases, Judgments, or other conveyances which may concern any of the land within the Said Precinct; and all Such conveyances not so entered or Registered shall not be of force against any person not privy to the Said contract or conveyance.

75. No man shall be Register of any Precinct who has not at least three hundred acres of Freehold within the Said Precinct.

76. The freeholders of every Precinct shall nominate three men, out of which three the Chief Justice court shall choose and Commission one to be Register of the Said precinct, whilst he shall well behave him self.

77. There shall be a Registry in every Colony, wherein shall be Recorded all the Births, Marriages, and deaths that shall happen within the said Colony.

78. No man shall be Register of a Colony that has not above fifty acres of Freehold within the said Colony.

79. The time of every one's Age shall be Recorded from the day that his Birth is entered in the Registry, and not before.

80. No Marriage shall be lawful, whatever Contract or Ceremonies they have used, till both the parties mutually own it before the Colony Register, and he enter it, with the names of the Father and mother of such party.

81. No man shall administer to the goods, or have right to them, or enter upon the Estate, of any person deceased till his death be Registered in the Colony Registry.

82. He that does not enter in the Colony Registry the death or [22] Birth of any person that dies in his house or ground shall pay to the said Register one shilling per week for each Such neglect, Reckoning from the time of each death or birth respectively to the time of Registering it.

83. In like manner, the births, Marriages, and deaths of the Lords Proprietors, Landgraves, and Caciques shall be Registered in the Chamberlain's Court.

84. There shall be in every Colony one Constable, to be Chosen annually by the Freeholders of the Colony, his Estate to be above one hundred acres of Freehold within the Said Colony; and Such Subordinate officers appointed for his assistance as the precinct court shall find requisite, and shall be Established by the Precinct court; the Election of the Subordinate annual officers shall be also in the Freeholders of the Colony.

85. All Towns incorporate shall be Governed by a Mayor, twelve Aldermen, and twenty four of the Common Council; the Said Common Council to be chosen by the present householders of the Said Town; and the Aldermen to be Chosen out of the Common Council, and the Mayor out of the Aldermen, by the Palatine and the Proprietors.

86. No man shall be permitted to be a Freeman of Carolina, or to have any Estate or habitation within it, that does not acknowledge a God, and that God is publicly and Solemnly to be worshipped.

87. But since the Natives of that place, who will be concerned in our Plantations, are utterly Strangers to Christianity, whose Idolatry, Ignorance, or mistake gives us no right to expel or use them ill; and those who remove from other parts to Plant there will unavoidably be of different opinions concerning matters of Religion, the liberty whereof they will expect to have allowed them, and it will not be reasonable for us, on this account, to keep them out; that Civil peace may be maintained amidst the diversity of opinions, and our agreement and compact with all men may be duly and faithfully observed, the violation whereof,

[22] *Penalty* was written after *or*, but was struck out.

upon what pretence soever, cannot be without great offence to Almighty God, and great Scandal to the true Religion that we profess; and also, that heathens, Jews, and other dissenters from the purity of Christian Religion may not be Scared and kept at a distance from it, but, by having an opportunity of acquainting them selves with the truth and reasonableness of its Doctrines, and the peaceableness and inoffensiveness of its professors, may, by good usage and persuasion,[23] and all those convincing Methods of Gentleness and meekness Suitable to the Rules and design of the Gospel, be won over to embrace and unfeignedly receive the truth: Therefore, any Seven or more persons agreeing in any Religion shall constitute a church or profession, to which they shall give Some name to distinguish it from others.

88. The terms of admittance and communion with any church or profession shall be written in a book and therein be Subscribed by all the members of the said church or profession.

89. The time of every one's Subscription and admittance shall be dated in the said book, or record.

90. In the terms of Communion of every church or profession, these following shall be three, without which no agreement or assembly of men upon pretence of Religion shall be accounted a Church or Profession within these Rules:

1. That there is a God.
2. That God is publicly to be worshipped.
3. That it is lawful, and the duty of every man, being thereunto called by those that Govern, to bear witness to truth; and that every church or profession shall, in their Terms of Communion, Set down the External way whereby they witness a truth as in the presence of God, whether it be by laying hands on and Kissing the Gospel, as in the Protestant and Papist Churches, or by holding up the hand, or any other Sensible way.

91. No person above seventeen years of Age shall have any benefit or protection of the law, or be capable of any place of profit or honor, who is not a member of Some church or profession, having his name recorded in Some one, and but one Religion Record at once.

92. The Religious Record of every church or profession shall be kept by the public Register of the Precinct where they reside.

[23] Originally *preservation,* but changed to *persuasion.*

93. No man of any other Church or profession shall disturb or molest any Religious Assembly.

94. No person whatsoever shall speak any thing in their Religious assembly Irreverently or Seditiously of the Government or Governors or States matters.

95. Any person Subscribing the terms of Communion of any church or profession in the Record of the said church before the Precinct Register and any one member of the church or profession shall be thereby made a member of the Said church or profession.

96. Any person striking out his own name out of any Record, or his name being struck out by any officer thereunto Authorized by any church or profession, shall cease to be a member of that Church or profession.

97. No person shall use any reproachful, Reviling, or abusive language against the Religion of any Church or Profession, that being the certain way of disturbing the public peace, and of hindering the conversion of any to the truth, by engaging them in Quarrels and animosities, to the hatred of the professors and that profession, which otherwise they might be brought to assent to.

98. Since Charity obliges us to wish well to the Souls of all men, and Religion ought to alter nothing in any man's civil Estate or Right, It shall be lawful for Slaves, as all others, to enter them selves and be of what church any of them shall think best, and thereof be as fully members as any freemen. But yet, no Slave shall hereby be exempted from that civil dominion his Master has over him, but be in all other things in the same State and condition he was in before.

99. Assemblies, upon what pretence soever of Religion, not observing and performing the above said Rules shall not be Esteemed as churches, but unlawful meetings, and be punished as other Riots.

100. No person whatsoever shall disturb, molest, or persecute another for his speculative opinions in Religion or his way of worship.

101. Every Freeman of Carolina shall have absolute Authority over his Negro Slaves, of what opinion or Religion soever.

102. No person whatsoever shall hold or claim any land in Carolina, by Purchase or gift or otherwise, from the Natives or any other per-

son whatsoever, but merely from and under the <Lords> Proprietors, upon pain of forfeiture of all his Estate, moveable or unmoveable, and perpetual Banishment.

103. Whoever shall possess[24] any Freehold in Carolina, upon what Title or grant soever, shall, at the farthest, from and after the year 1689, pay yearly unto the Proprietors for each acre of Land, English measure, as much fine Silver as is at this present in one English penny, or the Value thereof, to be as a Chief Rent and acknowledgment to the Proprietors, their heirs and Successors, for ever; and it shall be lawful for the proprietors, by their Officers, at any time, to take a new Survey of any man's land, not to out him of any part of his possession, but that, by Such a Survey, the Just number of acres he possesses may be known, and the Rent thereupon due may be paid by him.

104. All wrecks, mines, minerals, Quarries of Gems and precious stones, with whale fishing, <Pearl fishing>, and one half of all ambergris, by whom soever found, shall wholly belong to the Proprietors.

105. All Revenues and profits arising out of any thing but their distinct particular Lands and possessions shall be divided into ten parts, whereof the Palatine shall have three, and each Proprietor one; but if the Palatine shall Govern by a Deputy, his Deputy shall have one of those three tenths, and the Palatine the other two tenths.

106. All Inhabitants and freemen of Carolina above seventeen years of Age and under Sixty shall be bound to bear Arms and serve as Soldiers whenever the grand Council shall find it necessary.

108.[25] A true Copy of these Fundamental Constitutions shall be kept in a great book by the Register of every precinct, to be Subscribed before the said Register. Nor shall any person, of what condition or degree soever, above seventeen years Old, have any Estate or possession in Carolina, or protection or benefit of the law there, who has not Subscribed these fundamental constitutions in this form:

I, A. B., do promise to bear faith and true allegiance to our Sovereign Lord King Charles the Second; and will be true and faithful to the <Palatine and> Lords Proprietors of Carolina; and, with my utmost power, will defend them and maintain the Government, according to this Establishment in these fundamental constitutions.

---

[24] Originally *pass*, but changed to *possess*.

[25] The numbering skips from 106 to 108 in the manuscript.

109. And [26] whatsoever Alien shall, in this form, before any Precinct Register, Subscribe these fundamental Constitutions shall be thereby Naturalized.

110. In The Same manner shall every person at his admittance into any Office Subscribe these fundamental constitutions.

111. These fundamental constitutions, <in number 111>, and every part thereof, shall be, and remain as, the Sacred unalterable form and Rule of Government <of Carolina> for ever. Witness our hands and Seals, this twenty first day July, in the year of our Lord 1669.

[26] *And* was struck out.

[Transcribed from a photostatic copy of a manuscript in the British Public Record Office, London. Reference: PRO 30/24/47/No3. Photostatic copy deposited in the State Department of Archives and History, Raleigh, North Carolina.]

Revisions in the Version of July 21, 1669

Article 2 was struck out and the following was substituted:

The eldest of the Lords Proprietors shall [1] be Palatine; and upon the decease of the Palatine, the Eldest of the Seven Surviving Proprietors shall always succeed him.

Article 6 was revised to read as follows:

At any time before the year 1701, any of the Lords Proprietors shall have power to relinquish, Alienate, and dispose, to any other person, his Proprietorship, and all the Seigniories, powers, and Interest thereunto belonging, wholly and entirely together, and not otherwise. But after the year 1700, those who are then Lords Proprietors shall not have power to Alienate, make over, or let their proprietorship, with the Seigniories and privileges thereunto belonging, or any part thereof, to any person whatsoever, otherwise than as in article 18, but it shall descend unto their heirs male; and for want of heirs male, it shall descend on that Landgrave or Cacique of Carolina who is descended of the next heir female of the said Proprietor; and for want of Such heirs, it shall descend on the next heir general; and for want of Such heirs, the remaining Seven proprietors shall, upon the Vacancy, choose a Landgrave to succeed the deceased proprietor, who being chosen by the majority of the Seven Surviving proprietors, he and his heirs Successively shall be proprietors as fully, to all intents and purposes, as any of the rest.

Article 7 was revised to read as follows:

And that the number of eight Proprietors may be constantly kept, if, upon the vacancy of any Proprietorship, the Surviving Seven Proprietors shall not choose a Landgrave as a Proprietor before the Second Biennial Parliament after the vacancy, then the next Biennial Parliament but one after Such vacancy shall have power to choose any Landgrave to be Proprietor; but whosoever after the year 1700, either by inheritance or choice, shall Succeed any Proprietor in his proprietorship, and Seigniories thereunto belonging, shall be obliged to take the name and Arms of that proprietor whom he Succeeds, which from thenceforth shall be the name and Arms of his Family and their posterity.

---

[1] *Always* was inserted here, but was struck out.

Article 8 was struck out and the following was substituted:

Whatsoever Landgrave or Cacique shall any way come to be a Proprietor shall take the Seigniories annexed to the said Proprietorship, but his former dignity, with the Baronies annexed, shall devolve into the hands of the Lords Proprietors.

Article 10 was revised to read as follows:

The first Landgrave and Caciques of every County shall be nominated, not by the Joint election of the Proprietors all together, but the eight Proprietors shall, each of them separately, nominate and choose one Landgrave and two Caciques to be the eight Landgraves and the sixteen Caciques for the eight first Counties to be Planted; and when the said eight Counties shall be planted, the proprietors shall, in the same manner, nominate and Choose eight more Landgraves and sixteen Caciques for the eight next Counties to be planted; and so proceed, in the same manner, till the whole province of Carolina be set out and planted according to the proportions in these fundamental Constitutions.

Article 12 was revised to read as follows:

That the due number of landgraves and Caciques may be always kept up, if, upon the devolution of any Landgraveship or Caciqueship, The Palatine's Court shall not settle the devolved dignity, with the Baronies thereunto annexed, before the Second biennial Parliament after Such devolution, the next Biennial Parliament but one after such devolution shall have power to make any one Landgrave or Cacique in the Room of him, who dying with out heirs, his dignity and Baronies devolved.

Article 13 was revised to read as follows:

No one person shall have more than one dignity, with the Seigniories or Baronies thereunto belonging; but whensoever it shall happen that any one who is already Proprietor, Landgrave, or Cacique shall have any of those dignities descend to him by inheritance, it shall be at his choice to keep which of the two dignities, with the Lands annexed, he shall like best, but shall leave the other, with the lands annexed, to be enjoyed by him who, not being his heir apparent, and certain successor to his present dignity, is next of blood, unless when a Landgrave or Cacique comes to be proprietor, and then his former dignity and Baronies shall devolve as in Article 8.

Article 16 was revised to read as follows:

After the year 1700, whatsoever Landgrave or Cacique shall, without leave from the Palatine's Court, be out of Carolina during two successive biennial Parliaments shall, at the end of the second biennial Parliament after such his absence, be summoned by Proclamation; and if he come not into Carolina before the next biennial Parliament after Such Summons, then the Grand Council shall have power thence forward to receive all the rents and profits arising out of his Baronies until his return or death, and to dispose of the said profits as they shall think fit.

Article 17 was revised to read as follows:

In every Seigniory, Barony, and Manor, the respective Lord shall have power, in his own name, to hold Court there, for trying of all causes, both Civil and Criminal; But where it shall concern any [2] person being no inhabitant, vassal, or Leet man of the said Barony, Seigniory, or manor, he, upon paying down of forty shillings to the Lords Proprietors' use, shall have an appeal from [3] the Seigniory or Barony Court to the County Court, and from the Manor Court to the precinct Court.

Article 19 was revised to read as follows:

Every Manor shall consist of not less than three thousand Acres and not above twelve thousand Acres in one entire piece; but any three thousand acres or more in one piece and the possession of one Man shall not be a manor unless it be constituted a manor by the grant of the Palatine's Court.

Article 22 was revised to read as follows:

In every Seigniory, Barony, and manor, all the Leet men shall be under the Jurisdiction of the respective Lord of the said Seigniory, Barony, or Manor, without appeal from him; nor shall any Leet man or Leet woman have liberty to go off from the Land of his particular Lord and live any where else without Licences obtained from his Said Lord, under hand and Seal.

Article 24 was revised to read as follows:

No man shall be capable of having a Court Leet or Leet men but a Proprietor, Landgrave, or Cacique, or Lord of a Manor. Nor shall any

[2] *Other* was inserted here, but was struck out.

[3] *Thence to the County Court* was written after *from,* but was struck out.

man be a Leet man who has not voluntarily entered himself a Leet man in the Registry of the County Court.[4]

Article 25 was revised to read as follows:

Whoever is Lord of Leet men shall, upon the marriage of a Leet man or Leet woman of his, give them ten Acres of Land for their lives, they paying to him therefor not more than one eighth of all yearly produce and growth of the said ten acres.

Article 26 was struck out and the following was substituted:

No Landgrave or Cacique shall be tried for any criminal cause in any but in the Chief Justice Court,[5] and that by a jury of his peers.

Article 27 was revised to read as follows:

There shall be eight supreme Courts, the first, Called the Palatine's Court, consisting of the Palatine and the other Seven Proprietors. The other seven courts of the other seven great officers shall consist, each of them, of a Proprietor and six Councillors added to him; under each of these latter seven Courts shall be a College of twelve assistants. The twelve assistants of the Several Colleges shall be Chosen: two out of the Landgraves, by the Landgraves' Chamber; two out of the Caciques, by the Caciques' Chamber; two out of the Landgraves, Caciques, or Eldest sons of the Proprietors, by the Palatine's Court; four more of the twelve shall be chosen by the Commons' Chamber out of such as have been or are members of Parliament, Sheriffs, or Justices of the County Court; the other two shall be Chosen by the Palatine's Court out of the aforesaid members of Parliament, or Sheriffs, or Justices of the County Court, or the Eldest sons of Landgraves or Caciques, or younger Sons of Proprietors.

Article 28 was revised to read as follows:

Out of these Colleges shall be Chosen Six Councillors to be joined with each Proprietor in his Court; of which six, one shall be of those who were Chosen into any of the Colleges by the Palatine's Court out of the Landgraves, Caciques, or Eldest Sons of Proprietors; one out of those who were chosen by the Landgrave's Chamber; and one out of

---

[4] The added sentence was first written as follows: *Nor shall any man be a Leet man whose contract to be a Leet man is not entered in the Registry of the County Court.*

[5] *One of the Supreme* was written and struck out; *in the Chief Justice* was substituted.

those who were Chosen by the Caciques' Chamber; two out of those who were Chosen by the Commons' Chamber; and one out of those who were Chosen by the Palatine's Court out of the Proprietors' younger Sons, or Eldest Sons of Landgraves or Caciques, or Commons Qualified as aforesaid.

Article 30 was revised to read as follows:

No man being a member of the grand Council or of any of the seven Colleges shall be turned out but For misdemeanor, of which the grand Council shall be Judge; and the vacancy of the person so put out shall be filled, not by the Election of the grand Council, but by those who first chose him, and out of the same degree he was of who is expelled. But it is not hereby to be understood that the Grand Council has any power to turn out any one of the Lords Proprietors, or their Deputies, The Lords Proprietors having in themselves an inherent original right.[6]

Article 32 was revised to read as follows:

The Palatine's Court shall consist of the Palatine and Seven Proprietors, wherein nothing shall be acted without the presence and consent of the Palatine, or his Deputy, and three others of the Proprietors, or their deputies. This Court shall have power to call Parliaments, to pardon all Offences, to make Elections of all Officers in the Proprietors' dispose, to nominate and appoint port towns; and also, shall have power, by their Order to the Treasurer, to dispose of all public Treasure, excepting money granted by the Parliament and by them directed to some particular public use; and also, shall have a Negative upon all Acts, Orders, Votes, and Judgments of the grand Council and the Parliament, Except only as in Articles 7 and 12; and also, shall have a negative upon all Acts and orders of the Constable's Court and Admiral's Court relating to wars; And shall have all the powers granted to the Proprietors by their patent from our Sovereign Lord The King, except in such things as are limited by these fundamental constitutions.

Article 34 was revised to read as follows:

The Chancellor's Court, consisting of one of the Proprietors and his six Councillors, who shall be called vice-chancellors, shall have the Custody of the Seal of the Palatinate, under which all charters, of Lands or

[6] *Are not under the jurisdiction of the Grand Council* followed *inherent original right,* but was struck out.

otherwise, Commissions, and grants of the Palatine's Court shall pass, etc. And it shall not be lawful to put the Seal of the Palatinate to any Writing which is not signed by the Palatine, or his Deputy, and three other Proprietors, or their Deputies. To this Court, also, belongs all state matters, dispatches, and treaties, with the Neighbour Indians or any other, so far forth as is permitted by our Charter from our Sovereign Lord the King. To this Court, also, belongs all Invasions of the Law of Liberty of conscience, and all disturbances of the public peace upon pretence of Religion, as also, the Licence of printing. The twelve assistants belonging to this Court shall be called Recorders.

Article 37 was revised to read as follows:

The Admiral's Court, consisting of one of the Proprietors and his Six Councillors, called Consuls, shall have the care and inspection over all ports, Moles, and Navigable Rivers so far as the Tide flows; and also, all the public Shipping of Carolina, and stores thereunto belonging, and all maritime affairs. This Court, also, shall have the power of the Court of Admiralty, and also, to hear and try by Law-Merchant all cases in Matters of Trade between the Merchants of Carolina amongst them selves, arising without the limits of Carolina; as also, all controversies in Merchandising that shall happen between Denizens of Carolina and foreigners. The twelve Assistants belonging to this court shall be called proconsuls. In time of actual war, the High Admiral, whilst he is at Sea, Shall command in chief, and his Six Councillors, or such of them as the Palatine's Court shall for that time and service appoint, shall be the immediate great officers under him, and the proconsuls next to them.

Article 39 was revised to read as follows:

The High Steward's court, consisting of a proprietor and his six Councillors, who shall be called Comptrollers, shall have the care of all foreign and domestic Trade, Manufactures, public buildings and workhouses, high ways, passages by water above the flood of the Tide, drains, sewers and Banks against inundations, Bridges, Posts, Carriers, Fairs, Markets, and all things in order to trade and travel, and any thing that may corrupt, deprave, or infect the common Air or water, and all other things wherein the Public commerce or health is concerned; and also, the setting out and surveying of lands; and also, the setting out and appointing places for towns to be built on in the Precincts, and the prescribing and determining the Figure and bigness of the said Towns according to such Models as the said court shall order, contrary or dif-

fering from which Models it shall not be lawful for any one to build in any Town.

Another revision of Article 39 reads as follows:

The High Steward's court, consisting of a proprietor and his six Councillors, who shall be called Comptrollers, shall have the care of all foreign and domestic Trade, Manufactures, public buildings and work-houses, high ways, passages by water above the flood of the Tide, drains, sewers and Banks against inundations, Bridges, Posts, Carriers, Fairs, Markets, Corruptions or infections of the common air and water, and all things in order to public commerce and health. . . .[7]

Nothing in the manuscript indicates which revision of Article 39 was adopted, but the latter appears in the March 1, 1670, version.

Article 40 was first revised to read as follows:

This Court shall have power, also, to make any public building or any new high way, or enlarge any old high way, upon any Man's Land whatsoever; as also, to make cuts, Channels, Banks, locks, and Bridges, for making Rivers Navigable, for draining of Fens, or any other public uses; the damage the owner of such land, on or through which any such public thing shall be made, shall receive thereby shall be valued by a Jury of twelve men of the Precinct in which any such thing is done, and satisfaction shall be made accordingly by a Tax, either on the County or that particular precinct, as the grand Council shall think fit to order in that particular case. And if it be a Seigniory or Barony on or through which any such public thing shall be made, then the damage the owner of the said Seigniory or Barony shall receive thereby shall be valued by the High Steward's Court, and satisfaction shall be made accordingly by a tax on the County. The twelve assistants belonging to this Court shall be called Surveyors.

Article 40 was finally revised to read as follows:

This Court shall have power, also, to make any public building or any new high way, or enlarge any old high way, upon any Man's Land whatsoever; as also, to make cuts, Channels, Banks, locks, and Bridges, for making Rivers Navigable, for draining of Fens, or any other public uses; the damage the owner of such land, on or through which any such

[7] The remainder of the article, as thus revised, was unchanged.

public thing shall be made, shall receive thereby shall be valued, and satisfaction made, by such ways as the Grand Council [8] shall appoint. The twelve assistants belonging to this Court shall be called Surveyors.

Article 45 was struck out and the following was substituted:

In all the Proprietors' Courts, the Proprietor and any three of his Councillors shall make a Quorum; Provided always, that, for the better dispatch of business, it shall be in the power of the Palatine's Court to direct what sort of causes shall be heard and determined by a Quorum of any three.

Article 46 was revised to read as follows:

The grand Council shall consist of the Palatine, and Seven Proprietors, and the forty two Councillors of the Several Proprietors' Courts; who shall have power to determine any Controversies that may arise between any of the Proprietors' Courts about their respective Jurisdictions, or between the Members of one and the same Court about their manner and methods of proceeding; to make peace and war, Leagues, Treaties, etc., with any of the Neighbour Indians; To issue out their General Orders to the Constable's and Admiral's Court for the Raising, disposing, or disbanding the Forces, by land or by Sea; to prepare all matters to be proposed in Parliament; nor shall any matter whatsoever be proposed in Parliament but what has first passed the Grand Council, which, after having been read three several days in the Parliament, shall be passed or rejected.

Article 54 was revised to read as follows:

Each Proprietor's deputy shall be always one of their own Six Councillors respectively; And in case any of the Proprietors has not, in his absence out of Carolina, a Deputy in Carolina, commissioned under his hand and seal, the Eldest Nobleman of his Court shall of course be his Deputy.

Article 55 was struck out and the following was substituted:

In Every County there shall be a Court, consisting of a Sheriff and four Justices of the County Court, for Every precinct one. The Sheriff Shall be an inhabitant of this County and have at least five hundred acres of freehold within the said County; and the Justices Shall be in-

[8] *The High Steward's Court* was written and struck out; *Grand Council* was substituted.

habitants and have, each of them, five hundred acres apiece in the precinct for which they Serve respectively. These five Shall be chosen, commissioned from time to time by the Palatine's Court.[9]

Article 57 was revised to read as follows:

In every Precinct there shall be a Court, consisting of a Steward and four Justices of the Precinct, being Inhabitants and having three hundred Acres of Freehold within the said Precinct; who shall Judge all Criminal causes, except for Treason, Murder, and any other offences punished with death and all criminal causes of the Nobility; and all civil causes whatsoever, and in all personal actions not exceeding fifty pounds without appeal; but where the Cause shall exceed that Value, or concern a Title of land, and in all Criminal causes, there, either party, upon paying five pounds to the Proprietors' use, shall have Liberty of appeal unto the County Court.

Article 67 was revised to read as follows:

A new Parliament shall be assembled the first Monday of the Month of November every second year, and shall meet and Sit in the Town they last Sat in, without any Summons, unless by the Palatine's Court they be Summoned to meet at any other place; and if there shall be any occasion of a Parliament in these Intervals, it shall be in the power of the Palatine's Court to assemble them on forty days' notice, at Such time and place as the said Court shall think fit; and the Palatine's Court shall have power to dissolve the said Parliament when they Shall think fit.

Article 71 was revised to read as follows:

Any Proprietor, or his Deputy, may enter his Protestation against any act of the Parliament, before the Palatine or his deputy's consent be given as aforesaid, if he shall conceive the said act to be contrary to this Establishment or any of these Fundamental Constitutions of the Government; and in Such case, after a full and free debate, the several Estates shall retire into four several Chambers, the Palatine and Proprietors into one, the Landgraves into another, and the Caciques into another, and those Chosen by the Precincts into a fourth; and if the major part of any of these four Estates shall Vote that the law is not agreeable to this Establishment and these fundamental constitution of the Government, then it shall pass no further, but be as if it had never been proposed. The

[9] *And shall try and judge all appeals from any of the General Courts* followed *Palatine's Court,* but was struck out.

Quorum of the Parliament shall be one half of those who are members and capable of sitting in the house that present session of Parliament. The Quorum of each of the Chambers of Parliament shall be one half of the members of that Chamber.

Article 74 was revised to read as follows:

There shall be a Registry in every precinct, wherein shall be enrolled all deeds, Leases, Judgments, mortgages, or other conveyances which may concern any of the land within the Said Precinct; and all Such conveyances not so entered or Registered shall not be of force against any person not privy to the Said contract or conveyance.

Article 77 was revised to read as follows:

There shall be a Registry in every Seigniory, Barony, and Colony, wherein shall be Recorded all the Births, Marriages, and deaths that shall happen within the said Colony.

Article 79 was revised to read as follows:

The time of every one's Age that is born in Carolina shall be Reckoned from the day that his Birth is entered in the Registry, and not before.

Article 80 was revised to read as follows:

No marriage shall be lawful, whatever Contract or Ceremonies they have used, till both the parties mutually own it before the Register [10] where they were married, and he enter it, with the names of the Father and mother of each party.

Article 81 was revised to read as follows:

No man shall administer to the goods, or have right to them, or enter upon the Estate, of any person deceased till his death be Registered in the Respective Registry.

Article 82 was revised to read as follows:

He that does not enter in the respective Registry the death or Birth or any person that dies or is born in his house or ground shall pay to the said Register one shilling per week for each Such neglect, Reckoning

[10] *Of the place where they* ——— [illegible] *dwells* was inserted here, but was struck out, and *where they were married* was substituted.

from the time of each death or birth respectively to the time of Registering it.

Article 84 was revised to read as follows:

There shall be in every Colony one Constable, to be Chosen annually by the Freeholders of the Colony, his Estate to be above one hundred acres of Freehold within the Said Colony; and Such Subordinate officers appointed for his assistance as the County Court shall find requisite, and shall be Established by the said County court; the Election of the Subordinate annual officers shall be also in the Freeholders of the Colony.

Article 85 was revised to read as follows:

All Towns incorporate shall be Governed by a Mayor, twelve Aldermen, and twenty four of the Common Council; the Said Common Council to be chosen by the present householders of the Said Town; and the Aldermen to be Chosen out of the Common Council, and the Mayor out of the Aldermen, by the Palatine's Court.

Article 90 was revised to read as follows:

In the terms of Communion of every church or profession, these following shall be three, without which no agreement or assembly of men upon pretence of Religion shall be accounted a Church or Profession within these Rules:

1. That there is a God.
2. That God is publicly to be worshipped.
3. That it is lawful, and the duty of every man, being thereunto called by those that Govern, to bear witness to truth; and that every church or profession shall, in their Terms of Communion, Set down the External way whereby they witness a truth as in the presence of God, whether it be by laying hands on and Kissing the Bible, as in the Protestant and Papist Churches, or by holding up the hand, or any other Sensible way.

Article 95 was revised to read as follows:

Any person Subscribing the terms of Communion of any church or profession in the Record of the said church before the Precinct Register and any five members of the church or profession shall be thereby made a member of the Said church or profession.

Article 96 was revised to read as follows:

Any person striking out his own name out of any religious Record, or his name being struck out by any officer thereunto Authorized by Each church or profession respectively, shall cease to be a member of that Church or profession.

Article 101 was revised to read as follows:

Every Freeman of Carolina shall have absolute power and Authority over his Negro Slaves, of what opinion or Religion soever.

[See page 132, note, and page 152, note, for basis of transcription of revisions.]

Version of March 1, 1670

OUR Sovereign Lord The King having, out of His Royal Grace and Bounty, granted unto us the Province of Carolina, with all the Royalties, Proprieties, Jurisdictions, and Privileges of a County Palatine, as large and ample as the County Palatine of Durham, with other great Privileges; for the better settlement of the Government of the said Place, and establishing the Interest of the Lords Proprietors with Equality, and without Confusion; and that the Government of this Province may be made most agreeable to the Monarchy under which we live, and of which this Province is a part; and that we may avoid erecting a numerous Democracy: we, the Lords and Proprietors of the Province aforesaid, have agreed to this following Form of Government, to be perpetually established amongst us, unto which we do oblige our selves, our Heirs and Successors, in the most binding ways that can be devised.

1. The eldest of the Lords Proprietors shall be Palatine; and upon the Decease of the Palatine, the eldest of the seven surviving Proprietors shall always succeed him.

2. There shall be seven other chief Officers erected, viz., the Admiral's, Chamberlain's, Chancellor's, Constable's, Chief Justice's, High Steward's, and Treasurer's; which Places shall be enjoyed by none but the Lords Proprietors, to be assigned at first by Lot; and upon the vacancy of any one of the seven great Offices by Death, or otherwise, the eldest Proprietor shall have his choice of the said Place.

3. The whole Province shall be divided into Counties; each County shall consist of eight Seigniories, eight Baronies, and four Precincts; each Precinct shall consist of six Colonies.

4. Each Seigniory, Barony, and Colony shall consist of twelve thousand Acres, the eight Seigniories being the Share of the eight Proprietors, and the eight Baronies of the Nobility; both which Shares, being each of them one fifth part of the whole, are to be perpetually annexed, the one to the Proprietors, the other to the hereditary Nobility, leaving the Colonies, being three Fifths, amongst the People; that so, in Setting out and Planting the Lands, the Balance of the Government may be preserved.

5. At any time before the Year One thousand seven hundred and one, any of the Lords Proprietors shall have power to Relinquish, Alien-

ate, and Dispose, to any other Person, his Proprietorship, and all the Seigniories, Powers, and Interest thereunto belonging, wholly and entirely together, and not otherwise. But after the Year One thousand seven hundred, those who are then Lords Proprietors shall not have power to Alienate or Make over their Proprietorship, with the Seigniories and Privileges thereunto belonging, or any part thereof, to any Person whatsoever, otherwise than as in article 18, but it shall all Descend unto their Heirs Male; and for want of Heirs Male, it shall all Descend on that Landgrave or Cacique of Carolina who is Descended of the next Heirs Female of the said Proprietor; and for want of such Heirs, it shall Descend on the next Heir general; and for want of such Heirs, the remaining seven Proprietors shall, upon the Vacancy, choose a Landgrave to succeed the deceased Proprietor, who being chosen by the majority of the seven surviving Proprietors, he and his Heirs successively shall be Proprietors as fully, to all intents and purposes, as any of the rest.

6. That the number of eight Proprietors may be constantly kept, if, upon the vacancy of any Proprietorship, the seven surviving Proprietors shall not choose a Landgrave to be a Proprietor before the second biennial Parliament after the Vacancy, then the next biennial Parliament but one after such Vacancy shall have power to choose any Landgrave to be Proprietor.

7. Whosoever after the Year One thousand seven hundred, either by Inheritance or Choice, shall succeed any Proprietor in his Proprietorship, and Seigniories thereunto belonging, shall be obliged to take the Name and Arms of that Proprietor whom he succeeds, which from thenceforth shall be the Name and Arms of his Family and their Posterity.

8. Whatsoever Landgrave or Cacique shall any way come to be a Proprietor shall take the Seigniories annexed to the said Proprietorship, but his former Dignity, with the Baronies annexed, shall devolve into the Hands of the Lords Proprietors.

9. There shall be just as many Landgraves as there are Counties, and twice as many Caciques, and no more. These shall be the hereditary Nobility of the Province, and, by right of their Dignity, be Members of Parliament. Each Landgrave shall have four Baronies, and each Cacique two Baronies, hereditarily and unalterably annexed to and settled upon the said Dignity.

10. The first Landgraves and Caciques of the twelve first Counties to be Planted shall be nominated thus: that is to say, of the twelve Landgraves, the Lords Proprietors shall, each of them separately, for himself, nominate and choose one, and the remaining four Landgraves of the first twelve shall be nominated and chosen by the Palatine's Court; In like manner, of the twenty four first Caciques, each Proprietor, for himself, shall nominate and choose two, and the remaining eight shall be nominated and chosen by the Palatine's Court; and when the twelve first Counties shall be Planted, the Lords Proprietors shall again, in the same manner, nominate and choose twelve more Landgraves and twenty four Caciques for the twelve next Counties to be Planted, that is to say, two Thirds of each number by the single nomination of each Proprietor for himself, and the remaining one Third by the joint Election of the Palatine's Court; and so proceed, in the same manner, till the whole Province of Carolina be Set out and Planted according to the Proportions in these Fundamental Constitutions.

11. Any Landgrave or Cacique, at any time before the Year One thousand seven hundred and one, shall have power to Alienate, Sell, or Make over, to any other Person, his Dignity, with the Baronies thereunto belonging, all entirely together. But after the Year One thousand seven hundred, no Landgrave or Cacique shall have power to Alienate, Sell, Make over, or Let the Hereditary Baronies of his Dignity, or any part thereof, otherwise than as in article 18, but they shall all entirely, with the Dignity thereunto belonging, Descend unto his Heirs Males; and for want of Heirs Male, all entirely and undivided, to the next Heir general; and for want of such Heirs, shall devolve into the Hands of the Lords Proprietors.

12. That the due number of Landgraves and Caciques may be always kept up, if, upon the Devolution of any Landgraveship or Caciqueship, the Palatine's Court shall not settle the devolved Dignity, with the Baronies thereunto annexed, before the second biennial Parliament after such Devolution, the next biennial Parliament but one after such Devolution shall have power to make any one Landgrave or Cacique in the room of him, who dying without Heirs, his Dignity and Baronies devolved.

13. No one Person shall have more than one Dignity, with the Seigniories or Baronies thereunto belonging. But whensoever it shall happen that any one who is already Proprietor, Landgrave, or Cacique

shall have any of these Dignities descend to him by Inheritance, it shall be at his Choice to keep which of the Dignities, with the Lands annexed, he shall like best, but shall leave the other, with the Lands annexed, to be enjoyed by him who, not being his Heir Apparent, and certain Successor to his present Dignity, is next of Blood.

14. Whosoever, by Right of Inheritance, shall come to be Landgrave or Cacique shall take the Name and Arms of his Predecessor in that Dignity, to be from thenceforth the Name and Arms of his Family and their Posterity.

15. Since the Dignity of Proprietor, Landgrave, or Cacique cannot be divided, and the Seigniories or Baronies thereunto annexed must for ever, all entirely, descend with and accompany that Dignity, whensoever, for want of Heirs Male, it shall descend on the Issue Female, the eldest Daughter and her Heirs shall be preferred, and in the Inheritance of those Dignities, and in the Seigniories or Baronies annexed, there shall be no Coheirs.

16. In every Seigniory, Barony, and Manor, the respective Lord shall have power, in his own Name, to hold Court-Leet there, for Trying of all Causes, both Civil and Criminal; but where it shall concern any Person being no Inhabitant, Vassal, or Leetman of the said Seigniory, Barony, or Manor, he, upon paying down of forty Shillings to the Lords Proprietors' use, shall have an Appeal from the Seigniory or Barony Court to the County Court, and from the Manor Court to the Precinct Court.

17. Every Manor shall consist of not less than three thousand Acres and not above twelve thousand Acres in one entire Piece and Colony; but any three thousand Acres or more in one Piece and the Possession of one man shall not be a Manor unless it be Constituted a Manor by the Grant of the Palatine's Court.

18. The Lords of Seigniories and Baronies shall have power only of granting Estates, not exceeding three Lives or thirty one Years, in two Thirds of the said Seigniories or Baronies, and the remaining Third shall be always Demesne.

19. Any Lord of a Manor may Alienate, Sell, or Dispose, to any other Person, and his Heirs, for ever, his Manor, all entirely together, with all the Privileges and Leetmen thereunto belonging, so far forth as any other Colony Lands; but no Grant of any part thereof, either in Fee

or for any longer Term than three Lives or one and twenty Years, shall be good against the next Heir.

20. No Manor, for want of Issue Male, shall be divided amongst Coheirs, but the Manor, if there be but one, shall all entirely descend to the eldest Daughter and her Heirs. If there be more Manors than one, the eldest Daughter first shall have her choice, the second next, and so on, beginning again at the eldest, till all the Manors be taken up; that so, the Privileges which belong to Manors being indivisible, the Lands of the Manors to which they are annexed may be kept entire, and the Manor not lose those Privileges, which upon parcelling out to several Owners must necessarily cease.

21. Every Lord of a Manor, within his Manor, shall have all the Powers, Jurisdictions, and Privileges which a Landgrave or Cacique has in his Baronies.

22. In every Seigniory, Barony, and Manor, all the Leetmen shall be under the Jurisdiction of the respective Lords of the said Seigniory, Barony, or Manor, without Appeal from him. Nor shall any Leetman or Leetwoman have liberty to go off from the Land of their particular Lord and live any where else without Licence obtained from their said Lord, under Hand and Seal.

23. All the Children of Leetmen shall be Leetmen, and so to all Generations.

24. No Man shall be capable of having a Court-Leet or Leetmen but a Proprietor, Landgrave, Cacique, or Lord of a Manor.

25. Whoever shall voluntarily Enter himself a Leetman in the Registry of the County Court shall be a Leetman.

26. Whoever is Lord of Leetmen shall, upon the Marriage of a Leetman or Leetwoman of his, give them ten Acres of Land for their Lives, they paying to him therefor not more than one eighth part of all the yearly Produce and Growth of the said ten Acres.

27. No Landgrave or Cacique shall be Tried for any Criminal Cause in any but the Chief Justice's Court, and that by a Jury of his Peers.

28. There shall be eight Supreme Courts, The first, called The Palatine's Court, consisting of the Palatine and the other seven Proprietors. The other seven Courts of the other seven great Officers shall con-

sist, each of them, of a Proprietor and six Councillors added to him. Under each of these latter seven Courts shall be a College of twelve Assistants. The twelve Assistants of the several Colleges shall be chosen: two out of the Landgraves, Caciques, or eldest Sons of Proprietors, by the Palatine's Court; two out of the Landgraves, by the Landgraves' Chamber; two out of the Caciques, by the Caciques' Chamber; four more of the twelve shall be chosen by the Commons' Chamber, out of such as have been or are Members of Parliament, Sheriffs, or Justices of the County Court, or the younger Sons of Proprietors, or eldest Sons of Landgraves or Caciques; the two other shall be chosen by the Palatine's Court out of the same sort of Persons out of which the Commons' Chamber is to choose.

29. Out of these Colleges shall be chosen, at first by the Palatine's Court, six Councillors to be joined with each Proprietor in his Court; of which six, one shall be of those who were chosen into any of the Colleges by the Palatine's Court out of the Landgraves, Caciques, or eldest Sons of Proprietors; one out of those who were chosen by the Landgraves' Chamber; and one out of those who were chosen by the Caciques' Chamber; two out of those who were chosen by the Commons' Chamber; and one out of those who were chosen by the Palatine's Court out of the Proprietors' younger Sons, or eldest Sons of Landgraves, Caciques, or Commons Qualified as aforesaid.

30. When it shall happen that any Councillor dies, and thereby there is a Vacancy, the Grand Council shall have power to remove any Councillor that is willing to be removed out of any of the Proprietors' Courts to fill up the Vacancy, provided they take a Man of the same Degree and Choice the other was of whose vacant Place is to be filled up. But if no Councillor consent to be removed, or upon such Remove, the last remaining vacant Place in any of the Proprietors' Courts shall be filled up by the choice of the Grand Council, who shall have power to remove out of any of the Colleges any Assistant who is of the same Degree and Choice that Councillor was of into whose vacant Place he is to succeed. The Grand Council, also, shall have power to remove any Assistant that is willing out of one College into another, provided he be of the same Degree and Choice. But the last remaining vacant Place in any College shall be filled up by the same Choice, and out of the same Degree of Persons, the Assistant was of who is dead or removed. No Place shall be vacant in any Proprietors' Court above six Months. No Place shall be vacant in any College longer than the next Session of Parliament.

31. No Man being a Member of the Grand Council or of any of the seven Colleges shall be turned out but for Misdemeanor, of which the Grand Council shall be Judge; and the Vacancy of the Person so put out shall be filled, not by the Election of the Grand Council, but by those who first chose him, and out of the same Degree he was of who is expelled. But it is not hereby to be understood that the Grand Council has any power to turn out any one of the Lords Proprietors, or their Deputies, the Lords Proprietors having in themselves an inherent original Right.

32. All Elections in the Parliament, in the several Chambers of the Parliament, and in the Grand Council shall be Passed by Balloting.

33. The Palatine's Court shall consist of the Palatine and seven Proprietors, wherein nothing shall be acted without the Presence and Consent of the Palatine, or his Deputy, and three others of the Proprietors, or their Deputies. This Court shall have power to call Parliaments, to pardon all Offences, to make Elections of all Officers in the Proprietors' dispose, and to nominate and appoint Port-Towns; And also, shall have power, by their Order to the Treasurer, to dispose of all Public Treasure, excepting Money granted by the Parliament and by them directed to some particular public Use; And also, shall have a Negative upon all Acts, Orders, Votes, and Judgments of the Grand Council and the Parliament, except only as in articles 6 and 12. And shall have all the Powers granted to the Lords Proprietors by their Patent from Our Sovereign Lord The King, except in such things as are limited by these Fundamental Constitutions.

34. The Palatine himself, when he in Person shall be either in the Army or in any of the Proprietors' Courts, shall then have the Power of General or of that Proprietor in whose Court he is then present; and the Proprietor in whose Court the Palatine then Presides shall, during his presence there, be but as one of the Council.

35. The Chancellor's Court, consisting of one of the Proprietors and his six Chancellors [Councillors],[1] who shall be called Vice-Chancellors, shall have the custody of the Seal of the Palatinate, under which all Charters, of Lands or otherwise, Commissions, and Grants of the Palatine's Court shall pass. And it shall not be lawful to put the Seal of the Palatinate to any Writing which is not Signed by the Palatine, or

[1] Words in square brackets in this transcription were supplied from a copy of the March 1, 1670, Fundamental Constitutions printed about 1698.

his Deputy, and three other Proprietors, or their Deputies. To this Court, also, belongs all State Matters, Dispatches, and Treaties with the neighbor Indians. To this Court, also, belongs all Invasions of the Law of Liberty of Conscience, and all Disturbances of the Public Peace upon pretence of Religion, as also, the Licence of Printing. The twelve Assistants belonging to this Court shall be called Recorders.

36. Whatever passes under the Seal of the Palatinate shall be Registered in that Proprietors' Court to which the Matter therein contained belongs.

37. The Chancellor, or his Deputy, shall be always Speaker in Parliament and President of the Grand Council, and in his and his Deputy's absence, one of his Vice-Chancellors.

38. The Chief Justice's Court, consisting of one of the Proprietors and his six Chancellors [Councillors], who shall be called Justices of the Bench, shall Judge all Appeals, in Cases both Civil and Criminal, except all such Cases as shall be under the Jurisdiction and Cognizance of any other of the Proprietors' Courts, which shall be Tried in those Courts respectively. The Government and regulation of the Registries of Writings and Contracts shall belong to the Jurisdiction of this Court. The twelve Assistants of this Court shall be called Masters.

39. The Constable's Court, consisting of one of the Proprietors and his six Councillors, who shall be called Marshals, shall order and determine of all Military Affairs by Land, and all Land-Forces, Arms, Ammunition, Artillery, Garrisons, and Forts, etc., and whatever belongs unto War. His twelve Assistants shall be called Lieutenant-Generals.

40. In time of actual War, the Constable, whilst he is in the Army, shall be General of the Army, and the six Councillors, or such of them as the Palatine's Court shall for that time or Service appoint, shall be the immediate great Officers under him, and the Lieutenant-Generals next to them.

41. The Admiral's Court, consisting of one of the Proprietors and his six Councillors, called Consuls, shall have the care and inspection over all Ports, Moles, and Navigable Rivers so far as the Tide flows; and also, all the public Shipping of Carolina, and Stores thereunto belonging, and all Maritime Affairs. This Court, also, shall have the Power of the Court of Admiralty; and shall have power to Constitute Judges in Port-Towns to Try Cases belonging to Law-Merchant, as shall be most con-

venient for Trade. The twelve Assistants belonging to this Court shall be called Proconsuls.

42. In time of actual War, the Admiral, whilst he is at Sea, shall Command in Chief, and his six Councillors, or such of them as the Palatine's Court shall for that time and Service appoint, shall be the immediate great Officers under him, and the Proconsuls next to them.

43. The Treasurer's Court, consisting of a Proprietor and his six Councillors, called Under-Treasurers, shall take care of all Matters that concern the Public Revenue and Treasury. The twelve Assistants shall be called Auditors.

44. The High Steward's Court, consisting of a Proprietor and his six Councillors, called Comptrollers, shall have the care of all Foreign and Domestic Trade, Manufactures, public Buildings, Workhouses, Highways, Passages by Water above the Flood of the Tide, Drains, Sewers and Banks against Inundations, Bridges, Post, Carriers, Fairs, Markets, Corruption or Infection of the common Air or Water, and all things in order to the public Commerce and Health; also, Setting out and Surveying of Lands; and also, Setting out and appointing Places for Towns to be built on in the Precincts, and the prescribing and determining the Figure and bigness of the said Towns according to such Models as the said Court shall order, contrary or differing from which Models it shall not be lawful for any one to Build in any Town. This Court shall have power, also, to make any public Building or any new Highway, or enlarge any old Highway, upon any Man's Land whatsoever; as also, to make Cuts, Channels, Banks, Locks, and Bridges, for making Rivers Navigable, or for Draining Fens, or any other public Use. The Damage the Owner of such Lands, on or through which any such public thing shall be made, shall receive thereby shall be valued, and Satisfaction made, by such ways as the Grand Council shall appoint. The twelve Assistants belonging to this Court shall be called Surveyors.

45. The Chamberlain's Court, consisting of a Proprietor and his six Councillors, called Vice-Chamberlains, shall have the care of all Ceremonies, Precedency, Heraldry, Reception of public Messengers, Pedigrees; the Registry of all Births, Burials, and Marriages; Legitimation and all Cases concerning Matrimony or arising from it; and shall, also, have power to regulate all Fashions, Habits, Badges, Games, and Sports. To this Court, also, it shall belong to Convocate the Grand Council. The twelve Assistants belonging to this Court shall be called Provosts.

46. All Causes belonging to, or under the Jurisdiction of, any of the Proprietors' Courts shall in them respectively be Tried and ultimately Determined, without any farther Appeal.

47. The Proprietors' Courts shall have a power to mitigate all Fines and suspend all Executions in Criminal Causes, either before or after Sentence, in any of the other inferior Courts respectively.

48. In all Debates, Hearings, or Trials in any of the Proprietors' Courts, the twelve Assistants belonging to the said Courts respectively shall have liberty to be present, but shall not interpose unless their Opinions be required, nor have any Vote at all; but their Business shall be, by the direction of the respective Courts, to prepare such Business as shall be committed to them; as also, to bear such Offices and dispatch such Affairs, either where the Court is kept or elsewhere, as the Court shall think fit.

49. In all the Proprietors' Courts, the Proprietor and any three of his Councillors shall make a Quorum; Provided always, that, for the better dispatch of Business, it shall be in the power of the Palatine's Court to direct what sort of Causes shall be Heard and Determined by a Quorum of any three.

50. The Grand Council shall consist of the Palatine, and seven Proprietors, and the forty two Councillors of the several Proprietors' Courts; who shall have power to Determine any Controversies that may arise between any of the Proprietors' Courts about their respective Jurisdictions, or between the Members of the same Court about their Manner and Methods of Proceeding; To make Peace and War, Leagues, Treaties, etc., with any of the neighbor Indians; To Issue out their general Orders to the Constable's and Admiral's Courts for the Raising, Disposing, or Disbanding the Forces, by Land or by Sea.

51. The Grand Council shall prepare all Matters to be proposed in Parliament. Nor shall any Matter whatsoever be proposed in Parliament but what has first passed the Grand Council, which, after having been read three several Days in Parliament, shall, by majority of Votes, be Passed or rejected.

52. The Grand Council shall always be Judges of all Causes and Appeals that concern the Palatine, or any of the Lords Proprietors, or any Councillor of any Proprietors' Court in any Cause which otherwise

should have been Tried in the Court in which the said Councillor is Judge himself.

53. The Grand Council, by their Warrants to the Treasurer's Court, shall dispose of all the Money given by the Parliament and by them directed to any particular public Use.

54. The Quorum of the Grand Council shall be thirteen, whereof a Proprietor, or his Deputy, shall be always one.

55. The Grand Council shall meet the first Tuesday in every Month, and as much oftener as either they shall think fit or they shall be Convocated by the Chamberlain's Court.

56. The Palatine, or any of the Lords Proprietors, shall have power, under Hand and Seal, to be Registered in the Grand Council, to make a Deputy, who shall have the same power, to all intents and purposes, as he himself who deputes him, except in confirming Acts of Parliament, as in article 76, and except, also, in nominating and choosing Landgraves and Caciques, as in article 10. All such Deputations shall cease and determine at the end of four Years, and at any time shall be revocable at the pleasure of the Deputator.

57. No Deputy of any Proprietor shall have any power whilst the Deputator is in any part of Carolina, except the Proprietor whose Deputy he is be a Minor.

58. During the Minority of any Proprietor, his Guardian shall have power to Constitute and appoint his Deputy.

59. The eldest of the Lords Proprietors who shall be personally in Carolina shall of course be the Palatine's Deputy; and if no Proprietor be in Carolina, he shall choose his Deputy out of the Heirs Apparent of any of the Proprietors, if any such be there; and if there be no Heir Apparent of any of the Lords Proprietors, above one and twenty Years old, in Carolina, then he shall choose for Deputy any one of the Landgraves of the Grand Council; and till he have, by Deputation, under Hand and Seal, chosen any one of the forementioned Heirs Apparent or Landgraves to be his Deputy, the eldest Man of the Landgraves, and for want of a Landgrave, the eldest Man of the Caciques, who shall be personally in Carolina shall of course be his Deputy.

60. Each Proprietor's Deputy shall be always one of his own six Councillors respectively; and in case any of the Proprietors has not, in

his absence out of Carolina, a Deputy, Commissioned under his Hand and Seal, the eldest Nobleman of his Court shall of course be his Deputy.

61. In every County there shall be a Court, consisting of a Sheriff and four Justices of the County, for every Precinct one. The Sheriff shall be an Inhabitant of the County and have at least five hundred Acres of Freehold within the said County; and the Justices shall be Inhabitants and have, each of them, five hundred Acres apiece Freehold within the Precinct for which they serve respectively. These five shall be chosen and Commissioned from time to time by the Palatine's Court.

62. For any Personal Causes exceeding the value of two hundred Pounds Sterling, or in Title of Land, or in any Criminal Cause, either Party, upon paying twenty Pounds Sterling to the Lords Proprietors' use, shall have liberty of Appeal from the County Court unto the respective Proprietors' Court.

63. In every Precinct there shall be a Court, consisting of a Steward and four Justices of the Precinct, being Inhabitants and having three hundred Acres of Freehold within the said Precinct; who shall Judge all Criminal Causes, except for Treason, Murder, and any other Offences punishable with Death and except all Criminal Causes of the Nobility; and shall Judge, also, all Civil Causes whatsoever, and in all personal Actions not exceeding fifty Pounds Sterling without Appeal; But where the Cause shall exceed that value, or concern a Title of Land, and in all Criminal Causes, there, either Party, upon paying five Pounds Sterling to the Lords Proprietors' use, shall have liberty of Appeal to the County Court.

64. No Cause shall be twice Tried in any one Court, upon any reason or pretence whatsoever.

65. For Treason, Murder, and all other Offences punishable with Death, there shall be a Commission, twice a year at least, granted unto one or more Members of the Grand Council or Colleges, who shall come as itinerant Judges to the several Counties, and, with the Sheriff and four Justices, shall hold Assizes to Judge all such Causes; But upon paying of fifty Pounds Sterling to the Lords Proprietors' use, there shall be liberty of Appeal to the respective Proprietors' Court.

66. The Grand Jury at the several Assizes shall, upon their Oaths, and under their Hands and Seals, deliver in to the itinerant Judges a Presentment of such Grievances, Misdemeanors, Exigencies, or Defects

which they think necessary for the public good of the County; which Presentment shall, by the itinerant Judges, at the end of their Circuit, be delivered in to the Grand Council at their next Sitting. And whatsoever therein concerns the Execution of Laws already made, the several Proprietors' Courts, in the Matters belonging to each of them respectively, shall take Cognizance of it, and give such order about it as shall be effectual for the due Execution of the Laws. But whatever concerns the making of any new Law shall be referred to the several respective Courts to which that Matter belongs, and be by them prepared and brought to the Grand Council.

67. For Terms, there shall be Quarterly such a certain number of Days, not exceeding one and twenty at any one time, as the several respective Courts shall appoint. The time for the beginning of the Term in the Precinct Court shall be the first Monday in January, April, July, and October; in the County Court, the first Monday in February, May, August, and November; and in the Proprietors' Courts, the first Monday in March, June, September, and December.

68. In the Precinct Court, no Man shall be a Jury-man under fifty Acres of Freehold. In the County Court, or at the Assizes, no Man shall be a Grand Jury-man under three hundred Acres of Freehold, and no Man shall be a Petty Jury-man under two hundred Acres of Freehold. In the Proprietors' Courts, no Man shall be a Jury-man under five hundred Acres of Freehold.

69. Every Jury shall consist of twelve Men; and it shall not be necessary they should all agree, but the Verdict shall be according to the Consent of the Majority.

70. It shall be a base and vile thing to Plead for Money or Reward; nor shall any one, except he be a near Kinsman, not farther off than Cousin-german to the Party concerned, be permitted to Plead another Man's Cause till, before the Judge in open Court, he has taken an Oath that he does not Plead for Money or Reward, nor has nor will receive, nor directly nor indirectly Bargained with the Party, whose Cause he is going to Plead, for Money or any other Reward for Pleading his Cause.

71. There shall be a Parliament, consisting of the Proprietors, or their Deputies, the Landgraves and Caciques, and one Freeholder out of every Precinct, to be chosen by the Freeholders of the said Precinct respectively. They shall Sit all together in one Room, and have every Member one vote.

72. No Man shall be chosen a Member of Parliament who has less than five hundred Acres of Freehold within the Precinct for which he is chosen; nor shall any have a Vote in choosing the said Member that has less than fifty Acres of Freehold within the said Precinct.

73. A new Parliament shall be Assembled the first Monday of the Month of November every second Year, and shall meet and Sit in the Town they last Sat in, without any Summons, unless by the Palatine's Court they be Summoned to meet at any other Place. And if there shall be any occasion of a Parliament in these Intervals, it shall be in the power of the Palatine's Court to Assemble them in forty Days' notice, and at such Time and Place as the said Court shall think fit; and the Palatine's Court shall have power to Dissolve the said Parliament when they shall think fit.

74. At the opening of every Parliament, the first thing that shall be done shall be the reading of these Fundamental Constitutions, which the Palatine, and Proprietors, and the rest of the Members then present shall Subscribe. Nor shall any Person whatsoever Sit or Vote in the Parliament till he has, that Session, Subscribed these Fundamental Constitutions in a Book kept for that purpose by the Clerk of the Parliament.

75. In order to the due Election of Members for the Biennial Parliament, it shall be lawful for the Freeholders of the respective Precincts to meet the first Tuesday in September every two Years, in the same Town or Place that they last met in, to choose Parliament-men, and there choose those Members that are to Sit the next November following, unless the Steward of the Precinct shall, by sufficient notice thirty Days before, appoint some other Place for their Meeting in order to the Election.

76. No Act or Order of Parliament shall be of any force unless it be Ratified in open Parliament, during the same Session, by the Palatine, or his Deputy, and three more of the Lords Proprietors, and [or] their Deputies; and then not to continue longer in force but until the next Biennial Parliament, unless in the mean time it be Ratified under the Hands and Seals of the Palatine himself and three more of the Lords Proprietors themselves, and, by their Order, published at the next Biennial Parliament.

77. Any Proprietor, or his Deputy, may Enter his Protestation against any Act of the Parliament, before the Palatine or his Deputy's

Consent be given as aforesaid, if he shall conceive the said Act to be contrary to this Establishment or any of these Fundamental Constitutions of the Government. And in such case, after a full and free Debate, the several Estates shall retire into four several Chambers, the Palatine and Proprietors into one, the Landgraves into another, the Caciques into another, and those chosen by the Precincts into a fourth; and if the major part of any of the four Estates shall Vote that the Law is not agreeable to this Establishment and these Fundamental Constitutions of the Government, then it shall pass no farther, but be as if it had never been proposed.

78. The Quorum of the Parliament shall be one half of those who are Members and capable of Sitting in the House that present Session of Parliament. The Quorum of each of the Chambers of Parliament shall be one half of the Members of that Chamber.

79. To avoid multiplicity of Laws, which by degrees always change the right Foundations of the original Government, all Acts of Parliament whatsoever, in whatsoever Form Passed or Enacted, shall, at the end of a hundred Years after their Enacting, respectively cease and determine of themselves, and, without any Repeal, become null and void, as if no such Acts or Laws had ever been made.

80. Since multiplicity of Comments, as well as of Laws, have great inconveniences, and serve only to obscure and perplex, All manner of Comments and Expositions on any part of these Fundamental Constitutions, or any part of the Common or Statute Law of Carolina, are absolutely Prohibited.

81. There shall be a Registry in every Precinct, wherein shall be Enrolled all Deeds, Leases, Judgments, Mortgages, and other Conveyances which may concern any of the Land within the said Precinct; and all such Conveyances not so Entered or Registered shall not be of force against any Person nor Party of the said Contract or Conveyance.

82. No Man shall be Register of any Precinct who has not at least three hundred Acres of Freehold within the said Precinct.

83. The Freeholders of every Precinct shall nominate three Men, out of which three the Chief Justice's Court shall choose and Commission one to be Register of the said Precinct, whilst he shall well behave himself.

84. There shall be a Registry in every Seigniory, Barony, and Colony, wherein shall be Recorded all the Births, Marriages, and Deaths that shall happen within the respective Seigniories, Baronies, and Colonies.

85. No Man shall be Register of a Colony that has not above fifty Acres of Freehold within the said Colony.

86. The time of every one's Age that is born in Carolina shall be reckoned from the Day that his Birth is Entered in the Registry, and not before.

87. No Marriage shall be lawful, whatever Contract and Ceremony they have used, till both the Parties mutually own it before the Register of the Place where they were Married, and he Register it, with the Names of the Father and Mother of each Party.

88. No Man shall Administer to the Goods, or have right to them, or enter upon the Estate, of any Person deceased till his Death be Registered in the respective Registry.

89. He that does not Enter in the respective Registry the Birth or Death of any Person that is born or dies in his House or Ground shall pay to the said Register one Shilling per Week for each such Neglect, reckoning from the time of each Birth or Death respectively to the time of Registering it.

90. In like manner, the Births, Marriages, and Deaths of the Lords Proprietors, Landgraves, and Caciques shall be Registered in the Chamberlain's Court.

91. There shall be in every Colony one Constable, to be chosen annually by the Freeholders of the Colony; His Estate shall be above a hundred Acres of Freehold within the said Colony; and such subordinate Officers appointed for his Assistance as the County Court shall find requisite, and shall be established by the said County Court. The Election of the subordinate annual Officers shall be also in the Freeholders of the Colony.

92. All Towns Incorporate shall be Governed by a Mayor, twelve Aldermen, and twenty four of the Common-Council. The said Common-Council shall be chosen by the present Householders of the said Town. The Aldermen shall be chosen out of the Common-Council, and the Mayor out of the Aldermen, by the Palatine's Court.

93. It being of great consequence to the Plantation that Port-Towns should be built and preserved, Therefore, whosoever shall lade or unlade any Commodity at any other Place but a Port-Town shall forfeit to the Lords Proprietors for each Ton so laden or unladen the Sum of ten Pounds Sterling, except only such Goods as the Palatine's Court shall Licence to be laden or unladen elsewhere.

94. The first Port-Town upon every River shall be in a Colony, and be a Port-Town for ever.

95. No Man shall be permitted to be a Freeman of Carolina, or to have any Estate or Habitation within it, that does not acknowledge a God, and that God is publicly and solemnly to be Worshipped.

96. As the Country comes to be sufficiently Planted and Distributed into fit Divisions, it shall belong to the Parliament to take care for the building of Churches and the public Maintenance of Divines, to be employed in the Exercise of Religion according to the Church of England, which, being the only true and Orthodox, and the National Religion of all the King's Dominions, is so also of Carolina, and therefore, it alone shall be allowed to receive public Maintenance by Grant of Parliament.

97. But since the Natives of that Place, who will be concerned in our Plantation, are utterly Strangers to Christianity, whose Idolatry, Ignorance, or Mistake gives us no right to expel or use them ill; and those who remove from other Parts to Plant there will unavoidably be of different Opinions concerning Matters of Religion, the liberty whereof they will expect to have allowed them, and it will not be reasonable for us, on this account, to keep them out; that Civil Peace may be maintained amidst the diversity of Opinions, and our Agreement and Compact with all Men may be duly and faithfully observed, the violation whereof, upon what pretence soever, cannot be without great offence to Almighty God, and great scandal to the true Religion, which we profess; and also, that Jews, Heathens, and other Dissenters from the purity of Christian Religion may not be scared and kept at a distance from it, but, by having an opportunity of acquainting themselves with the truth and reasonableness of its Doctrines, and the peaceableness and inoffensiveness of its Professors, may, by good usage and persuasion, and all those convincing Methods of gentleness and meekness suitable to the Rules and Design of the Gospel, be won over to embrace and unfeignedly receive the Truth: Therefore, any seven or more Persons

agreeing in any Religion shall Constitute a Church or Profession, to which they shall give some Name to distinguish it from others.

98. The Terms of Admittance and Communion with any Church or Profession shall be written in a Book and therein be Subscribed by all the Members of the said Church or Profession; which Book shall be kept by the public Register of the Precinct where they reside.

99. The Time of every one's Subscription and Admittance shall be Dated in the said Book, or religious Record.

100. In the Terms of Communion of every Church or Profession, these following shall be three, without which no Agreement or Assembly of Men upon pretence of Religion shall be accounted a Church or Profession within these Rules:

1. That there is a God.
2. That God is publicly to be Worshipped.
3. That it is lawful, and the Duty of every Man, being thereunto called by those that Govern, to bear Witness to Truth; and that every Church or Profession shall, in their Terms of Communion, set down the external Way whereby they witness a Truth as in the presence of God, whether it be by laying Hands on or kissing the Bible, as in the Church of England, or by holding up the Hand, or any other sensible way.

101. No Person above seventeen Years of Age shall have any benefit or protection of the Law, or be capable of any Place of Profit or Honor, who is not a Member of some Church or Profession, having his Name Recorded in some one, and but one religious Record at once.

102. No Person of any other Church or Profession shall disturb or molest any religious Assembly.

103. No Person whatsoever shall speak any thing in their religious Assembly irreverently or seditiously of the Government or Governors or State Matters.

104. Any Person Subscribing the Terms of Communion in the Record of the said Church or Profession before the Precinct Register and any five Members of the said Church or Profession shall be thereby made a Member of the said Church or Profession.

105. Any Person striking out his own Name out of any religious Record, or his Name being struck out by any Officer thereunto author-

ized by each Church or Profession respectively, shall cease to be a Member of that Church or Profession.

106. No Man shall use any reproachful, reviling, or abusive Language against the Religion of any Church or Profession, that being the certain way of disturbing the Peace, and of hindering the Conversion of any to the Truth, by engaging them in Quarrels and Animosities, to the hatred of the Professors and that Profession, which otherwise they might be brought to assent to.

107. Since Charity obliges us to wish well to the Souls of all Men, and Religion ought to alter nothing in any Man's Civil Estate or Right, it shall be lawful for Slaves, as well as others, to Enter themselves and be of what Church or Profession any of them shall think best, and thereof be as fully Members as any Freeman. But yet, no Slave shall hereby be exempted from that Civil Dominion his Master has over him, but be in all other things in the same State and Condition he was in before.

108. Assemblies, upon what pretence soever of Religion, not observing and performing the abovesaid Rules shall not be esteemed as Churches, but unlawful Meetings, and be punished as other Riots.

109. No Person whatsoever shall disturb, molest, or persecute another for his speculative Opinions in Religion or his Way of Worship.

110. Every Freeman of Carolina shall have absolute Power and Authority over his Negro Slaves, of what Opinion or Religion soever.

111. No Cause, whether Civil or Criminal, of any Freeman shall be Tried in any Court of Judicature without a Jury of his Peers.

112. No Person whatsoever shall hold or claim any Land in Carolina, by Purchase or Gift or otherwise, from the Natives or any other whatsoever, but merely from and under the Lords Proprietors, upon pain of forfeiture of all his Estate, moveable or immoveable, and perpetual banishment.

113. Whosoever shall possess any Freehold in Carolina, upon what Title or Grant soever, shall, at the farthest, from and after the Year One thousand six hundred eighty nine, pay yearly, unto the Lords Proprietors, for each Acre of Land, English Measure, as much fine Silver as is at this present in one English Penny, or the value thereof, to be as a Chief Rent and Acknowledgment to the Lords Proprietors, their Heirs and Successors, for ever. And it shall be lawful for the Palatine's Court, by their Officers, at any time, to take a new Survey of any Man's Land, not

to out him of any part of his Possession, but that, by such a Survey, the just number of Acres he possesses may be known, and the Rent thereupon due may be paid by him.

114. All Wrecks, Mines, Minerals, Quarries of Gems and Precious Stones, with Pearl-fishing, Whale-fishing, and one half of all Ambergris, by whomsoever found, shall wholly belong to the Lords Proprietors.

115. All Revenues and Profits belonging to the Lords Proprietors in common shall be divided into ten Parts, whereof the Palatine shall have three, and each Proprietor one; but if the Palatine shall Govern by a Deputy, his Deputy shall have one of those three Tenths, and the Palatine the other two Tenths.

116. All Inhabitants and Freemen of Carolina above seventeen Years of Age and under sixty shall be bound to bear Arms and Serve as Soldiers whenever the Grand Council shall find it necessary.

117. A true Copy of these Fundamental Constitutions shall be kept in a great Book by the Register of every Precinct, to be Subscribed before the said Register. Nor shall any Person, of what Condition or Degree soever, above seventeen Years old, have any Estate or Possession in Carolina, or protection or benefit of the Law there, who has not, before a Precinct Register, Subscribed these Fundamental Constitutions in this Form:

I, A. B., do promise to bear Faith and true Allegiance to our Sovereign Lord King Charles the Second; and will be true and faithful to the Palatine and Lords Proprietors of Carolina; and, with my utmost power, will defend them and maintain the Government, according to this Establishment in these Fundamental Constitutions.

118. Whatsoever Alien shall, in this Form, before any Precinct Register, Subscribe these Fundamental Constitutions shall be thereby Naturalized.

119. In the same manner shall every Person at his Admittance into any Office Subscribe these Fundamental Constitutions.

120. These Fundamental Constitutions, in number a hundred and twenty, and every part thereof, shall be, and remain, the sacred and unalterable Form and Rule of Government of Carolina for ever. Witness our Hands and Seals, the first Day of March, 1669.[2]

[2] In present-day reckoning, 1670. From the twelfth century until September, 1752, England used the Julian Calendar, according to which the new year began March 25. The period from January 1 through March 24, therefore, was included in the year preceding that to which it belongs in the Gregorian Calendar.

Rules of Precedency

1. The Lords Proprietors, the eldest in Age first, and so in order.
2. The eldest Sons of the Lords Proprietors, the eldest in Age first, and so in order.
3. The Landgraves of the Grand Council, he that has been longest of the Grand Council first, and so in order.
4. The Caciques of the Grand Council, he that has been longest of the Grand Council first, and so in order.
5. The seven Commoners of the Grand Council that have been longest of the Grand Council, he that has been longest of the Grand Council first, and so in order.
6. The youngest Sons of Proprietors, the eldest first, and so in order.
7. The Landgraves, the eldest in Age first, and so in order.
8. The seven Commoners who, next to those before mentioned, have been longest of the Grand Council, he that has been longest of the Grand Council first, and so in order.
9. The Caciques, the eldest in Age first, and so in order.
10. The seven remaining Commoners of the Grand Council, he that has been longest of the Grand Council first, and so in order.
11. The Male Line of the Proprietors.

The rest shall be determined by the Chamberlain's Court.

[Transcribed from a copy printed about 1670.]

Version of January 12, 1682

OUR Sovereign Lord the King having, out of his most Royal Grace and Bounty, granted unto us the Province of Carolina, with all the Royalties, Proprieties, Jurisdictions, and Privileges of a County Palatine, as large and ample as the County Palatine of Durham, with other great Privileges; for the better settlement of the Government of the Said Place, and establishing the Interest of the Lords Proprietors with Equality, and without Confusion; and that the Government of this Province may be made most agreeable to the Monarchy under which we live, and of which this Province is a part; and that we may avoid erecting a numerous Democracy: we, the Lords and Proprietors of the Province aforesaid, have agreed to this following Form of Government, to be perpetually established amongst us, unto which we do Oblige ourselves, our Heirs, Assigns, and Successors, in the most binding ways that can be devised.

1. The eldest of the Lords Proprietors shall be Palatine; and upon the Decease of the Palatine, the eldest of the seven surviving Proprietors shall always succeed him.

2. There shall be Seven other chief Offices erected, Viz., the Admiral's, [Chamberlain's],[1] Chancellor's, Constable's, Chief Justice's, High Steward's, Treasurer's; which Places shall be enjoyed by none but the Lords Proprietors, to be assigned at first by Lot; and upon the Vacancy of any one of the seven great Offices by Death, or otherwise, the eldest Proprietor shall have his choice of the said Place.

3. The whole Province shall be divided into Counties; each County shall consist of eight Seigniories, eight Baronies, and four Precincts; each Precinct shall Consist of six Colonies.

4. Each Seigniory, Barony, and Colony shall consist of twelve Thousand acres, the eight Seigniories being the share of the eight Proprietors, and the eight Baronies of the Nobility; both which Shares, being each of them one fifth part of the whole, are to be perpetually annexed, the one to the Proprietors, the other to the hereditary Nobility, leaving the Colonies, being three Fifths, amongst the People; that so, in

[1] The words in square brackets in this transcription have been supplied from a copy of the January 12, 1682, version printed in 1682.

Setting out and planting the Lands, the Balance of the Government may be preserved.

5. At any time before the year One thousand seven hundred and one, any of the Lords Proprietors shall have power to Relinquish, Alienate, and Dispose, to any other Person, his Proprietorship, and all the Seigniories, Powers, and Interest thereunto belonging, wholly and entirely together, and not otherwise. But after the year One thousand seven hundred, those who are then Lords Proprietors shall not have power to Alienate or make over their Proprietorship, with the Seigniories and Privileges thereunto belonging, or any part thereof, to any Person whatsoever, otherwise than as in page [article] 18, but it shall all descend unto their Heirs Male; and for want of Heirs Male, it shall all descend on that Landgrave or Cacique of Carolina who is descended of the next Heir Female of the Said Proprietor; and for want of such Heirs, the Remaining seven Proprietors shall, upon the Vacancy, choose A Landgrave to succeed the deceased Proprietor, who being Chosen by the majority of the Seven Surviving proprietors, he and his Heirs successively shall be Proprietors as fully, to all intents and purposes, as any of the rest.

6. That the number of eight Proprietors may be constantly Kept, if, upon the vacancy of any proprietor, the seven Surviving proprietors shall not choose a Landgrave to be A Proprietor before the Second biennial Parliament after the Vacancy, then the next Biennial Parliament but one after such Vacancy shall have power to Choose any Landgrave to be Proprietor.

7. Whosoever after the year one thousand seven hundred, either by inheritance or Choice, shall succeed any Proprietor in his proprietorship, and Seigniory thereunto belonging, shall be obliged to take the Name and Arms of that Proprietor whom he succeeds, which from thence forth shall be the Name and Arms of his Family and their Posterity.

8. Whatsoever Landgrave or Cacique shall any way come to be a proprietor shall take the Seigniories annexed to the Said Proprietorship, but his former Dignity, with the Baronies annexed, shall devolve into the Hands of the Lords Proprietors.

9. There shall be just as many Landgraves as there are Counties, and [twice] as many Caciques, and no more. These shall be the heredi-

tary Nobility of the Province, and, by right of their dignity, be Members of Parliament. Each Landgrave shall have four Baronies, and each Cacique two Baronies, hereditarily and unalterably annexed to and settled upon the said Dignity.

10. The first Landgraves and Caciques of the twelve first Counties to be Planted shall be nominated thus: that is to say, of the twelve Landgraves, the Lords proprietors shall, each of them separately, for himself, nominate and choose one, and the Remaining four Landgraves of the first twelve shall be nominated and chosen by the Palatine's Court. In Like manner, of the twenty four first Caciques, each Proprietor, for himself, shall nominate and choose two, and the Remaining eight shall be nominated and chosen by the Palatine's Court; and when the twelve first Counties shall be Planted, the Lords Proprietors shall again, in the Same manner, nominate and choose twelve more Landgraves and twenty four Caciques for the twelve next Counties to be Planted, that is to say, two Thirds of each number by the Single nomination of each Proprietor for himself, and the Remaining one third by the joint Election of the Palatine's Court; and so proceed, in the same manner, till the whole Province of Carolina be Set out and planted according to the Proportions in these fundamental constitutions.

11. Any Landgrave or Cacique, at any time before the year one thousand seven hundred and one, shall have power to Alienate, Sell, or make over, to any one person, his dignity, with the Baronies thereunto belonging, all entirely together. But after the Year One thousand seven hundred, no Landgrave or Cacique shall have power to Alienate, sell, make over, or let the Hereditary Baronies of his dignity, or any part thereof, otherwise than as in page [article] 18, but they shall all entirely, with the dignity thereunto belonging, descend unto his Heirs Males; and for want of Heirs Male, all entirely and undivided, to the next Heir General; for want of such Heirs, shall devolve into the hands of the Lords Proprietors.

12. That the due number of Landgraves and Caciques may be always Kept up, if, upon the Devolution of any Landgraveship or Caciqueship, the Palatine's Court shall not settle the devolved dignity, with the Baronies thereunto annexed, before the Second biennial Parliament after such Devolution, the next biennial Parliament but one after such Devolution Shall have power to make any one Landgrave or Cacique in the room of him, who dying without Heirs, his dignity and Baronies devolved.

13. No one person shall have more than one Dignity, with the Seigniories or Baronies thereunto belonging. But whensoever it shall happen that any one who is already Proprietor, Landgrave, or Caciques shall have any of these Dignities descend to him by Inheritance, it shall be at his Choice to Keep which of the Dignities, with the Lands annexed, he shall like best, but shall leave the other, with the Lands annexed, to be enjoyed by him who, not being his Heir Apparent, and certain Successor [to his present Dignity, is next of Blood.]

14. Whosoever, by Right of Inheritance, shall come to be Landgrave or Cacique shall take the Name and Arms of his Predecessor in that Dignity, to be from thence forth the Name and Arms of his Family and their Posterity.

15. Since The Dignity of Proprietor, Landgrave, or Cacique Cannot be divided, and the Seigniories or Baronies thereunto annexed must for ever, all entirely, descend with and accompany that Dignity, whensoever, for want of Heirs Male, it Shall [descend on the Issue Female, the eldest Daughter and her Heirs shall] be preferred, and in the Inheritance of those Dignities, and in the Seigniories or baronies annexed, there shall be no Coheirs.

16. In every Seigniory, Barony, and Manor, the Respective Lord shall have power, in his own Name, to hold Court-Leet there, for Trying of all Causes, both Civil and Criminal; but where it shall concern any Person being no Inhabitant, Vassal, or Leet-man of the Said Seigniory, Barony, or Manor, he, upon paying down of forty Shillings to the Lords Proprietors' use, shall have an Appeal from the Seigniory or Barony Court to the County Court, and from the Manor Court to the Precinct Court.

17. Every Manor shall consist of not less than three thousand Acres and not above twelve thousand Acres in one entire Piece and Colony; but any three thousand Acres or more in one Piece and the Possession of one Man Shall not be a Manor unless it be Constituted A Manor by the Grant of the Palatine's Court.

18. The Lords of Seigniories and Baronies shall have power only of granting Estates, not exceeding three lives or thirty one years, in two Thirds of the Said Seigniories or Baronies, and the Remaining third shall be always Demesne.

19. Any Lord of a Manor may Alienate, Sell, or Dispose, to any other person, and his Heirs, for ever, his manor, all entirely together,

with all the Privileges and Leet-men thereunto belonging, so far forth as any other Colony Lands; but no Grant of any part thereof, either in Fee or for any longer Term than three Lives or one and twenty Years, shall be good against the next Heir.

20. No Manor, for want of Issue Male, shall be divided amongst Coheirs, but the Manor, if there be but one, shall all entirely descend to the eldest Daughter and her Heirs. If there be more Manors than one, the eldest Daughter first shall have her choice, the Second next, and so on, beginning again at the eldest, till all the Manors be taken up; that so, the Privileges which belong to Manors being indivisible, the Lands of the Manors to which they are annexed may be kept entire, and the Manor not lose those Privileges, which upon parcelling out to several Owners must necessarily cease.

21. Every Lord of a Manor, within his Manor, shall have all the Powers, Jurisdictions, and Privileges which A Landgrave or Cacique has in his Baronies.

22. In every Seigniory, Barony, and Manor, all the Leet-men shall be under the Jurisdiction of the respective Lords of the said Seigniory, Barony, or Manor, without Appeal from him. Nor shall any Leet-man or Leet-woman have liberty to go off from the Land of their particular Lord and live any where else without License obtained from their said Lord, under Hand and Seal.

23. All the Children of Leet-men shall be Leet-men, and so to all Generations.

24. No Man shall be Capable of having A Court-leet or Leet-Men but A Proprietor, Landgrave, Cacique, or Lord of a Manor.

25. Whoever shall voluntarily Enter himself a Leet-man in the Registry of the County Court Shall be a Leet-man.

26. Whoever is Lord of Leet-men shall, upon the Marriage of a Leet-man or Leet-woman of his, give them ten Acres of Land for their Lives, they paying to him therefor not more than one eighth part of all the yearly Produce and Growth of the said ten Acres.

27. No Landgrave or Cacique shall be Tried for any Criminal Cause in any but the Chief Justice's Court, and that by a Jury of his Peers.

28. There shall be eight Supreme Courts, The first, called The Palatine's Court, consisting of the Palatine and the other seven Proprietors. The other seven Courts of the other seven great Officers shall consist, each of them, of a Proprietor and six Councillors added to him. Under each of these latter seven Courts shall be a College of twelve Assistants. The twelve Assistants of the several Colleges shall be Chosen: two out of the Landgraves, Caciques, or eldest sons of the Proprietors, [by the Palatine's] Court; two out of the Landgraves, by the Landgraves' Chamber; two out of the Caciques, by the Caciques' Chamber; Four more of the twelve shall be chosen by the Commons' Chamber, out of such as have been or are Members of the Parliament, Sheriffs, or Justices of the County Court, or the younger Sons of Proprietors, or eldest Sons of Landgraves or Caciques; the two other shall be chosen by the Palatine's Court out of the same sort of Persons out of which the Commons' Chamber is to Choose.

29. Out of these Colleges shall be chosen, at first by the Palatine's Court, six Councillors to be joined with each Proprietor in his Court; of which six, one shall be of those who were chosen in any of the Colleges by the Palatine's Court out of the Landgraves, Caciques, or eldest Sons of Proprietors; one out [of] those who were chosen by the Landgraves' Chamber; and one out of those who were chosen by the Caciques' Chamber; two out of those who were chosen by the Commons' Chamber; and one out of those who were chosen by the Palatine's Court out of the Proprietors' younger Sons, or eldest sons of the Landgraves [or] Caciques, or Commons Qualified as aforesaid.

30. When it shall happen that any Councillor dies or is removed, and thereby there is a Vacancy, he that has been Longest a Councillor in any of the Proprietors' Courts, of the same degree or Choice the other was of whose Vacant place is to be filled up, shall have his choice, whether he will remove into the place of the person that is dead or removed; But if he refuse to remove, the next in Seniority of the same degree and Choice shall have his choice; and so of Course the Rest in order. And the Last remaining Vacant place in any of the foresaid Proprietors' Courts shall be filled up by him that has been longest of any of the Colleges, being of the same degree and choice with him that is dead or removed; and he that is next of Seniority in the same degree and Choice shall have power to remove himself, if he please, in any College where any place shall be Vacant; and so of course the rest, as in case of Councillors; but the last remaining Vacant place in any College shall be

filled up by the Same Choice and out of the same degree of Persons that he was of who is dead or removed. No place shall be Vacant in any of the proprietors' Courts or Colleges longer than the next Sessions of Parliament.

31. No Man being a Member of the Grand Council or of any of the Seven Colleges shall be turned out but for Misdemeanor, of which the Grand Council shall be Judge; and the Vacancy of the person so put out shall be filled as is provided in case of the Death of any Councillor. But it is not hereby to be understood that the Grand Council has any power to turn out any one of the Lords proprietors, or their deputies, the Lords Proprietors having in themselves an inherent original Right.

32. All Elections in the Parliament, in the several Chambers of the Parliament, and in the Grand Council shall be passed by Balloting.

33. The Palatine's Court shall consist of the Palatine and seven Proprietors, wherein nothing shall be acted without the Presence and Consent of the Palatine, or his Deputy, and three others of the Proprietors, or their Deputies. This Court shall have power to call Parliaments, to pardon all Offences, to make Elections of all Officers in the Proprietors' dispose, and to nominate and appoint Port-Towns; and also, shall have power, by their Order to the Treasurer, to dispose of the public Treasure, excepting money granted by the Parliament and by them directed to some particular public Use; and also, shall have a Negative upon all acts, Orders, Votes, and Judgements of the grand Council, except only as in Page [articles] 6, 12. And shall have all the Power granted to the Lords Proprietors by their Patent from Our Sovereign Lord the King, except such things as are limited by these Fundamental Constitutions.

34. The Palatine himself, when he in person shall be either in the Army or in any of the Proprietors' Courts, shall then have the Power of General or of that Proprietor in whose Court he is then present; and the Proprietor in whose Court the palatine then presides shall, during his presence there, be but as one of the Council.

35. The Chancellor's Court, Consisting of one of the Proprietors and his six Councillors, who shall be called Vice Chancellors, shall have the custody of the Seal of the Palatinate, under which all Charters of Lands and other Commissions and Grants of the Palatine's Court shall pass; and it shall not be lawful to put the Seal of the Palatinate to any

writing which is not Signed by the Palatine, or his Deputy, and three other Proprietors, or their Deputies. To this Court, also, belongs all states Matters, Dispatches, and Treaties with the neighbour Indians. To this Court, also, belongs all Invasions of the Law of Liberty of Conscience, and all disturbances of the Public Peace upon pretence of Religion, as also, the License of Printing. The twelve Assistants belonging to this Court shall be called Recorders.

36. Whatever passes under the Seal of the Palatinate shall be Registered in that Proprietors' Court to which the Matter therein Contained belongs.

37. The Chancellor, or his Deputy, shall be always Speaker in Parliament and President of the Grand Council, and in [his and] his Deputy's absence, one of his Vice Chancellors.

38. The Chief Justice's Court, consisting of one of the Proprietors and [his] six Councillors, who shall be called Justices of the Bench, shall Judge all Appeals, in Cases both Civil and Criminal, except all such Cases as shall be under the Jurisdiction and Cognizance of any other of the Proprietors' Courts, which shall be tried in those Courts respectively. The Government and Regulation of the Registries of writings and Contracts shall belong to the Jurisdiction of this Court. The twelve Assistants of this Court shall be called Masters.

39. The Constable's Court, consisting of one of the Proprietors and his six Councillors, who shall be called Marshals, shall order and determine of All Military Affairs by Land, and all Land-Forces, Arms, Ammunition, Artillery, Garrisons, and Forts, and whatever belongs unto war. His twelve Assistants shall be called Lieutenant Generals.

40. In time of actual War, the Constable, whilst he is in the Army, shall be General of the Army, and the six Councillors, or such of them as the Palatine's Court shall for that time or Service appoint, shall be the immediate great Officers under him, and the Lieutenant Generals next to them.

41. The Admiral's Court, Consisting of one of the Proprietors and his six Councillors, called Consuls, shall have the care and inspection over all Ports, Moles, and Navigable Rivers so far as the Tide flows; and also, all the Public Shipping of Carolina, and Stores thereunto belonging, and all Maritime Affairs. This Court, also, shall have the power of the Court of Admiralty; and shall have power to Constitute Judges in Port-

Towns to try cases belonging to Law-Merchant, as shall be most convenient for Trade; the twelve assistants belonging to this Court shall be called Proconsuls.

42. In time of actual War, the Admiral, whilst he is at Sea, shall Command in Chief, and his six Councillors, or such of them as the Palatine's [Court] shall for that time and Service appoint, shall be the immediate great Officers under him, and the Proconsuls next to them.

43. The Treasurer's Court, consisting of a proprietor and his six Councillors, Called Under-Treasurers, shall take care of all Matters that Concern the Public Revenue and Treasury. The twelve Assistants shall be called Auditors.

44. The High Steward's Court, consisting of a Proprietor and his six Councillors, called Comptrollers, shall have the care of all Foreign and Domestic Trade, Manufactures, public Buildings and work houses, Highways, Passages by Water above the Flood of the Tide, Drains, Sewers and Banks against inundations, Bridges, Post, Carriers, Fairs, Markets, Corruption or Infection of the common Air or Water, and all things in order to the Public commerce and health; also, Setting out and Surveying of Lands; and also, setting out and appointing Places for towns <according to such Models as the said Court shall order, contrary> [2] to be built on in the Precincts, and the prescribing and determining the figure and bigness of the said Towns according to such models as the said Court shall order, contrary or differing from which Models it shall not be lawful for any one to Build in any Town. This Court shall have power, also, to make any Public Building or any new highway, or enlarge any old Highway, upon any man's Land whatsoever; as also, to make Cuts, Channels, Banks, Locks, and Bridges, for making Rivers Navigable, or for draining Fens, or any other public Use. The Damage the Owner of such Lands, on or through which any such public thing shall be made, shall Receive thereby shall be valued, and satisfaction made, by such ways as the grand Council shall appoint. The twelve Assistants belonging to this Court shall be called Surveyors.

45. The Chamberlain's Court, consisting of a proprietor and his six Councillors, called Vice-Chamberlains, shall have the Care of all Ceremonies, Precedency, Heraldry, Reception of public Messengers, Pedi-

[2] The passage in angle brackets is not in the 1682 printed copy with which this manuscript was collated; it appears to be an accidental insertion of a passage occurring a few lines below it.

grees; the Registry of all Births, Burials, and Marriages; Legitimation and all Cases concerning Matrimony or arising from it; and shall, also, have power to regulate all fashions, Habits, Badges, Games, and Sports. To this Court, also, it shall belong to Convocate the Grand Council. The twelve Assistants belonging to this Court shall be called Provosts.

46. All Causes belonging to, or under the Jurisdiction of, any of the Proprietors' Courts shall in them respectively to be tried and Ultimately Determined, without any further Appeal.

47. The Proprietors' Courts shall have a power to mitigate all Fines and suspend all executions in Criminal Causes, either before or after Sentence, in any of the other inferior Courts respectively.

48. In all Debates, Hearings, or Trials in any of the Proprietors' Courts, the twelve assistants belonging to the said Courts Respectively shall have liberty to be present, but shall not interpose unless their Opinions be required, nor have any Vote at all; but their Business shall be, by the Direction of the respective Courts, to prepare such Business as shall be committed to them; as also, to bear such Offices and dispatch such Affairs, either where the Court is Kept or elsewhere, as the Court shall think fit.

49. In all the Proprietors' Courts, the Proprietors and any three of his Councillors shall make a Quorum; provided always, that, of the better dispatch of Business, it shall be in the power of the Palatine's Court to direct what sorts of Causes shall be heard and Determined by a Quorum of any three.

50. The Grand Council shall consist of the Palatine, and seven Proprietors, and the forty two Councillors of the Several Proprietors' Courts; who shall have power to Determine any Controversies that may arise between any of the Proprietors' Courts about their Respective Jurisdictions, or between the Members of the Same Court about their Manner and Methods of Proceedings; To make Peace and War, Leagues, Treaties, etc., with any of the neighbour Indians; To Issue out their general Orders to the Constable and Admiral's Courts for the Raising, Disposing, or Disbanding the Forces, by Land or by Sea.

51. The Grand Council shall prepare all Matters to be proposed in Parliament. Nor shall any Matters whatsoever be proposed in Parliament, except as in part 66, but what has first passed the Grand Council; which, after having been read three several days in the Grand Council, and there

carried by majority of Votes, shall be proposed to the Parliament, and in such Proposal it shall not be necessary to have the Consent of the Palatine's Court; which Law so proposed by the Grand Council, having been read three several days in Parliament, shall, by majority of Votes, be there passed or rejected.

52. The Grand Council shall always be Judges of all Causes and Appeals that concern the Palatine, or any of the Lords Proprietors, or any Councillor of any proprietors' Court in any Cause which otherwise should have been Tried in the Court in which the said Councillor is Judge himself.

53. The Grand Council, by their Warrants to the Treasurer's Court, shall dispose of all the Money Given by the Parliament and by them directed to any particular public Use.

54. The Quorum of the Grand Council shall be Thirteen, whereof a proprietor, or his deputy, shall be always one.

55. The Grand Council shall meet the first Tuesday in every Month, and as much oftener as either [they] shall think fit or they shall be Convocated by the Chamberlain's Court.

56. The Palatine, or any of the Lords Proprietors, shall have power, under Hand and Seal, to be Registered in the grand Council, to make A Deputy, who shall have the same power, to all intents and purposes, as he himself who deputes him, except in Confirming Acts of Parliament, as in part 76, and except, also, in nominating and choosing Landgraves and Caciques, as in part 10. All such Deputations shall cease and determine at the end of four years, and at any time shall be revocable at the pleasure of the Deputator.

57. No Deputy of any proprietor shall have any power whilst the Deputators are in any part of Carolina, except the proprietor whose Deputy he is be A Minor.

58. During the Minority of any Proprietor, his Guardian shall have power [to] Constitute and appoint his Deputy.

59. The eldest of the Lords proprietors who were Proprietors the first of March, one thousand six hundred sixty and nine, who shall be personally in Carolina shall of course be the palatine's deputy; and if no such proprietor be in Carolina, he that has been Longest a proprietor and is in Carolina, and of the Age of Twenty one years, shall be his deputy;

but after the year one thousand Seven hundred, and the decease of those that were proprietors the first of March, one thousand six hundred sixty and nine, the eldest man of the then Lords proprietors shall be always the Palatine's Deputy; but if no proprietor be in Carolina, he shall choose his deputy out of the Heirs Apparent of any of the Proprietors, if any such be there; and if there be no Heir Apparent of any of the Lords Proprietors, above one and twenty years old, in Carolina, then he shall choose for Deputy any one of the Landgraves or Caciques of the Grand Council; and till he have, by Deputation, under hand and Seal, chosen any one of the forementioned Heirs Apparent or Landgraves to be his deputy, the eldest Man of the Landgraves, and for want of a Landgrave, the eldest man of the Caciques, who shall be personally in Carolina shall of course be his Deputy.

60. Each Proprietor's Deputy shall be always one of his own Six Councillors respectively; and in case any of the Proprietors has not, in his absence out of Carolina, a Deputy, Commissioned under his hand and seal, the eldest Nobleman of his Court shall of course be his Deputy.

61. In every County there shall be A Court, consisting of A sheriff and four Justices of the County, for every precinct one. The sheriff shall be an Inhabitant of the County and have at least five hundred Acres of Freehold within the said County; and the Justices shall be inhabitants and have, each of them, five hundred acres Apiece Freehold within the Precinct for which they serve respectively. These five shall be Chosen and Commissioned from time to time by the Palatine Court.

62. For any personal Causes exceeding the value of two hundred Pounds sterling, or in title of Land, or in any Criminal Cause, either Party, upon paying twenty pounds Sterling to the Lords proprietors' use, shall have Liberty of Appeal from the County Court unto the Respective Proprietors' Court.

63. In every precinct there shall be A Court, Consisting of a Steward and four Justices of the Precinct, being inhabitants and having three hundred Acres of Freehold within the said Precinct; who shall Judge all Criminal Causes, except for Treason, Murder, or any other offences punishable with death and except all Criminal Causes of the Nobility; shall Judge, also, all Civil Causes whatsoever, and in all personal Actions not exceeding fifty Pound Sterling without appeal; but where the Cause shall exceed that Value, or concern a [Title of Land, and in all Criminal Causes, there, either Party, upon] paying five pounds

Sterling to the Lord Proprietors' use, shall have liberty of Appeal to the County Court.

64. No Cause shall be Tried twice in any one Court, upon any reason or pretence whatsoever.

65. For Treason, Murder, and all other Offences punishable with death, there shall be A Commission, Twice a year at least, granted unto one or more Members of the Grand Council or Colleges, who shall come as itinerant Judges to the Several Counties, and, with the Sheriff and four Justices, shall hold Assizes to Judge all such Causes; but upon paying of fifty pounds sterling to the Lords proprietors' use, there shall be liberty of Appeal to the respective Proprietors' Court.

66. The Grand Jury at the Several Assizes shall, upon their Oaths, and under their Hands and Seals, deliver in to the itinerant Judges a Presentment of Such Grievances, Misdemeanors, Exigencies, or defects which they think necessary for the Public good of the County; which Presentment shall, by the itinerant Judges, at the end of their Circuit, be delivered in to the Grand Council at their next Sitting; and whatsoever therein concerns the Execution of Laws already made, the Several proprietors' Courts, in the Matters belonging to each of them respectively, shall take Cognizance of it, and give such order about it as shall be effectual for the due Execution of the Laws; whatever concerns the making of any new Laws shall be referred to the Several Respective Courts to which the Matter belongs, and be by them prepared and brought to the Grand Council; and if the major part of the Grand Juries of the Respective Counties shall present any thing as necessary to be passed into a Law and the Grand Council does not propose the Same to the Parliament [at their first Sitting which shall happen six Months after such Presentment] made by the Major part of the Grand Juries, then it shall be Lawful to be proposed in any of the Chambers of Parliament, and having been there carried three several days by majority Votes, shall be proposed in Parliament, to be Passed into a bill as in other Cases.

67. For terms, there shall be Quarterly such a certain number of days, not exceeding one and twenty at any one time, as the several respective Courts shall appoint. The time for the beginning of the Term in the Precinct Court shall be the first Monday in January, April, July, and October; in the County Court, the first Monday in February, May, August, and November; and in the Proprietors' Courts, the first Monday in March, June, September, and December.

68. In the Precinct Court, no Man shall be a Juryman under fifty Acres of Freehold. In the County Court, or at the Assizes, no Man shall be a Grand Juryman under three hundred Acres freehold, and [no Man] shall be A Petty Juryman under two hundred Acres of Freehold. In the Proprietor Courts, no man shall be a Juryman under five hundred Acres of Freehold.

69. Every Jury shall consist of twelve Men; and it shall not be necessary they should all Agree, but the Verdict shall be according to the Majority.

70. It shall be a base and Vile thing to Plead for money or Reward; nor shall any one, except he be A near Kinsman, not farther off than Cousin-German to the Party Concerned, be Permitted to Plead another Man's Cause till, before the Judge in open Court, he has taken An Oath that he does not Plead for Money or Reward, nor has nor will Receive, nor directly nor indirectly Bargained with the Party, whose Cause he is going to Plead, for money or any other reward for pleading his Cause.

71. There shall be A Parliament, consisting of the Proprietors, or their Deputy, the Landgraves and Caciques, and one Freeholder out of every Precinct, to be chosen by the freeholders of the said Precinct respectively; they shall Sit all together in one Room, and have every Member one Vote.

72. No Man shall be chosen a Member of Parliament who has less than five hundred Acres of Freehold within the precinct for which he is chosen; nor shall any have a Vote in choosing the said Member that has less than fifty Acres of Freehold within the said precinct.

73. A new Parliament shall be Assembled the first Monday of the Month of November every Second year, and shall meet and sit in the Town they Last sat in, without any Summons, unless by the Palatine's Court they be Summoned to meet at any other Place; and if there shall be any occasion of A Parliament in their Intervals, it shall be in the Power of the Palatine's Court to Assemble them in forty Days' Notice, and at such time and place as the said Court shall think fit; and the Palatine's court shall have Power to Dissolve the said Parliament when they shall think fit.

74. At the Opening of every Parliament, the first thing that shall be done shall be the Reading of these Fundamental Constitutions, which the Palatine, and Proprietors, and the Rest of the Members then present

shall Subscribe. Nor shall any Person whatsoever Sit or Vote in the Parliament till he has, that Session, Subscribed these Fundamental Constitutions in A Book Kept for that purpose by the Clerk of the Parliament.

75. In order the due election of Members for the Biennial Parliament, it shall be lawful for the freeholders of the respective Precincts to meet the [first] Tuesday in September every two years, in the Same Town or Place that they Last met in, to choose Parliament-men, and there Choose those members that are to Sit the next November following, unless the Steward of the Precinct shall, by sufficient notice thirty days before, appoint Some other place for their Meeting in order to the Election.

76. No Act or Order of Parliament shall be of any Force unless it be Ratified in open Parliament, during the Same Session, by the Palatine, or his deputy, and three more Lords Proprietors, or their deputies; and then not to continue Longer in force but until the Next Biennial Parliament, unless in the mean time it be Ratified under the hands and Seals of the Palatine himself and three more of the Lords Proprietors themselves, and, by their Order, published at the Next biennial Parliament.

77. Any Proprietor, or his deputy, may enter his Protestation against any Act of Parliament, before the Palatine or his Deputy's Consent be given as aforesaid, if he shall conceive the Said Act to be contrary to this Establishment or any of these Fundamental Constitutions of the Government; and in such case, after a full and free Debate, the several Estates shall retire into four Several Chambers, the Palatine and Proprietors into one, the Landgraves into another, the Caciques into another, and those Chosen by the Precincts unto A fourth; and if the major part of any of the four Estates shall Vote that the Law is not agreeable to the Fundamental Constitutions of the Government, then it shall pass no further, but be as if it had never been proposed.

78. The Quorum of the Parliament shall be one half of those who are members and capable of sitting in the house that Present Session of Parliament. The Quorum of each of the Chambers of Parliament shall be one half of the Members of that Chamber.

79. To avoid multiplicity of Laws, which by degrees always Change the Right Foundations of the Original Government, all acts of Parliament, in whatsoever Form Passed or Enacted, shall, at the end of

A hundred years after the enacting, respectively cease and determine of themselves, and, without any Repeal, become null and Void, as if no such Act or Laws had ever been made.

80. Since multiplicity of Comments, as well as of Laws, have great inconveniences, and serve only to obscure and perplex, all manner of Comments and expositions on any part of these Fundamental Constitutions, or any part of the Common or Statute law of Carolina, are absolutely Prohibited.

81. There shall be a Registry in every Precinct, wherein shall be Enrolled all Deeds, Leases, Judgements, Mortgages, and other Conveyances which may Concern any of the Land within the said Precincts; and all such Conveyances not so Entered or Registered shall not be of force against any person nor Party to the said Contract or Conveyance.

82. No man shall be Register of any Precinct who has not at least three hundred Acres of Freehold within the said Precinct.

83. The Freeholders of every Precinct shall nominate three Men, out of which three the Chief Justice's Court shall Choose and Commission one to be Register of the said Precinct, whilst he well behave himself.

84. There shall be A Registry in every Seigniory, Barony, and Colony, wherein shall be Recorded all the Births, Marriages, and Deaths that shall happen within the Respective Seigniories, Baronies, and Colonies.

85. No Man shall be Register of a Colony that has not above fifty Acres of Freehold within the said Colony.

86. The time of every one's Age that is born in Carolina shall be reckoned from the day that his Birth is Entered in the Registry, and not before.

87. No Marriage shall be lawful, whatever Contract and Ceremony they have used, till both the Parties mutually own it before the Register of the Place where they were married, and he register it, with the Names of the Father and Mother of each Party.

88. No Man shall administer to the Goods, or have right to them, or enter upon the Estate, of any Person deceased till his death be registered in the Respective Registry.

89. He that does not enter in the Respective Registry the Birth or death of any Person that is born and dies in his house or Ground shall pay to the said Register one shilling per Week for each such Neglect, reckoning from the time of each Birth or death respectively to the time of Registering it.

90. In like manner, the Births, Marriages, and deaths of the Lords Proprietors, Landgraves, and Caciques shall be Registered in the Chamberlain's Court.

91. There shall be in every Colony one Constable, to be chosen annually by the Freeholders of the Colony; His estate shall be above a hundred Acres of Freehold within the said Colony; and such subordinate Officers appointed for his Assistance as the County Court shall find Requisite, and shall be established by the said County Court; the election of the Subordinate annual Officers shall be also in the Freeholders of the Colony.

92. It being of great consequence to the Plantation that Port-Towns should be built and preserved, Therefore, whosoever shall lade or unlade any Commodity at any other Place but A Port-Town shall forfeit to the Lord Proprietors for each Ton So Laden or unladen the Sum of ten Pound Sterling, except only such Goods as the Palatine's Court shall License to be Laden or unladen elsewhere.

93. The first Port-Town upon every River shall be in A Colony, and be A Port-Town for ever.

94. No Man shall be permitted to be a Freeman of Carolina, or to have any estate or habitation within it, that does not acknowledge a God, and that God is publicly and solemnly to be worshipped, and that there is a future being after this Life.

95. As the Country comes to be sufficiently Planted and distributed into fit Divisions, it shall belong to the Parliament to take care for the Building of Churches and for the Public maintenance of Divines, to be employed In the exercise of Religion according to the Church of England, which, being the Religion of the Government of England, it alone shall be allowed to receive public maintenance by Grant of Parliament.

96. But Since the Natives of that place, who will be concerned in our Plantation, are utterly strangers to Christianity, whose Idolatry, Ignorance, or Mistake gives us no right to expel or use them ill; and those

who remove from other parts to plant there will unavoidably be of different Opinions Concerning Matters of Religion, the liberty whereof they will expect to have Allowed them, and it will not be reasonable for us, on this account, to keep them out; that Civil Peace may be maintained amidst the diversity of Opinions, and our agreement and Compact with all men may be faithfully observed, the Violation whereof, upon what pretence soever, cannot be without great Offence to Almighty God, and great Scandal to the true Religion, which we profess; and Also, that Jews, Heathens, and other dissenters from the Purity of Christian Religion may not be scared and kept at a distance from it, but, by having an opportunity of acquainting themselves with the truth and reasonableness of its Doctrines, and the Peaceableness and Inoffensiveness of Its profession, may, by good usage and persuasion, and all those Convincing Methods of gentleness and meekness suitable to the Rules and designs of the gospel, be won over to Embrace and unfeignedly receive the truth: Therefore, any Seven or more Persons agreeing in Religion Shall Constitute A Church or Profession, to which they shall give some name to distinguish It from others.

97. The Terms of Admittance and Communion with any Church or Profession shall be written in a book and therein be Subscribed by all the Members of the Said Church or Profession; which Book shall be kept by the Public Register of the Precinct where they Reside.

98. The time of every one's Subscription and admittance shall be dated in the said Book, or Religious Record.

99. In the Terms of Communion of every Church or Profession, these following be three, without which no Agreement or assembly of Men upon Pretence of Religion shall be accounted a Church or profession within these Rules:

1. That there is A God.
2. That God is publicly to be worshipped.
3. That it is Lawful, and the Duty of every man, being thereunto Called by those that Govern, to bear Witness to the Truth; and every Church and Profession shall, in their terms of Communion, set down the External way whereby they witness a truth as in the Presence of God, whether it be by Laying hands on or kissing the Bible, as in the Church of England, or holding up the hand, or any other sensible way.

100. No Person above seventeen years of age shall have any benefit or protection of the Law, or be Capable of any place of Profit or Hon-

our, who is not A member of some Church or Profession, having his name Recorded in some one, and but one Religious Record at once.

101. No Person of any other Church or Profession shall disturb or molest any Religious Assembly.

102. No person whatsoever shall speak any thing in their Religious Assembly irreverently or seditiously of the Government or Governors or of State Matters.

103. Any person Subscribing the terms of Communion in the record of the said Church or Profession before the Precinct Register and any five Members of the said church or Profession shall be thereby made A Member of the said Church or Profession.

104. Any Person striking out his own name out of any Religious Record, or his name being struck out by any Officer thereunto authorized by each Church or Profession [respectively, shall cease to be a Member of that Church or Profession.]

105. No man shall use any Reproachful, Reviling, or abusive Language against the Religion of any Church or Profession, that being the Certain way of disturbing the Peace, and of hindering the Conversion of any to the truth, by engaging them In Quarrels and Animosities, to the hatred of the Professors and that Profession, which otherwise they might be brought to Assent to.

106. Since Charity obliges us to wish well to the Souls of all men, and Religion ought to alter nothing in any man's Civil Estate or Right, it shall be Lawful for slaves, as well as others, to enter themselves and be of what Church or profession any of them shall think best, and thereof be as Fully members as any Freeman. But yet, no Slave shall hereby be exempted from that Civil dominion his Master has over him, but in all other things in the Same State and Condition he was in before.

107. Assemblies, upon what pretence soever of Religion, not observing and performing the above Said Rules shall not be esteemed as Churches, but unlawful Meetings, and be punished as other Riots.

108. No person whatsoever shall disturb, molest, or persecute another for his speculative Opinions in Religion or his way of worship.

109. Every Freeman of Carolina shall have absolute Power and authority over Negro Slaves, of what Opinion or Religion Soever.

110. No Cause, whether Civil or Criminal, of any Freeman Shall be Tried in any Court of Judicature without A Jury of his peers.

111. No person whatsoever shall hold or Claim any Land in Carolina, by purchase or gift or otherwise, from the Natives or any other whatsoever, but merely from and under the Lords Proprietors, upon pain of forfeiture of all his estate, Moveable or immoveable, and perpetual Banishment.

112. Whosoever shall possess any Freehold in Carolina, upon what title or Grant soever, shall, at the Farthest, from and after the Year One thousand six hundred eighty nine, pay yearly, unto the Lords Proprietors, for each acre of Land, English Measure, as much fine Silver as is at this Present in one English Penny, or the Value thereof, to be as a Chief [Rent] and Acknowledgment to the Lords Proprietors, their Heirs and Successors, for ever, except such persons with whom the Lords Proprietors have made some other agreement, under their hands and Seals; and it shall be Lawful for the Palatine's Court, by their Officers, at any time, to take a new Survey of any man's Lands, not to out him of any part of his Possession, but that, by such a Survey, the Just number of Acres he possesses may be Known, and the Rents thereupon due may be paid by him.

113. All Wrecks, Mines, Minerals, Quarries of Gems and Precious stones, with Pearl-fishing, Whale-fishing, and one half of All Ambergris, by whomsoever found, shall wholly belong to the Lords Proprietors.

114. All Revenues and Profits belonging unto the Lords Proprietors, except for Lands and Rents sold in common, shall be divided into ten parts, whereof the Palatine shall have three, and each Proprietor one; but if the Palatine shall Govern by a Deputy, his deputy shall have one of those three tenths, and the Palatine the other two tenths.

115. All inhabitants and Freemen of Carolina above seventeen years of Age and under Sixty shall be bound to bear Arms and Serve as Soldiers whenever the Grand Council shall find it necessary.

116. A true Copy of these Fundamental Constitutions shall be kept in a great Book by the Register of the Precinct, to be Subscribed before the said Register. Nor shall any person, of what Condition or Degree soever, above Seventeen years of age, have any estate in Carolina, or Protection or benefit of the Law there, who has not, before a Precinct Register, Subscribed these Fundamental Constitutions in this form:

117. I, A. B., do promise to bear Faith and true Allegiance to our Sovereign Lord King Charles the Second, his Heirs and Successors; and will be true and faithful to the Palatine and Lord Proprietors of Carolina, their Heirs and Successors; and, with my utmost power, will defend and maintain the Government, according to the Establishment in these Fundamental Constitutions.

118. Whatsoever Alien shall, in this Form, before any Precinct Register, Subscribe these Fundamental Constitutions shall be there [by] Naturalized.

119. In the Same manner shall every person at his Admittance into any office Subscribe these Fundamental Constitutions.

120. Whosoever, by Succession or otherwise, shall come to be Proprietor of Carolina shall not be admitted to exercise any of the Powers of Jurisdictions belonging to a Lord Proprietor of the aforesaid Province, to receive any of the Revenues or Profits belonging to the Same, until he has, either in England or Carolina, subscribed these Fundamental Constitutions in this Form:

I, A. B., do promise to bear Faith and true Allegiance to our Sovereign Lord King Charles the Second, his Heirs and Successors; and will be true and faithful to my Brethren, the Palatine and Lords Proprietors of Carolina, in defence of their Rights; and, with my utmost Power, will maintain the Government, according to the Establishment in these Fundamental Constitutions.

These Fundamental Constitutions, in number a hundred and twenty, and every part thereof, shall be, and Remain, the Sacred and unalterable Form and Rule of Government of Carolina for ever. Witness our hands and Seals, the Twelfth day of January, one thousand six hundred Eighty one.[8]

Rules of Precedency

1. The Lords Proprietors, the eldest in age first, and so in order.
2. The eldest Sons of the Lords Proprietors, the eldest in age first, and so in order.
3. The Landgraves of the Grand Council, he that has been Longest of the Grand Council first, and so in order.
4. The Caciques of the Grand Council, he that has been Longest of the Grand Council first, and so in order.

[8] In present-day reckoning, 1682. From the twelfth century until September, 1752, England used the Julian calendar, according to which the new year began on March 25. The period from January 1 through March 24, therefore, was included in the year preceding that to which it belongs in the Gregorian calendar.

5. The seven Commoners of the Grand Council that have been Longest of the Grand Council, he that has been Longest of the Grand Council first, and so in order.
6. The younger Sons of Proprietors, the eldest first, and so in order.
7. The Landgraves, the eldest in Age first, and so in order.
8. The Seven Commoners who, next to those before mentioned, have been Longest of the Grand Council, he that has been Longest of the Grand Council first, and so in order.
9. The Caciques, the eldest in Age first, and so in order.
10. The Seven remaining Commoners of the Grand Council, he that has been Longest of the Grand Council first, and so in order.
11. The Male Line of the Proprietors.

The rest shall be determined by the Chamberlain's Court.

[Transcribed from a photostatic copy of a manuscript in the British Public Record Office, London. Reference: C. O. 5/287. Photostatic copy deposited in the State Department of Archives and History, Raleigh, North Carolina.]

Version of August 17, 1682

OUR Sovereign Lord the King having, out of his Royal grace and bounty, granted unto us the Province of Carolina, with all the Royalties, Proprieties, Jurisdictions, and privileges of A County Palatine, as Large and ample as the County palatine of Durham, with other great Privileges; for the better Settlement of the government of the said Province, and Establishing the Interest of the Lords proprietors with equality, and without Confusion; and that the Government of this Province may be made most Agreeable to the monarchy under which we Live, and of which this Province is A part; and that we may avoid Erecting A Numerous Democracy: we, the Lords and Proprietors of the Province aforesaid, having [have] [1] agreed to this following form of Government, to be perpetually established amongst us, unto which we do Oblige our selves, our heirs, Assigns, and Successors, in the most binding ways that Can be devised.

1. The Eldest of the Lords proprietors shall be Palatine; and upon the decease of the Palatine, the Eldest of those who were proprietors the first of March, one thousand six hundred sixty and nine, shall succeed him; and when none of them are living, he that has been Longest A Proprietor shall Succeed; but after the year one thousand Seven hundred, and the death of all those who were Proprietors the first of March, one thousand six hundred Sixty and nine, the Eldest man of the then Lords proprietors shall always be Palatine.

2. There shall be Seven Other Chief Offices Erected, viz., the Admiral's, Chamberlain's, Chancellor's, Constable's, Chief Justice's, High Steward's, and Treasurer's; which Places shall be enjoyed by none but the Lords Proprietors, to be assigned at first by lot; and upon the Vacancy of any one of the Seven great offices by death, or otherwise, the Eldest of those who were proprietors the first of March, one thousand six hundred sixty nine, shall have his Choice; and when none of them are Living, he that has been Longest a proprietor shall have his Choice; but after the year one thousand Seven hundred, if none of those that were Proprietors in the year one thousand six hundred sixty and nine are then

[1] All words in square brackets in this transcription were taken from a photostatic copy of a manuscript in the British Public Record Office, labeled "Fourth Constitutions (17, Aug. 1682)." Reference: P. R. O. 30/24/48. This copy does not contain in the final article the date of adoption, and it has other differences in wording from the copy transcribed. These differences, which are slight, are shown only where they seem needed to clarify the copy transcribed.

living, the Eldest man of the then Lords Proprietors shall have his Choice.

3. The Whole province shall be divided into Counties; each County shall Consist of Eight Seigniories, Eight Baronies, and four precincts. Each precinct shall consist of Six Colonies.

4. Each seigniory, Barony, and Colony shall consist of twelve thousand Acres, the Eight seigniories being the Share of the Eight Proprietors, and the Eight Baronies of the Nobility; both which shares, being each of them one fifth part of the Whole, are to be perpetually Annexed, the one to the Proprietors, the other to the hereditary nobility, leaving the Colonies, being three fifths, among the people; that so, in setting out and planting the Land, the Balance of the government may be preserved.

5. At any time before the year one thousand seven hundred and one, any of the Lord proprietors shall have power to Relinquish, alienate, and dispose, to any other person, his proprietorship, and All the seigniories, powers, and interest thereunto belonging, wholly and entirely together, and not otherwise; but after the year one thousand seven hundred, those who are then Lords Proprietors shall not have power to Alienate or make over their Proprietorship, with the Seigniories and privileges thereunto belonging, or any part thereof, to any person whatsoever, otherwise than as in paragraph 17, but it shall all descend unto their heirs male; and for want of heirs Male, it shall all descend on that Landgrave or Cacique of Carolina who is descended of the Next heir female of the said proprietor; and for want of Such heirs, it shall all descend on the Next heir General; and for want of Such heirs, the Remaining seven Proprietors shall, upon the vacancy, Choose a Landgrave to Succeed the deceased proprietor, who being Chosen by the majority of the Surviving Proprietors, he and his heirs Successively shall be Proprietors as full, to all intents and Purposes, as any of the Rest.

6. That the number of Eight proprietors may be constantly Kept, if, upon the Vacancy of any Proprietorship, the Seven Surviving Proprietors shall not choose A landgrave to be A Proprietor before the Second Biennial Parliament after the Vacancy, then the Next Biennial Parliament but one after such Vacancy shall have power to Choose any landgrave to be A Proprietor.

7. Whosoever after the year one thousand Seven hundred, Either by Inheritance or Choice, shall succeed any Proprietor in his proprietor-

ship, and Seigniory thereunto belonging, shall be Obliged to take the name and Arms of that Proprietor whom he succeeds, which from thenceforth shall be the Name and Arms of his family and their posterity.

8. There shall be Just as many Landgraves as there are counties, and twice as many Caciques, and no more. These shall be the Hereditary Nobility of the province, and, by Right of their dignity, be members of Parliament. Each Landgrave shall have four Baronies, Each Cacique two Baronies, Hereditarily and unalterably settled upon and Annexed to the said dignity.

9. The first landgraves and Caciques of the twelve first Counties to be planted shall be nominated thus: that is to say, of the twelve Landgraves, the Lord Proprietors shall, Each of them Separately, for himself, nominate and Choose one, and the Remaining four Landgraves of the first twelve shall be nominated and chosen by the Palatine's Court; in the like manner, of the twenty four first Caciques, Each Proprietor, for himself, shall Nominate and Choose two, and the remaining eight shall be nominated and Chosen by the Palatine's Court; and when the twelve first Counties shall be planted, the Lords Proprietors shall again, in the Same manner, nominate and Choose twelve more Landgraves and twenty four Caciques for the twelve next Counties to be planted, that is to say, two thirds of Each number by the Single Nomination of Each Proprietor for himself, and the Remaining one third by the Joint election of the palatine's Court; and so Proceed, in the Same manner, till the whole province of Carolina be settled out and planted according to the proportions in these fundamental Constitutions.

10. Any Landgrave or Cacique, at any time before the year one thousand seven hundred and one, shall have power to Alienate, sell, or make over, to any other person, his dignity, with the Baronies thereunto belonging, all entirely together; but after the year one thousand seven hundred, no Landgrave or Cacique shall have power to Alienate, sell, make over, or let the Hereditary Baronies of his dignity, or any part thereof, otherwise than as in paragraph 17, but they shall entirely, with the dignity thereto belonging, descend unto his heir male; and for want of heirs male, all entirely and undivided, to the next heir general; and for want of Such heirs, shall devolve into the hands of the Lords Proprietors.

11. That the due number of Landgraves and Caciques may be always kept up, If, upon the devolution of any Landgraveship or Cacique-

ship, the palatine's Court shall not settle the devolved dignity, with the Baronies thereunto annexed, before the Second biennial Parliament after such devolution, the next Biennial Parliament but one after such devolution shall have power to make any one Landgrave or Cacique in the Room of him, who dying without heirs, his dignity and Baronies Devolved.

12. No one person shall have more than one dignity, with the Seigniories or Baronies thereunto belonging; but whensoever it shall happen that any one who is already Proprietor, Landgrave, or Cacique shall have any of these dignities descend to him by Inheritance, it shall be at his choice to keep which of the dignities, with the Lands annexed, he shall like best, but shall leave the other, with the Lands annexed, to be enjoyed by him who, not being his heir apparent, and certain successor to his Present dignity, is next of Blood.

13. Whosoever, by right of inheritance, shall come to be Proprietor, Landgrave, or Cacique shall take the name and arms of his predecessor in that dignity, to be from thenceforth the name and arms of his family and their posterity.

14. Since the dignity of proprietors, Landgraves, or Caciques cannot be divided, and the Seigniories or Baronies thereunto annexed must forever, all entirely, descend with and accompany that dignity, whresoever, for want of heirs male, it shall descend on the Issue female, the Eldest daughter and their [her] heirs shall be preferred, and in the inheritance of those dignities, and in the Seigniories or Baronies annexed, there shall be no Coheirs.

15. In Every Seigniory, Barony, and manor, the Respective Lord Shall have power, in his own name, to hold Court leet there, for trying all causes, both civil and criminal; but where it shall concern any person being no Inhabitant, vassal, or Leetman of the said Seigniory, Barony, or manor, he, upon paying down of forty shillings to the Lords Proprietors' use, shall have appeal from the Seigniory or Barony Court to the County Court, and from the Manor Court to the Precinct Court.

16. Every Manor shall consist of not less than three thousand acres and not above twelve thousand acres in one entire Piece and colony; but any three thousand acres or more in one piece and the possession of one man shall not be a manor unless it be constituted a manor by the grant of the Palatine's Court.

17. The Lords of Seigniories and Baronies shall have power only of granting Estates, not Exceeding three Lives or thirty one years, in two thirds of the said Seigniories or Baronies, and the Remaining one third shall be always demesne.

18. Any Lord of A Manor may alien, sell, or dispose, to any other Person, and his heirs, forever, his manor, all entirely together, with all the Privileges and leetmen thereunto belonging, so far forth as any other colony lands; but no grant of any part thereof, either in fee or for any longer term than three lives or one and twenty years, shall be good against the next heir.

19. No Manor, for want of Issue Male, shall be divided amongst Coheirs, but the manor, if there be but one, shall all entirely descend to the eldest Daughter and her heirs; if there be more manors than one, the Eldest daughter first shall have her choice, the Second next, and so on, beginning again at the Eldest, till all the manors be taken up; that so, the Privileges which belong to the manors being Indivisible, the Lands of the manors to which they are annexed may be kept entire, and the manor not lose those Privileges, which upon Parcelling out to several owners must necessarily cease.

20. Every lord of a manor, within his manor, shall have all the powers, Jurisdictions, and privileges which A Landgrave or Cacique has in his Baronies.

21. In Every Seigniory, Barony, and Manor, all the leetmen shall be under the Jurisdiction of the Respective Lord of the Said Seigniory, Barony, or Manor, without appeal from him; nor shall any leetman or leetwoman have liberty to go off from the Land of their Particular Lords and live any where else without licence obtained from their said Lord, under hand and seal.

22. All the Children of leetmen shall be leetmen, and so to all generations.

23. No man shall be capable of having A Court leet or leetmen but A Proprietor, Landgrave, Cacique, or lord of A manor.

24. No man shall be A leetman but such as voluntarily enters himself leetman in the County Court, in Open Court, and there so registers himself.

25. Whoever is lord of leetmen shall, upon the Marriage of A leetman or leetwoman of his, give them ten Acres of Land for their Lives,

they paying to him therefor not more than one eighth part of all the yearly produce and growth of the said ten acres.

26. No Landgrave or Cacique shall be tried for any criminal cause in any but the Chief Justice's Court, and that by A Jury of his peers, drawn by lot out of all the Nobility, after the manner of other Juries; but when there is not A Sufficient number of the nobility in Carolina, then the Jury for the trial of any Landgrave or Cacique shall be made up by Lot with such of the Commons as are qualified to Serve as Jury men in the proprietors' Court.

27. There shall be eight supreme Courts, the first, called the Palatine's Court, consisting of the Palatine and the Seven other proprietors; the other Seven Courts of the other Seven great officers shall consist, each of them, of A Proprietor and six Councillors added to him; under each of these latter seven courts shall be a College of twelve assistants; the twelve assistants of the Several colleges shall be chosen: two out of the Landgraves, Caciques, or Eldest Sons of Proprietors, by the Palatine's Court; Two out of the Landgraves, by the Landgraves' Chamber; Two out of the Caciques, by the Caciques' Chamber; four more of the twelve shall be Chosen by the Commons' Chamber, out of Such as have been or are members of the Parliament, Sheriffs, or Justices of the County Court, or the younger sons of Proprietors, or Eldest Sons of Landgraves or Caciques; the two other shall be chosen by the palatine's Court out of the Same sort of Persons out of which the Commons' Chamber is to Choose.

28. Out of these Colleges shall be chosen, at first by the palatine's Court, six Councillors to be Joined with Each Proprietor in his Court; of which six, one shall be of those who were Chosen into any of the Colleges by the Palatine's Court out of the Landgraves, Caciques, or Eldest Sons of proprietors; One out of those who were Chosen by the Landgraves' Chamber; and one out of those who were Chosen by the Caciques' Chamber; two out of those who were Chosen by the Commons' Chamber; one out of those who were Chosen by the Palatine's court out of the Proprietors' younger Sons, or eldest sons of Landgraves, Caciques, or commons qualified as aforesaid.

29. When it shall happen that any Councillor dies or is removed, and thereby there is A Vacancy, he that has been Longest A Councillor in any of the Proprietors' courts, of the Same degree and choice the other was of whose vacant place is to be filled up, shall have his Choice,

whether he will Remove into the place of the person that is dead or Removed; but if he Refuse to Remove, the next in Seniority of the Same degree and choice shall have his choice; and so of course the Rest in Order; and the last Remaining vacant place in any of the foresaid Proprietors' Courts shall be filled up by him that has been longest of any of the Colleges, being of the Same degree and choice with him that is dead or Removed; and he that is next of Seniority in the Same degree and choice shall have power to Remove himself, if he please, into the College where any place shall be vacant; and so of course the rest, as in case of Councillors; but the Last remaining vacant place in any college shall be filled up by the Same Choice and out of the Same degree of Persons that he was of who is dead or Removed; no place shall be Vacant in any of the Proprietors' courts or Colleges longer than the next session of Parliament.

30. No Man being a member of the grand council or of any of the seven colleges shall be turned out but for misdemeanor, by the Vote of three fifths of the grand council, three several days, or by sentence in parliament, as in paragraph 81; and the vacancy of the Person so put out shall be filled as is Provided in case of the death of any councillor; but it is not hereby to be understood that the grand council has any power to turn out any one of the Lords Proprietors, or their deputies, the Lords Proprietors having in themselves an inherent Original right.

31. All elections in the parliament, in the several Chambers of the Parliament, and in the grand council shall be passed by balloting.

32. The Palatine's Court shall consist of the Palatine and the Seven other Proprietors, wherein nothing shall be acted without the presence and consent of the Palatine, or his deputy, and three other of the Proprietors, or their deputies. This Court shall have power to call parliaments, to make Election of all Officers in the Proprietors' dispose, to nominate and appoint port towns, and, with the consent of the grand council, to pardon all offences, except of such Persons as are for maladministration of any public charge condemned or any way sentenced by the parliament, whose sentence on such malfactors no body shall have power to suspend, remit, or mitigate but the parliament itself; and also, shall have power, by their orders to the treasurer, to dispose of all public treasure, excepting money granted by the Parliament and by them directed to some Particular public use; and also, shall have a Negative upon all acts, orders, and votes of the grand Council and the parliament, except in Judgments and Judicial proceedings as in paragraph 6, 11, 30, and 81;

and shall have power to displace any officer of the militia; and shall have all the powers granted to the Lords Proprietors by their patent from Our Sovereign Lord the King, except in such things as are Limited by these fundamental Constitutions.

33. The Palatine himself, or his Vice palatine or Deputy, when he in Person shall be either in the Army or in any of the Proprietors' Courts, shall then have the power of General or of that Proprietor in whose Court he is then present; and the Proprietor in whose Court the Palatine, or his deputy, then presides shall, during his presence there, be but as one of the Council.

34. The Chancellor's Court, consisting of one of the Proprietors and his six Councillors, who shall be called Vice chancellors, shall have the Custody of the seal of the Palatinate, under which all charters, of Lands or otherwise, Commissions, and grants of the Palatine's court shall pass; and it shall not be lawful to put the Seal of the Palatinate to any writing which is not signed by the Palatine, or his deputy, and three other Proprietors, or their deputies; to this Court, also, belongs all state matters, dispatches, and treaties with the neighbour Indians; to this court, also, belongs all invasions of the Law of Liberty of conscience, and all disturbances of the public peace upon Pretence of Religion. The twelve assistants belonging to this Court shall be called Recorders.

35. Whatsoever passes under the seal of the Palatinate shall be registered in that Proprietors' Court to which the matter therein contained belongs.

36. The Chancellor, or his deputy, shall be always speaker in Parliament and President of the Grand Council, and in his and his deputy's absence, one of his Vice Chancellors.

37. The Chief Justice's court, Consisting of one of the Proprietors and his six Councillors, who shall be called Justices of the bench, shall Judge all appeals, in cases both Civil and criminal, except all such cases as shall be under the Jurisdiction and Cognizance of any other of the Proprietors' Courts, which shall be tried in those courts respectively. The government and Regulation of the Registry of writings and Contracts shall belong to the Jurisdiction of this Court. The twelve assistants of this court shall be called Masters.

38. The Constable's Court, consisting of one of the Proprietors and his six Councillors, who shall be called marshalls, shall order and deter-

mine of all military Affairs by land, and all Land forces, arms, ammunition, artillery, Garrisons, and forts, etc., and whatever belongs unto war. His twelve assistants shall be called Masters of the Ordnance.

39. In time of actual war, the Constable, while he is in the army, shall be General of the army, except the Palatine be there in person, or his deputy, who, when present, shall be General, as In paragraph 33.

40. The Admiral's Court, consisting of one of the Proprietors and his six Councillors, called Consuls, shall have the care and Inspection over all ports, moles, and navigable rivers so far as the tide flows; and also, all the public shipping of Carolina, and stores thereunto belonging, and all maritime affairs. This court, also, shall have the power of the court of Admiralty; and Shall have power to constitute Judges in port towns to try cases belonging to law merchant, as shall be most convenient for trade. The twelve assistants belonging to this court shall be called Proconsuls.

41. The Treasurer's court, consisting of a Proprietor and his six Councillors, called under treasurers, shall take care of all matters that concern the Public revenue and treasury. The twelve assistants shall be called auditors.

42. The High steward's court, consisting of a Proprietor and his six Councillors, called Comptrollers, shall have the care of all foreign and domestic trade, manufactures, public Buildings, work houses, high ways, passages By water above the flood of the tide, drains, Sewers and Banks against inundations, Bridges, Post, Carriers, fairs, markets, Corruption or infection of the common Air or water, and all things in order to the Public commerce and health; also, setting out and Surveying of Land; also, setting out and appointing places for towns to be built on in the Precincts, and the Prescribing and determining the figure and bigness of the said towns according to such models as the said Court shall order, Contrary or differing from which models it shall not be lawful for any one to build any town. This Court shall have power, also, to make any public building or any new high way, or enlarge any old high way, upon any man's land whatsoever; as also, to make cuts, channels, banks, locks, and Bridges, for making Rivers navigable, or for draining fens, or any other Public use. The damage the owner of such land, on or through which any such public thing shall be made, shall Receive thereby shall be valued, and satisfaction made, by such ways as the grand Council

shall appoint. The twelve assistants belonging to this Court shall be called Surveyors.

43. The chamberlain's Court, consisting of a Proprietor and six Councillors, called Vice chamberlains, shall have the care of all Ceremonies, Precedency, heraldry, reception of public messengers, Pedigrees; the Registering of all births, burials, and marriages; Legitimation and all cases concerning matrimony or arising from it; and shall, also, have power to regulate all fashions, habits, Badges, games, and sports. To this Court, also, it shall belong to convocate the grand Council. The twelve assistants belonging to this court shall be called Provosts.

44. All Causes belonging to, or under the Jurisdiction of, any of the Proprietors' Courts shall in them respectively be tried and ultimately determined, without any further appeal.

45. The Proprietors' Courts shall have power to mitigate all fines and suspend all Executions in criminal Causes, either before or after sentence, in any of the other inferior courts respectively.

46. In all debates, hearings, and trials in any of the Proprietors' courts, the twelve assistants belonging to the said Courts respectively shall have liberty to be Present, but shall not interpose unless their opinion be required, nor have any Vote at all; but their business shall be, by the direction of the Respective Courts, to Prepare such business as shall be committed to them; as also, to bear such office and to dispatch such Affairs, either where the Court is kept or elsewhere, as the Court shall think fit.

47. In all the Proprietors' Courts, the Proprietor and any three of his Councillors shall make A Quorum; provided always, that, for the Better dispatch of business, it shall be in the Power of the palatine's Court to direct what sort of Causes shall be heard and determined by A Quorum of any three.

48. The Grand Council shall Consist of the Palatine, and seven Proprietors, and the forty two Councillors of the Several Proprietors' Courts; who shall have power to determine any controversy that may Arise between any of the Proprietors' Courts about their respective Jurisdictions, or between the members of the same court about their manner and method of Proceeding; to make peace and war, Leagues, treaties, etc., with any of the neighbour Indians; to Issue out their General orders to the Constable's and admiral's Court for the Raising, dispos-

ing, or disbanding the forces, by Land or by sea, or themselves disband any forces when they see fit, by Proclamation or otherwise; and to Choose the Colonels and other inferior officers and Commanders of the militia or posse of Carolina, and Present them to the Palatine to be Commissioned by him.

49. The grand Council shall always be Judges of all causes and appeals that Concern the Palatine, or any of the Lords Proprietors, or any Councillor of any Proprietors' Court in any cause which otherwise should have been tried in the Court in which the Said Councillor is Judge himself; and their Votes in such Cases shall be by Ballot.

50. The Grand council, by their warrant to the treasurer's court, shall dispose of all the money given by the Parliament and by them directed to any Particular public use.

51. The Quorum of the grand council shall be thirteen, whereof a Proprietor, or his deputy, shall be always one.

52. The Grand council shall meet the first Tuesday in every month, and as much oftener as either they shall think fit or they shall be convocated by the Chamberlain's Court.

53. The Palatine, or any of the lords Proprietors, shall have power, under hand and seal, to be Registered in the grand Council, to make A deputy, who shall have the Same power, to all intents and purposes, as he himself who deputes him, except in Confirming acts of Parliament, as in Paragraph 83, and Except, also, in nominating and Choosing Landgraves and Caciques, as in paragraph 9. All such deputations shall cease and determine at the end of four years, and at any time shall be Revocable at the pleasure of the deputator.

54. No Deputy of any Proprietor shall have any power whilst the deputator is in any part of Carolina, except the Proprietor whose deputy he is be a Minor.

55. During the minority of any proprietor, his Guardian shall have Power to Constitute and appoint his deputy.

56. The Eldest of the Lords Proprietors who were Proprietors the first of March, one thousand six hundred sixty and nine, who shall be personally in Carolina shall of Course be the Palatine's deputy, or vice palatine; and if no such proprietor be in Carolina, he that has been Longest a Proprietor and is in Carolina, and of the age of one and twenty years, shall be the palatine's deputy, or Vice palatine; but after the year

one thousand seven hundred, and the decease of those that were Proprietors the first of March, one thousand six hundred sixty nine, the eldest man of the then Lords Proprietors shall be always Vice Palatine; but if no Proprietor be in Carolina, the Eldest man of the Heirs apparent of any of the Proprietors, that is past twenty one years of age, if any such there be, shall be Vice palatine; and when ever there is a vice palatine as aforesaid, the Palatine shall have power to choose for his deputy as proprietor any one of the Landgraves or Caciques of the Grand council, that so the number of eight may always be Preserved and the Palatine may always have one in Carolina to take care of his business, who shall have the Same power as one of the other Proprietors' deputies, and no more; but if there be no Proprietor in Carolina, nor his heir apparent, as aforesaid, above twenty one years old, then the Palatine shall choose for Vice Palatine, and deputy, any one of the Landgraves or Caciques of the grand Council; and till he have, by deputation, under hand and seal, Chosen any one of the Landgraves or Caciques to be his deputy, the Eldest man of the Landgraves, and for want of a Landgrave, the Eldest man of the Caciques, who shall be Personally in Carolina shall of Course be his deputy.

57. Each Proprietor's deputy shall be always one of his own six Councillors respectively; and in case any of the Proprietors has not, in his absence out of Carolina, a deputy, commissioned under his hand and seal, the Eldest nobleman of his Court shall of course be his deputy; and in case he refuse to act, then the next in age that will.

58. In Every County there shall be a court, consisting of a sheriff and four Justices of the County, for every Precinct one. The sheriff shall be an inhabitant of the County and have at least five hundred Acres of freehold within the said County; and the Justices shall be inhabitants and have, each of them, four hundred [five hundred] Acres apiece freehold within the precinct for which they serve respectively. These five shall be chosen and commissioned from time to time by the Palatine's court.

59. For any personal causes exceeding the value of two hundred pounds sterling, or in title of land, or in any criminal cause, either party, upon paying twenty pounds sterling to the Lords Proprietors' use, shall have liberty of appeal from the County court unto the Respective proprietors' courts.

60. In every Precinct there shall be a Court, consisting of a Steward and four Justices of the precinct, being inhabitants and having three hun-

dred acres of freehold within the said precinct; who shall Judge all criminal causes, except for treason, murder, and any other Offences punishable with death and except all criminal causes of the nobility; and shall Judge, also, all Civil causes whatsoever, and in all personal actions not exceeding fifty pounds sterling without appeal; but where the Cause shall exceed that value, or concern a Title of Land, and in all criminal causes, there, either party, upon paying five pounds sterling to the Lords Proprietors, shall have Liberty of appeal to the County court.

61. No cause shall be twice tried in any one court, upon any reason or Pretense whatsoever.

62. For treason, murder, and all other offences punishable with death, there shall be a commission, twice a year at least, granted unto one or more members of the grand council or colleges, who shall come as Judges Itinerant to the Several counties, and, with the sheriff and four Justices, shall hold assizes to Judge all such causes.

63. The Grand Jury at the Several assizes shall, upon their oath, and under their hands and Seals, deliver unto the Itinerant Judges a presentment of such grievances, misdemeanors, exigencies, or defects which they think necessary for the Public good of the county; which Presentment shall, by the Itinerant Judges, at the end of their Circuit, be delivered in to the grand council at their next sitting; and whatsoever therein concerns the Execution of Laws already made, the Several Proprietors' courts, in the matter belonging to each of them respectively, shall take cognizance of it, and give such order about it as shall be effectual for the due execution of the Laws; but whatever concerns the making of any new Laws shall be Referred unto the several Respective courts to which the matter belongs, and be by them prepared and brought to the grand Council; and if the major part of the grand Juries of the Respective Counties shall present anything as necessary to be passed into a law and the grand council does not propose the Same to the parliament at the first sitting which shall happen Six months after such presentment made by the major part of the grand Juries, then it shall be lawful to be proposed in any of the Chambers of the parliament, and having been there carried three several days by majority of Votes, shall be proposed in parliament, to be passed into a bill as in other cases.

64. For Terms, there shall be quarterly such a certain number of days, not Exceeding One and Twenty at any one time, as the several respective Courts shall appoint. The time for the beginning of the term in

the precinct court shall be the first Monday in February, May, August, and November; in the County Court, the first Monday In January, April, July, and October; and in the Proprietors' court, the first Monday in March, June, September, and December.

65. In the Precinct court, no man shall be a Jury man under fifty acres of freehold; in the County court, or at the assizes, no man shall be A grand Jury man under three hundred acres of freehold, and no man shall be a petty Jury man under two hundred acres of freehold. In the proprietors' Court, no man shall be a Jury man under five hundred acres of freehold.

66. All the names of freeholders who have not less than fifty Acres nor above two hundred in the precinct shall be put into the precinct court bag for Jury men at the precinct court and assizes. All the names of freeholders of Three hundred Acres of Land and upward shall be put into the grand Jury bag for grand Jury men at the County Court and assizes. All the names of the freeholders of five hundred Acres and upwards shall be put into the Proprietors' Court bag, to be Jury men In the Proprietors' Court.

67. At every precinct court, before they Rise, the names of all the freeholders who are to serve as Jury men in the Precinct court, writ in Little pieces of parchment of Equal bigness and rolled up, shall be taken out of the bag and compared with the freeholders' Book, to see that none be omitted and none double; and then all shall be put into a box and shaken together; and then, by a child under ten years old, so many names shall be drawn out as will be sufficient for so many Juries as the Court shall think they shall have need of the next term, who thereupon shall have Summons to attend.

68. The same order shall be observed in drawing Jurors to Serve in the Proprietors' Courts and on grand and petty Juries at the County court and assizes respectively.

69. If there be not freeholders' names enough in any Bag for the Service of Jurors in that Court, it shall be supplied by drawing out of the next superior bag.

70. The Names of those who were summoned to serve any one term and do appear shall again be put into a box at the opening of the term, and in Court, by a child as before, shall be drawn out so many dozens as there are for so many petty Juries; which shall serve in their

turns for the Causes to be heard that day, the first which was drawn first, and so on for the first term; and after that, that Jury to be next taken which gave in its Verdict first; every morning, at the Setting of the Court, the names shall be drawn anew, unless any Jury be not then ready with their Verdict, and then that Jury shall remain the Same until the next day.

71. Each Court shall allot such an allowance to be paid by each party for whom there is a verdict as may be sufficient to defray the Charges of their Journey and attendance honourably.

72. In civil causes, each party shall have Liberty to Challenge when they are called, and before they are sworn, as many of his Jury as he has Just Exception against; and the number shall be made up by drawing new names out of the Jury men of that term who are not then actually upon any Jury.

73. In Criminal Causes of life and death, each prisoner at the Bar shall have liberty to challenge as many without showing Reason as is permitted in England, and as many more as he can show Just reason for; and the number shall be supplied by drawing new names out of the freeholders who, having appeared, are not then upon any Jury.

74. It shall be a base and vile thing to plead for money or reward; nor shall any one, except he be a near kinsman, not farther off than Cousin German to the party concerned, be permitted to plead another man's cause till, before the Judge in open court, he has taken an oath that he does not plead for money or reward, nor has nor will receive, nor directly nor indirectly bargained with the party, whose cause he is going to plead, for money or any other reward for pleading his cause.

75. There shall be a parliament, consisting of the proprietors, or their deputies, the Landgraves and Caciques, and one freeholder out of every precinct, to be chosen by the freeholders of the said precinct respectively; they shall sit all together in one Room, and have every member one Vote.

76. No man shall be chosen a member of parliament which has less than five hundred acres of freehold within the precinct for which he is chosen; nor shall any have a vote in choosing the said member that has Less than fifty acres of freehold within the said precinct.

77. A new parliament Shall be assembled the first Monday of the month of November every Second year, and shall meet and sit in the

town they Last sat in, without any Summons, unless by the Palatine's Court they be summoned to meet at any other place; and if there shall be any Occasion of a parliament in these intervals, it shall be in the power of the palatine's court to assemble them in forty days' notice, and at such time and place as the said Court shall think fit; and the Palatine's court shall have power to dissolve the said parliament at the end of two months, or Sooner if the complaints brought in the first ten days and the bills brought in by the grand council be all dispatched.

78. At the Opening of every parliament, the first thing that shall be done shall be the reading of these fundamental Constitutions, which the Palatine, and the Proprietors, and the Rest of the members then Present shall Subscribe; nor shall any person whatsoever sit or Vote in the parliament till he has, that Session, subscribed these fundamental constitutions in a book kept for that Purpose by the clerk of Parliament.

79. In order to the due Election of members for the Biennial parliament, it shall be lawful for the freeholders of the Respective precincts to meet the first Tuesday in September every two years, in the Same Town or place that they last met in, to choose parliament men, and there, by ballot, choose those members that are to sit next November following, unless the Steward of the precinct shall, by sufficient notice thirty days before, appoint some other place for their meeting in order to the Election.

80. Controversies about election of members of parliament shall be tried in any of the Proprietors' Courts by Juries drawn by Lot out of all uncontroverted members of parliament, as well Noblemen as commons; but nobody's claim against returned members shall be admitted who has not, within three days after the Election, given Notice, under his hand, to the contrary party, upon what heads he intends to proceed in his claim; nor shall any claim be admitted but what is, before the opening of the parliament, put into the grand council, which shall transmit the said Claims to the Several proprietors' Courts, to be tried there as soon as the parliament shall meet, that So, by the ending of Controverted Elections, the house may be quickly Settled; for till that be done, no bills or sentence are to pass in the house; and the time of the two months for the house to sit is to be reckoned to Commence from the Settling all Elections.

81. The Grand council shall prepare all matters of legislature to be proposed in parliament; nor shall any bill or matter to be passed into a

Law, except as in paragraph 63, be proposed in parliament But what has first passed the grand council; which, after having been read three several days in the grand council, and there carried by Majority of Votes, shall be proposed to the parliament, and in such proposal it shall not be necessary for the grand council to have the consent of the Palatine's court; which law or bill so proposed by the grand council shall not be passed but by Reading three several days in open parliament, and upon each reading being consented to by three fifths of the members Present, and after that, another day, read again in the Chamber of the Nobility (who, in the Passing of Bills and Judicial proceedings, shall, both Landgraves and Caciques, make but one Chamber) and the chamber of the Commons, and, in each of these chambers, passed again by the majority. But whatever complaints shall be brought into the Parliament, during the first ten days of their sitting, against any person under the degree of a proprietor, who are not any of them to be liable to any censures in the parliament, in writing and Signed by the person who brings in such complaint, for any Misdemeanor in the Execution of any office the person so complained of has borne or does bear, provided the time of such complaint be not after two biennial parliaments have sat after such fact was committed, the parliament shall have liberty to take Cognizance thereof, although it be not proposed to them by the grand council; and if the party accused has two several days been found guilty of the misdemeanor laid to his charge, by three fifths of the house there present, and afterwards, another day, by the major part of the Chamber of the nobility and the major part of the Chamber of the Commons, the parliament shall then, after the Same manner, two Several days in the whole house and one day in each of the Chambers, Proceed to Vote what punishment he shall undergo for the misdemeanor he has been voted guilty of, and accordingly to sentence him; nor shall it be in the power of the palatine's court, nor any other person or persons in Carolina, but only of the parliament itself, to suspend, remit, or mitigate the Execution of any such sentence; and the parliament shall have liberty to sit until they have determined of all such complaints, provided it be not above two months, after which time it shall be in the power of the palatine's Court to Adjourn, prorogue, or dissolve it; and furthermore, there is not required the consent or concurrence of the Palatine, or any of the Proprietors, in such Judicial proceedings against any person for misdemeanor in any office they have borne, but they shall be valid without it; always provided, that such Sentence extend not to the taking away of Life or member, or be not to turn out any of the Lords proprietors' depu-

ties, who, being entrusted by the Respective Proprietors to see that nothing is done contrary to their interest, are not to be hindered from sitting and Voting as Deputies.

82. No Judgment shall be given in the house against any one, nor sentence passed, when there are Less than sixty members present.

83. No act or order of parliament shall be of any force unless it be ratified in open parliament, during the Same session, by the Palatine, or his deputy, and three more of the Lords proprietors, and [or] their deputies; and then not to continue longer in force but till the next biennial parliament, unless in the mean time it be ratified under the hands and seals of the palatine himself and three more of the Lords Proprietors themselves, and, by their order, published at the Next Biennial Parliament.

84. Any proprietor, or his deputy, or any three members of parliament, may Enter his or their protestation against any act of parliament, before it be passed into a law as aforesaid, if he or they shall conceive the said act to be contrary to this Establishment or any of these fundamental Constitutions of the government; and in such case, after a full and free debate, the several Estates shall retire into four several chambers, the Palatine and proprietors into one, the Landgraves into another, the Caciques into another, and those chosen by the precincts into A Fourth; and if the major part of any of the four Estates shall Vote that the Law is not agreeable to this establishment and these fundamental constitutions of the Government, then it shall pass no further, but be as if it never had been proposed.

85. The Quorum of the parliament shall be half of those who are members and Capable of Sitting in that house that presents the Session [in the House that present Session] of Parliament; the Quorum of Each of the Chambers of the parliament shall be one half of the members of that Chamber.

86. To avoid multiplicity of laws, which by degrees always change the right foundation of the Original Government, all acts of parliament whatsoever, in whatsoever form passed or enacted, shall, at the end of one hundred years after their Enacting, respectively cease and determine of themselves, and, without any Repeal, become null and Void, as if no such acts or laws had ever been made.

87. Since multiplicity of Comments, as well as laws, have great inconveniences, and serve only to Observe [obscure] and perplex, all man-

ner of Comments and Expositions, in writing or print, on any part of these fundamental Constitutions, or any part of the Common or Statute Law of Carolina, are absolutely prohibited.

88. There shall be a registry in every precinct, wherein shall be enrolled all deeds, Leases, Judgments, mortgages, and other conveyances which may concern any of the Land within the said precinct; and all Conveyances not so entered or registered shall not be of force against any person not party to the said Contract or Conveyance.

89. No man shall be Register of any Precinct who has not at least three hundred acres of freehold within the said Precinct.

90. The freeholders of every Precinct shall nominate three men, out of which three the chief Justice's court shall choose and Commission one to be Register of the said precinct, whilst he shall well behave himself.

91. There shall be a Registry in every seigniory, Barony, and Colony, wherein shall be Recorded all the births, marriages, and deaths that shall happen within the Respective Seigniories, Baronies, and Colonies; and in registering births, the name of the father and mother of the Child, and the places where their births were Registered, shall be set down, by which means men's pedigrees will be certainly Kept.

92. No man shall be Register of a Colony that has not above fifty acres of freehold within the said Colony.

93. All marriages performed in Carolina shall be owned by both the parties before the Register of the place where they were married, who thereupon shall Register it, with the names of the father and mother of each party; and whosoever shall neglect to Register his marriage shall forfeit, for every week it remains unregistered, one shilling, Provided it be not the fault of the said Register it be not Registered.

94. No man shall administer to the goods, or have right to them, or enter upon the estate, of any Person deceased till his death be Registered in the respective Registry.

95. He that does not enter into the Respective registry the birth or death of any person that is Born or dies in his house or ground shall pay unto the said Register one shilling per week for each such neglect, reckoning from the time of each birth or death Respectively to the time of Registering it.

96. In like manner, the Births, marriages, and deaths of the Lords Proprietors, Landgraves, and Caciques shall be registered in the Chamberlain's Court.

97. There shall be in every colony one constable, to be chosen annually by the freeholders of the said colony; his estate shall be above one hundred Acres of freehold within the said colony; and such subordinate Officers appointed for assistants at [as] the County Court shall find requisite, and shall be established by the said County Court; the Election of the Subordinate annual officers shall be also in the freeholders of the Colony.

98. It being of great consequence to the plantation that port towns should be built and preserved, therefore, whosoever shall lade or unlade any commodity at any other place but a port town shall forfeit to the Lords proprietors for each Ton so Laden or unladen the Sum of Ten pounds sterling, except only such goods as the Palatine's court shall Licence to be laden or unladen elsewhere.

99. The first port Town upon every River shall be in A colony, and be a port town forever.

100. No man shall be permitted to be a freeman of Carolina, or to have any estate or habitation within it, that does [does not] acknowledge a God, and that God is publicly and solemnly to be worshipped, and that There is a future being after this life, of happiness or misery.

101. As the Country comes to be sufficiently planted and distributed into fit divisions, it shall belong to the parliament to take care of the building of churches and the public maintenance of divines, to be employed in the exercise of Religion according to the Church of England, which being the Religion of the government of England, it alone shall be allowed to receive public maintenance by grant of parliament; which said public maintenance is to arise out of lands or rents assigned voluntarily, contributions, or such other ways whereby no man shall be chargeable to pay out of his particular Estate that is not conformable to the church as aforesaid;[2] but every church or Congregation of Christians, not of the communion of the Church of Rome, shall have power to lay a tax on its own members, not exceeding a penny per acre on their

[2] In the copy with which this manuscript was compared, the passage reads as follows: *which said public Maintenance is to arise out of Lands or Rents assigned, voluntary Contributions, or Such other ways whereby No Man shall be chargeable to pay out of his particular estate that is not conformable to the Church as aforesaid.*

Lands and twelve per head per annum, for the maintenance of their public ministers; and of all money so paid and disbursed they shall keep an account, which the grand council, or any authorized by them, shall have liberty from time to time to Inspect.

102. No ordained minister, or that receives any maintenance as minister of any congregation or Church, shall be member of parliament, or have any civil office, but wholly attend his ministry.

103. But since the Natives of that place, who will be concerned in our plantation, are utterly strangers to Christianity, whose Idolatry, Ignorance, or mistake gives us no right to Expel or use them ill; and those who remove from other parts to plant there will unavoidably be of different opinions concerning matters of Religion, the liberty whereof they will expect to have allowed them, and it will not be Reasonable for us, on this account, to keep them out; that civil peace may be maintained amidst the diversity of opinions, and our agreement and compact with all men may be duly and faithfully observed, the volution [violation] whereof, upon what pretense soever, cannot be without great offence to Almighty God, and great scandal to the true Religion, which we profess; and also, that Jews, heathens, and other dissenters from the purity of Christian Religion may not be scared and kept at a distance from it, but, by having an opportunity of acquainting themselves with the truth and Reasonableness of its doctrine, and the peaceableness and Inoffensiveness of Its professors, may, by good usage and persuasion, and all those Convincing methods of Gentleness and meekness suitable to the Rules and design of the gospel, be won over to embrace and unfeignedly Receive the truth: therefore, any Seven or more persons agreeing in any Religion shall constitute a church or profession, to which they shall give some name to distinguish it from others.

104. The Terms of Communion or admittance with any church or profession shall be written in a book and therein be subscribed by all the members of said church or profession; which book shall be kept by the public Register of the precinct where they reside.

105. The time of Every One's Subscription or admittance shall be dated in the said book, or Religious Record.

106. In the terms of communion of every Church or Profession, these following shall be three, without which no agreement or assembly of men upon pretense of Religion shall be accounted a Church or profession within these Rules:

1. That there is a God.
2. That God is publicly to be worshipped.
3. That it is lawful, and the duty of every man, being thereunto called by those that govern, to bear witness to truth; and that every church or profession shall, in their terms of Communion, set down the External way whereby they witness a truth as in the presence of God, whether it be by laying hands on or kissing the Bible, as in the church of England, or by holding up the hand, or any other sensible way.

107. No person above seventeen years of age shall have any benefit or protection of the law, or be capable of any place of profit or honour, who is not a member of Some church or profession, having his name recorded in Some one, and but one religious Record at once.

108. No person of any other church shall disturb or molest any Religious Assembly.

109. No person whatsoever shall speak anything in their religious assembly irreverently or seditiously of the Government or the Governors or of state matters.

110. Any person subscribing the terms of Communion in the Record of the said Church or profession before the Precinct register and any five members of the said Church or profession shall be thereby made a member of the said church or profession.

111. Any person striking out his name out of any Religious Record, or his name being struck out by any officer thereunto authorized by each church or profession respectively, shall cease to be a member of that church or profession.

112. No man shall use any reproachful, reviling, or abusive language against the Religion of any church or profession, that being the Certain way of disturbing the peace, and of hindering the conversion of any to the truth, by engaging them in quarrels and animosities, to the hatred of the Professors and that profession, which otherwise they might be brought to assent to.

113. Since Charity obliges us to wish well to the Souls of all men, and Religion ought to alter nothing in any man's civil estate or right, it shall be Lawful for Slaves, as well as others, to enter themselves and be of what Church and profession any of them shall think best, and thereof be as full members as any freemen; but yet, no slave shall thereby be Exempted from that Civil dominion his master has over him, but be in all other things in the Same state and condition he was in before.

114. Assemblies, upon what pretense soever of Religion, not observing and performing the above said Rules shall not be esteemed as churches, but unlawful meetings, and be punishable as other Riots.

115. No person whatsoever shall disturb, molest, or persecute another for his Speculative opinions in Religion or his way of worship.

116. No Cause, whether Civil or Criminal, of any freeman shall be tried in any Court of Judicature without a Jury of his peers.

117. No person whatsoever shall hold or claim any Land in Carolina, by Purchase, gift, or otherwise, from the natives or any other whatsoever, but merely from and under the Lords proprietors, upon pain of forfeiture of all his estate, moveable or immoveable, and perpetual Banishment.

118. Whosoever shall possess any freehold in Carolina, upon title or grant soever, shall, at the farthest, from and after the year one thousand six hundred eighty-nine, pay yearly unto the Lords Proprietors for each acre of Land, English measure, as much fine silver as is at this present in one English penny, or the value thereof, to be as chief Rent and acknowledgement to the Lords proprietors, their heirs and successors, forever, except such persons with whom the Lords proprietors have made, or shall make, some other agreement, under their hands and seals; and it shall be Lawful for the Palatine's court, by their officers, at any time, to take a new survey of any man's lands, not to out him of any part of his possession, but that, by such A survey, the Just number of acres he possesses may be known, and the Rent thereupon due may be paid by him.

119. All wrecks, Mines, Minerals, Quarries of Gems and precious stones, with Pearl fishing, whale fishing, and one half of Ambergris, by whomsoever found, shall wholly belong to the Lords Proprietors.

120. All revenues and profits belonging to the Lords Proprietors, except for lands and Rents sold in common, shall be divided into ten parts, whereof the palatine shall have three, and each proprietor one; but if the Palatine shall govern by a deputy or Vice palatine, his deputy or Vice palatine shall have one of those three tenths, and the palatine the other two tenths; and all Lands or mines or other thing whatsoever held in common by the Lords proprietors shall descend to the succeeding proprietors in common, and no benefit be taken by those who outlive the rest by survivorship; but the Respective part of all the Land, mines, and other profits and things that are held in common shall come to the suc-

cessors of that proprietor who is deceased as fully and amply as if the proprietor deceased had conveyed the Same during his life time.

121. Every freeman of Carolina above seventeen years of age and under sixty shall be bound to have and bear arms, and all the freemen, being formed into troops, Companies, and Regiments, shall be at Convenient times mustered and exercised; this militia or posse of the County shall be bound to assist the Civil magistrates or officers in execution of the Laws or keeping the peace; and there must never be in Carolina a select militia, wherein one part of the people shall be armed and the other not, nor any standing forces in pay, except only in such frontier garrisons, with such number of Soldiers in them, as the palatine's court, with the Consent of the grand council and parliament, shall appoint.

122. A true copy of these fundamental constitutions shall be kept in a great book by the Register of every precinct, to be subscribed before the said Register; nor shall any person, of what condition or degree soever, above seventeen years old, have any estate or possession in Carolina, or protection or benefit of the Law there, who has not, before a precinct Register, subscribed these fundamental Constitutions in this form:

I, A. B., do promise to bear faith and true allegiance unto our Sovereign Lord King Charles the Second, his heirs and successors; and will be true and faithful unto the Palatine and Lords Proprietors of Carolina, their heirs and successors; and, with my utmost power, will defend them and their fundamental Constitutions.

123. Whatsoever Alien shall, in this form, before any precinct register, subscribe these fundamental constitutions shall be thereby naturalized.

124. In the Same manner shall every person at his admittance into any office subscribe these fundamental Constitutions.

125. Whosoever, by succession or otherwise, shall come to be a proprietor in Carolina shall not be admitted to exercise any power or Jurisdiction belonging to A lord proprietor of the foresaid province, or receive any of the revenues or profits belonging unto the Same, until he has, either in England or Carolina, subscribed these fundamental constitutions in this form:

I, A. B., do promise to bear faith and true Allegiance to our Sovereign Lord King Charles the Second, his heirs and successors; and will be true and faithful to my Brethren, the Palatine and Lords Proprietors of Carolina, in defence of their Rights; and, with my utmost power, will maintain the government, according to this Establishment in these fundamental Constitutions.

These fundamental Constitutions, in number one hundred twenty six articles, and every part thereof, shall be, and Remain, the sacred and unalterable form and Rule of government of Carolina forever, unless, in the variety of human affairs, any future Exigency should Require any addition or alteration to be made in any part of them; in such case, any new articles confirmed by the hands and seals of all the Proprietors, all the members of Grand Council, all the members of parliament two successive parliaments, shall be added to these constitutions, and from thenceforth to be Esteemed as part of them, to all intents and Purposes. Witness, our hands and Seals, and the great seal of our province, this seventeenth day of August, in the year of our Lord God one thousand six hundred eighty and two.

Rules of Precedency

1. The Lords Proprietors, the eldest in age first, and so in order.
2. The eldest sons of the Lords proprietors, the eldest in age first, and so in order.
3. The Landgraves of the grand council, he that has been longest of the grand council first, and so in order.
4. The Caciques of the grand council, he that has been longest of the grand council first, and so in order.
5. The seven commons of the grand Council, he that has been longest of the grand Council first, and so in order.
6. The youngest Sons of proprietors, the Eldest first, and so in order.
7. The Landgraves, the Eldest in age first, and so in order.
8. The seven Commoners who, next to those before mentioned, have been longest of the grand council, he that has been Longest of the grand council first, and so in order.
9. The Caciques, the eldest in age first, and so in Order.
10. The seven Remaining Commoners of the grand Council, he that has been longest of the grand Council first, and so in order.
11. The male Line of the Proprietors.

The rest shall be determined by the Chamberlain's Court.

Mentioned, that before the Signing and Sealing hereof, these following words were interlined.

In the 13 Line of 42 section (*or Enlarge any old high way*).

In the 3d line of 47 Section (*the power of*).

In the 5 line of the 120 Section (*and the palatine the other two tenths*).

In the 4 line of 122 Section (*or degree soever*).

In the 10 line of the Same Section (*and will be true and faithful to the Palatine and Lords proprietors of Carolina their heirs and Successors*).

Craven Pt.
Albemarle
Bathe for the Lord Carteret
P. Colleton

[Transcribed from a photostatic copy of a manuscript in the British Public Record Office, London. Reference: C. O. 5/287. Photostatic copy deposited in the State Department of Archives and History, Raleigh, North Carolina.]

Version of April 11, 1698

OUR late Sovereign Lord King Charles the Second having, out of his Royal Grace and Bounty, granted unto Us the Province of Carolina, with all the Royalties, Proprieties, Jurisdictions, and Privileges of a County Palatine, as large and ample as the County Palatine of Durham, with other great privileges; for the better Settlement of the Government of the said place, and Establishing the Interest of the Lords Proprietors with Equality, and without Confusion; and that the Government may be made most agreeable to the Monarchy under which we live, and of which this Province is a part; and that we may avoid Erecting a numerous Democracy: We, the Lords Proprietors of the Province aforesaid, with the advice and consent of the Landgraves and Caciques and Commons in this present Parliament assembled, have agreed to this following form of Government, to be perpetually established amongst us, Unto which We do Oblige ourselves, our heirs and Successors, in the most Binding ways that can be devised.

1. THE Proprietors' Court shall consist of the Palatine and Seven Proprietors, wherein nothing shall be acted without the presence and consent of the Palatine and three others of the Lords Proprietors. This Court shall have power to call and Dissolve Parliaments, to pardon all Offences, to make Elections of all Offices in the Proprietors' Disposal, to nominate and appoint Port towns; and also, shall have power, by their order to the Treasurer, to dispose of all public Treasure, Excepting money granted by the Parliament and by them Directed to some particular public Use; and also, shall have a negative upon all Acts, Orders, Votes, and Judgments of the Parliament; and shall have all power granted to the Lords Proprietors by their Patent from our Sovereign Lord the King, Except in such things as are limited by these Fundamental Constitutions.

2. DURING the absence of the Palatine and Proprietors from Carolina, the Governor, Commissionated by the Proprietors, together with their respective Deputies, shall be the Proprietors' Court there, and shall have all the Powers above mentioned, Excepting in pardoning Offences and Constituting Port towns.

3. IN the Proprietors' Court, the Palatine and any Three of the Proprietors, or the Governor and any three of the Proprietors' Deputies, shall make a Quorum.

4. No Deputy of any Proprietor shall have any power whilst the Deputator is in any Part of Carolina, Except the Proprietor whose Deputy he is be a Minor.

5. DURING the Minority of any Proprietor, his Guardian shall have power to Constitute and appoint his Deputy.

6. THERE shall be a Parliament, consisting of the Proprietors, or their Deputies by themselves, the Landgraves, and Caciques in the upper house, and the Freeholders out of every County, to be chosen by the Freeholders of the said Counties respectively, together with the Citizens and Burgesses, to be Elected by the Cities and Boroughs (which shall be hereafter Created), in the lower House.

7. AND since all Power and Dominion is most naturally founded in Property, and that it is reasonable that every man who is Empowered to dispose of the Property and Estate of others should have a Property of his own, whereby he is tied in Interest to the Good and Welfare of that place and Government whereby he is Entrusted with such Power, it is, therefore, Declared and appointed that no person shall be admitted, or shall continue to Sit or vote, in Parliament as a Landgrave who has not actually taken up, and has in his possession, at least ____[1] acres, part of the land granted him in his Patent, and ____ Slaves, or in the possession of his Tenants ____ acres of Land, and whose real and personal Estate shall not be worth at least ____ pounds; nor as a Cacique to sit or vote in parliament who has not actually taken up, and has in his possession, at least ____ acres, part of the land Granted him in his Patent, and ____ Slaves, or in the possession of his Tenants ____ acres of land, and whose real and personal Estate shall not be worth at least ____ pounds.

8. No Person shall be admitted, or continue to sit or vote, in Parliament as a Representative of the Commons of Carolina who is not possessed of at least ____ acres of land, and whose real and personal Estate is not worth ____ pounds.

9. No person shall be capable of giving his voice for the Election of a Member to Serve in Parliament that is not actually possessed of ____ acres of land, and is a Householder, and has a family, and whose real and personal Estate does not amount to ____ pounds.

10. THE present number of the Representatives of the Commons shall be ____, who, as the Country shall Increase, shall also proportion-

[1] A blank in the manuscript is indicated thus: ____.

ably be Increased, if the Commons do so desire, But shall in no future time be Increased beyond one hundred.

11. AND pursuant to that Just Maxim of Government above mentioned, and for the preservation of the Balance of Power according to the proportion of the Property, it is Declared and appointed that the Number of the Representatives of the people to be sent from any County or place shall be more or less according to the charges borne and money paid by each respective Division of the country in the last General assessment foregoing such Election.

12. THE Landgraves and Caciques who compose the upper house shall not at any time Exceed half the number of the Commons.

13. THE Landgraves and Caciques shall be created by the Lords Proprietors' Letters Patents, under their Great Seal, by the Joint Election of the Proprietors, or a Quorum of them; which shall be the Hereditary Nobility of the Province of Carolina, and, by right of their Dignity, be Members of the upper house of Parliament. Each Landgrave shall have ——— acres of land to be taken up in ——— Several Counties, and Each Cacique ——— acres of land to be taken up in ——— Several Counties. And the said honour and dignity shall descend to the eldest son unless by Deed or Will Devised to any other of the sons; or for want of sons, to the Eldest Daughter unless as aforesaid; and for want of such, to the next Heir unless devised, as aforesaid, by Deed or will (to be attested by three credible Witnesses, whereof one, at least, to be of the nobility) to any other Person.

14. AND to the End that such an Order of persons, being made noble and Invested with great powers and privileges, whereby to Engage them in a more particular affection towards this Settlement and Country of Carolina, may not fall into Contempt or be any ways Injurious to the Constitution of the Government, it is Declared and appointed that whatsoever Landgrave or Cacique, his heirs and Successors, shall not be qualified as in Article 7, and so be Excluded from the aforesaid Privilege of Sitting and voting in the upper House, and shall continue Defective in the said qualification for the Space of forty years Successively, Such Landgrave or Cacique, his Heirs and Successors, shall from thenceforth be for ever utterly Excluded, and his or their Dignity, honour, Privilege, and Title of Landgrave or Cacique shall Cease and be utterly lost, and the Letters Patents of Creation of such Dignity shall be vacated.

15. AND in order to the due Election of Members for the Biennial Parliament, it shall be lawful for the Freeholders of the respective Precinct to meet the first Tuesday in September every two years, in the same town or place they last met in, to choose Parliament men, and there to choose those Members that are to sit next November following, unless the Proprietors' Court shall, by sufficient notice —— days before, appoint some other place for their meeting.

16. A New Parliament shall be assembled the first Monday of the Month of November every Second year, and shall meet and Sit in the Town they last sat in, without any Summons, unless by the Proprietors' Court in Carolina they be Summoned to meet at any other place; and if there shall be occasion of a Parliament in these Intervals, it shall be in the power of the Proprietors' Court to assemble them in —— days' notice, and at such time and place as the Court shall think fit.

17. AT the opening of every Parliament, the first thing that shall be done shall be the reading of these Fundamental Constitutions, which the Palatine, and the Proprietors, and the Members then present shall subscribe; nor shall any person whatsoever Sit or vote in the Parliament till he has, in that Session, Subscribed these Fundamental Constitutions in a Book kept for that purpose by the Clerk of the Parliament.

18. ANY act or order of Parliament that is ratified in open Parliament, during the same Session, by the Governor and three more of the Lords Proprietors' Deputies, shall be in force, and continue till the Palatine himself and three more of the Lords Proprietors themselves Signify their Dissent to any of the said acts or orders, under their hands and Seals; But if ratified under their hands and Seals, then to continue according to the time limited in such act.

19. THE whole Province shall be divided into Counties by the Parliament.

20. No Proprietor, Landgrave, or Cacique shall hereafter take up a Seigniory or Barony that shall exceed Four thousand acres, or thereabout, for a Proprietor or Landgrave, and two thousand acres, or thereabout, for a Cacique, in one County.

21. No Cause, whether Civil or Criminal, of any Freeman shall be tried in any Court of Judicature without a Jury of his Peers.

22. No Landgrave or Cacique shall be tried for any criminal cause in any but the chief Justice's court, and that by a Jury of his Peers, un-

less a sufficient number of such cannot be legally had, and then to be supplied by the best and most sufficient Freeholders.

23. If, upon the Decease of the Governor, no person be appointed by the Lords Proprietors to succeed him, then the Proprietors' Deputies shall meet and choose a Governor till a new Commission be sent from the Lords Proprietors, under their hands and Seals.

24. Balloting shall be continued in all Elections of the Parliament, and in all other Cases where it can conveniently be used.

25. No man shall be permitted to be a Freeman of Carolina, or to have any Estate or habitation within it, that does not acknowledge a God, and that God is publicly and solemnly to be worshipped.

26. As the Country comes to be sufficiently planted and Distributed into fit Divisions, it shall belong to the Parliament to take care for the building of Churches and the public maintenance of Divines, to be Employed in the Exercise of Religion according to the Church of England, which, being the only true and orthodox, and the National Religion of the King's Dominions, is so also of Carolina; and therefore, it alone shall be allowed to receive public Maintenance by Grant of Parliament.

27. Any Seven or more persons agreeing in any Religion shall constitute a Church or Profession, to which they shall give some name to distinguish it from others.

28. The Terms of admittance and Communion with any Church or profession shall be written in a Book, and therein be subscribed by all the Members of the said Church or Profession, which shall be kept by the public Register of the Precinct wherein they reside.

29. The time of every one's subscription and admittance shall be dated in the said Book of religious Records.

30. In the Terms of Communion of every Church or Profession, these following shall be Three, without which no agreement or assembly of men upon pretence of Religion shall be accounted a Church or Profession within these Rules:

1. That there is a God.
2. That God is publicly to be worshipped.
3. That it is lawful, and the Duty of every man, being thereunto called by those that govern, to bear witness to truth; and that every Church or Profession shall, in their terms of Communion, Set down the Ex-

ternal way whereby they witness a truth as in the presence of God, whether it be by laying hands on or kissing the Bible, as in the Church of England, or by holding up the hand, or any sensible way.

31. No Person above Seventeen years of age shall have any benefit or protection of the Law, or be capable of any Place of profit or honour, who is not a Member of some Church or Profession, having his name recorded in some one, and but one religious Record at once.

32. No person of any Church or Profession shall Disturb or molest any Religious assembly.

33. No person whatsoever shall speak any thing in their Religious assembly Irreverently or seditiously of the Government or Governor or of State matters.

34. Any person subscribing the terms of Communion in the Record of the said Church or Profession before the Precinct Register and any Five Members of the said Church or Profession shall be thereby made a Member of the said Church or Profession.

35. Any person striking out his own name out of any Religious Records, or his name being struck out by any officer thereunto authorized by Each Church or Profession respectively, shall cease to be a Member of that Church or Profession.

36. No man shall use any reproachful, reviling, or abusive Language against the Religion of any Church or Profession, that being the certain way of disturbing the Peace, and of hindering the conversion of any to the Truth, by Engaging them in quarrels and animosities, to the hatred of the Professors and that Profession, which otherwise they may be brought to assent to.

37. Since Charity obliges us to wish well to the Souls of all Men, and Religion ought to alter nothing in any man's civil Estate or Right, it shall be Lawful for Slaves, as well as others, to enter themselves and be of what Church or profession any of them shall think best, and thereof be as fully Members as any Freeman. But yet, no Slave shall hereby be Exempted from that Civil Dominion his Master has over him, but be in all other things in the same State and condition he was in before.

38. Assemblies, upon what pretence soever of Religion, not observing and performing the abovesaid Rules shall not be Esteemed as Churches, but unlawful Meetings, and be punished as other Riots.

39. No person whatsoever shall disturb, molest, or persecute another for his Speculative opinions in Religion or his way of worship.

40. Every Freeman of Carolina shall have absolute power and authority over his Negro slaves, of what opinion or Religion soever.

41. Any person at his Admittance into any office, or Place of Trust whatsoever, shall subscribe these Fundamental Constitutions in this Form:

I, A. B., do promise to bear faith and true allegiance to our Sovereign Lord King William; and will be true and faithful to the Palatine and Lords Proprietors of Carolina, their heirs and Successors; and, with my utmost power, will defend them and maintain the Government, according to this Establishment in these Fundamental Constitutions.

These Fundamental Constitutions, in number Forty one, and every part thereof, shall be, and remain, the Inviolable Form and Rule of Government of Carolina, for ever. Witness, our hands and Seals, this Eleventh day of April, 1698.

Bathe, Palatine
A. Ashley
Craven
Bathe, for the Lord Carteret
Wm. Thornburgh for Sir John Colleton
Tho. Amy
Wm. Thornburgh

[Transcribed from a photostatic copy of a manuscript in the British Public Record Office, London. Reference: C. O. 5/288. Photostatic copy deposited in the State Department of Archives and History, Raleigh, North Carolina.]

Index

INDEX

THE COLONIAL RECORDS OF NORTH CAROLINA

Mattie Erma Edwards Parker, *Editor*

ADVISORY EDITORIAL BOARD

John Alden
Mrs. Memory F. Blackwelder
Christopher Crittenden
Cecil Johnson
Hugh T. Lefler
Brig. Gen. John D. F. Phillips, USA (Ret.)
William S. Powell
Sam Ragan
Robert H. Woody

W9-CZT-346